T0184691

Communications in Computer and Information Science 572

Commenced Publication in 2007
Founding and Former Series Editors:
Alfredo Cuzzocrea, Dominik Ślęzak, and Xiaokang Yang

More information about this series at http://www.springer.com/series/7899

Xing Zhang · Zhonghai Wu
Xingmian Sha (Eds.)

Embedded System Technology

13th National Conference, ESTC 2015
Beijing, China, October 10–11, 2015
Revised Selected Papers

 Springer

Editors
Xing Zhang
School of Software and Microelectronics
Peking University
Beijing
China

Zhonghai Wu
School of Software and Microelectronics
Peking University
Beijing
China

Xingmian Sha
College of Computer Science
Chongqing University
Chongqing
China

ISSN 1865-0929 ISSN 1865-0937 (electronic)
Communications in Computer and Information Science
ISBN 978-981-10-0420-9 ISBN 978-981-10-0421-6 (eBook)
DOI 10.1007/978-981-10-0421-6

Library of Congress Control Number: 2015958314

Preface

The 13th National Embedded System Technology Conference (ESTC 2015) was successfully held at Peking University during October 10–11, 2015. More than 200 scholars, specialists, engineers, and graduates of embedded systems in China attended the two-day conference, with a focus on "Trusted Embedded Computing and Intelligent Hardware." The conference was organized by the China Computer Federation (CCF) and the School of Software and Microelectronics, Peking University.

ESTC 2015 covered a board range of related fields, including three main subjects this year, smart hardware, system and networks, and applications and algorithms. These three subjects focus on research about real-world applications. The research is not limited to academia but also comes from industry and business with different solutions for end-user applications and enabling technologies, in a diversity of communication environments.

ESCT 2015 received 63 papers in total. These papers demonstrate a number of innovative ideas and solutions related to real-world applications. To evaluate each submission, the conference adopted a method of concealed evaluation: each paper was reviewed by at least three experts from the Technical Program Committee. The selection process strictly abided to the conference criteria and only 18 papers were accepted and orally presented at ESTC 2015.

Thanks to all the attendees for their participation and thanks to all the authors for their contributions. We are especially grateful to the keynote speakers and authors of invited papers for their inspiring work. Due to the excellent technical program and the organizers' hard work, we had a successful and enjoyable ESTC 2015.

November 2015

Xing Zhang
Zhonghai Wu
Xingmian Sha

Organization

The 13th National Embedded System Technology Conference (ESTC 2015) was sponsored by the China Computer Federation and Peking University. It was organized by the Technical Committee of Embedded Systems, China Computer Federation, and School of Software & Microelectronics, Peking University German (Germany).

Conference Co-chairs

Xing Zhang   Peking University, China
Pranav Mehta   Intel Lab, USA

Program Committee Co-chairs

Zhonghai Wu   Peking University, China
Xingmian Sha   Chongqing University, China (American)

Program Committee Members

Bin Guo   Sichuan University, China
Chuanfeng Yuan   Nanjing University, China
Dong Liu   Accenture Technology Lab Beijing, China
                         (Corporate America)
Dongshen Wang   Tsinghua University, China
Gang Cui   Harbin Institute of Technology, China
Jian Kuang   Beijing University of Posts and Telecommunications, China
Jianfeng Yang   Wuhan University, China
Letian Jiang   Shanghai Jiao Tong University, China
Linxiang Zheng   Xiamen University, China
Mingquan Zhou   Beijing Normal University, China
Minsong Chen   East China Normal University, China
Pin Tao   Tsinghua University, China
Qingfeng Zhuge   Chongqing University, China (American)
Qingguo Zhou   Lanzhou University, China
Quan Wang   Xidian University, China
Renfa Li   Hunan University, China
Wanggeng Wan   Shanghai University, China
Weiguo Wu   Xian Jiao Tong University, China
Wenzhi Chen   Zhejiang University, China
Xiang Liu   Peking University, China (Singaporean)
Xinan Wang   Peking University, China
Xingshe Zhou   Northwestern Polytechnical University, China
Xixin Cao   Peking University, China
Yi Yan   Hangzhou Dianzi University, China

Ying Li	Peking University, China
Yinong Chen	Arizona State University, USA
Ying Huang	Lenovo Research Lab, China (American)
Yixiang Chen	East China Normal University, China
Yunwei Dong	Northwestern Polytechnical University, China
Zhiming Gu	Beijing Institute of Technology, China

Contents

Applications and Algorithm

Smart Hardware

System and Network

Applications and Algorithm

Noise Reduction Method for MEMS Gyroscope Based on Evolved Adaptive Kalman Filter

Youcong Ni[(⊠)], Fengping Ang[(⊠)], and Xin Du[(⊠)]

Faculty of Software, Fujian Normal University, Fuzhou 350108, Fujian, China
youcongni@foxmail.com, {afp1020,xindu79}@126.com

Abstract. It's a difficult problem to filter MEMS gyroscope random noise in a dynamic state. Aiming at this problem, a method named EAKFA is proposed in this paper. The EAKFA method selects adaptive Kalman filter algorithm as a fading factor. Furthermore, the fading factor is optimized by evolutionary algorithms. Finally, the effectiveness of EAKFA is validated by comparing EAKFA with a general adaptive Kalman filter algorithm. The results show that the error mean and the standard deviation of the MEMS gyroscope are reduced by 2.5 % and 55.7 % after filtered, respectively.

Keywords: MEMS gyroscope · Random noise · Adaptive Kalman filter · Evolutionary algorithms · Fading factor

1 Introduction

As the advantages of low cost, small size, low power consumption, high impact resistance, and easy to mass production, etc., MEMS gyroscope has been widely used in low-cost inertial system [1]. However, due to the influence of the manufacturing process, the use of the environment and other factors, the precision of the MEMS gyroscope is still low, which limits its further application. Studies have shown that both deterministic noise and random noise are important factors that affect the precision of MEMS gyroscope [2]. Deterministic noise is often a regular pattern, and all types of error coefficients can be determined by the turntable calibration, so the noise can be compensated accurately. But the random noise is uncertain which often more complex than deterministic noise and difficult to be eliminated by the conventional methods of real-time compensation. Thus filtering the random noise is the key to improve the precision of the gyroscope.

Recently, many noise reduction methods for MEMS gyroscope have emerged, such as neural networks [3], wavelet analysis [4] and Kalman filter [5–10]. Although the neural network method has the advantages of self-learning and fast optimization, it still has the problem of over-fitting, local minima and complex grid structure. Wavelet analysis method has good localization characteristics in time domain and frequency domain, and it is possible to separate the valid signal and noise depending on the different characteristics of signal and noise in wavelet domain. However, the wavelet analysis method is lack of adaptive capability, and the wavelet function is difficult to determine. In addition, neural network method and wavelet analysis method are

X. Zhang et al. (Eds.): ESTC 2015, CCIS 572, pp. 3–12, 2015.
DOI: 10.1007/978-981-10-0421-6_1

computation-intensive and time-consuming, and the resulting models often have a higher order, which are difficult to be applied in low-cost systems for real-time online estimation [11]. In view of the shortcomings of these two methods, the Kalman filter which widely used in the industrial field is applied to the random noise processing of MEMS gyroscope in [5–10]. Firstly, the random noise of MEMS gyroscope is modeled by the method of time series analysis, and then the Kalman filter is designed for filtering noise. Kalman filtering is simple in use, and the resulting model is comparatively precise. This method can effectively eliminate the random noise in the static case, but its filter effect in a dynamic environment is not ideal. To solve this problem, an adaptive Kalman filter algorithm is proposed in [12–15]. However, the filtering quality of conventional adaptive Kalman filter algorithm (GAKFA) rely on a parameter that needs to be determined by experiment and experience, which lead to its application affected to a certain extent. Aiming at this problem, this paper proposed an evolved adaptive Kalman filter algorithm (EAKFA) based on AR (1) model, and then proposed a new noise reduction method for MEMS gyroscope. The method selected adaptive Kalman filter algorithm with a fading factor that optimized by evolution algorithms, which can provide a useful way to improve the filtering effect of the random noise of MEMS gyroscope in a dynamic environment.

This paper is organized as follows. Section 2 describes the AR (1) model of the random noise of MEMS gyroscope; The random noise filtering method based on EAKFA algorithm for MEMS gyroscope is given in Sect. 3; In Sect. 4, the proposed method in this paper is compared with GAKFA algorithm through simulation experiments; Finally, Sect. 5 consists of the conclusion for this study and the future work.

2 AR (1) Model of the Random Noise for MEMS Gyroscope

AR (1) model is comparatively precise and has high operational efficiency [16]. In this paper, we consider the Akaike Information Criterion (AIC), the applicability of the model and the real-time requirement of the system. Firstly fitting the model from the simplest model, and then, the AR (1) model was determined as the random noise model of MEMS gyroscope according to the numerical value of the residual error after fitting.

A stationary random sequences $\{x_n\}$ normally distributed can be represented by the Auto-Regressive-Moving-Average (ARMA) model, p, q are the order of the model. AR (1) model is a special case of ARMA (p, q) when p = 1 and q = 0. The definition of ARMA (p, q) model is given in Eqs. (1) and (2).

$$X_n = -\left(a_1 x_{n-1} + a_2 x_{n-2} + \ldots + a_p x_{n-p}\right) + \varepsilon_n + b_1 \varepsilon_{n-1} + b_2 \varepsilon_{n-2} + \ldots + b_q \varepsilon_{n-q}. \quad (1)$$

$$\varepsilon_i \sim W\left(0, \sigma^2\right). \quad (2)$$

In Eq. (1), $a_i < 1 (i = 1, 2,\ldots, p)$ and $b_i < 1 (i = 1, 2,\ldots,q)$ are referred to as autoregressive coefficient and autoregressive moving coefficient respectively; ε_n is a discrete white noise sequence, whose mean is zero and variance is σ^2.

When q = 0, the model is simplified to Eq. (3)

$$x_n = -(a_1 x_{n-1} + a_2 x_{n-2} + \ldots + a_p x_{n-p}) + \varepsilon_n \tag{3}$$

This model is called p-order autoregressive model, namely AR (p). AR (1) is the first-order autoregressive model, as shown in Eq. (4).

$$x_n = -a_1 x_{n-1} + \varepsilon_n \tag{4}$$

Equation (4) shows that the observed value x_n of the moment is only correlated with the observed value x_{n-1} of the previous time.

After the random noise of MEMS gyroscope described by AR (1) model, Eq. (4) can be changed into the state space model defined in Eq. (5)

$$X_n = -a_1 X_{n-1} + \varepsilon_n = \Phi_n X_{n-1} \tag{5}$$

In Eq. (5), X_n and ε_n are state vector and observation noise of the angular velocity measured by MEMS gyroscope respectively. Q_n is the variance of $\{\varepsilon_n\}$; Φ_n is the state transition matrix.

3 Filtering Algorithm of Random Noise for MEMS Gyroscope (EAKFA)

In this paper, we designed an algorithm for filtering the random noise of MEMS gyroscope called EAKFA based on the noise model described in Eq. (5). Firstly, the fading factor was optimized by the evolution algorithm (EA4FF), and then we substituted the factor into the adaptive Kalman filter algorithm (AKFA) for filtering out the random noise of MEMS gyroscope. As the AKFA needs to be called during the process of solving fitness in EA4FF, the paper firstly gave out the design of AKFA, and the specific steps of EA4FF was described subsequently.

3.1 AKFA

AKFA is an optimal state estimation algorithm. The state equation and measurement equation of the system should be determined firstly to prepare for the subsequent estimation process in AKFA.

Equation (5) has given the system's state equation. The system's state is measured by using MEMS gyroscope, and measurement noise also exists in the process of data collecting. The system's measurement equation is shown in Eq. (6)

$$Z_n = H_n X_n + v_n \tag{6}$$

In Eq. (6), Z_n is measurement vector of the angular velocity; H_n is measurement matrix; v_n is measurement noise of the MEMS gyroscope; R_n is the variance of $\{v_n\}$.

We set α as the fading factor and gave the recurrence equations of AKFA shown in Eqs. (7) to (11) based on Eqs. (5) and (6).

From Eq. (7), we can get that the angular velocity of MEMS gyroscope for the current moment is predicted by the estimated value of the angular velocity at the last moment. And Eq. (8) shows that the error covariance of the current time is predicted by the estimated value of the error covariance at the last time. $X_{k|k-1}$ and $P_{k|k-1}$ are the intermediate results.

$$X_{k|k-1} = \Phi_{k|k-1} X_{k-1} \tag{7}$$

$$P_{k|k-1} = \Phi_{k|k-1} P_{k-1} \Phi_{k|k-1}^T + \alpha Q_{k-1} \tag{8}$$

The calculation of the matrix of Kalman filter gain is defined by Eq. (9)

$$K_k = P_{k|k-1} H_k^T \left(H_k \alpha P_{k|k-1} H_k^T + \alpha R_k \right)^{-1} \tag{9}$$

Then update $X_{k|k-1}$ by inputting the original measured value of angular velocity of MEMS gyroscope and the angular velocity after filtering is obtained. Z_k and X_k are original measured value and updated value respectively. This step is called state filtering, and the corresponding renewal equation of state is Eq. (10)

$$X_k = X_{k|k-1} + K_k \left(Z_k - H_k X_{k|k-1} \right) \tag{10}$$

Equation (11) defines an update to the error covariance of the angular velocity of MEMS gyroscope at the present moment, which is prepared for the next iteration.

$$P_k = \left[(I - K_k H_k) P_{k|k-1} \right] / \alpha \tag{11}$$

The specific process of AKFA algorithm is shown in Table 1.

Table 1. AKFA Algorithm

Input: n groups of original measurements of MEMS gyroscope, fading factor **Output**: an array of the angular velocity of MEMS gyroscope after filtering (KX)	
1:	Initialize the initial value X_0, and the system parameters of filtering algorithm, such as P_0, Q_0, and the like;
2:	The current time k←1;
3:	While k<n do
4:	According to the estimated value at the moment k-1, estimate the angular velocity of MEMS gyroscope at the moment k by Eq. (7). The new estimated value $X_{k|k-1}$ is a intermediate result;
5:	By Eq. (8), forecast the error variance matrix of angular velocity of MEMS gyroscope at the moment k;
6:	Based on $P_{k|k-1}$, calculate the matrix of Kalman filter gain at the moment k by Eq. (9);
7:	Update $X_{k|k-1}$ for state filtering based on K_k and the original measurements of MEMS gyroscope at the moment k, and the angular velocity of MEMS gyroscope after filtering is stored in an array KX;
8:	Based on $P_{k|k-1}$ and K_k, update error covariance by Eq. (11);
9:	k←k+1 ;
10:	end while ;
11:	Output KX, algorithm ends.

3.2   EA4FF

EA4FF algorithm is used to optimize the fading factor in Eqs. (8) and (9). The value of α should be between 0.5 and 1. Therefore, we choose real coding as the encoded mode of EA4FF algorithm, then the length of chromosome is set to 1, and the value of chromosome should between 0.5 and 1. Crossover operator selection for real arithmetic crossover, mutation operator choose conventional mutation operator, the selection strategy adopts the roulette selection with elite reserved, and the evolutional generation is 50. The process definition of EA4FF algorithm is shown in Table 2.

Table 2. EA4FF Algorithm

Input: population size   n; crossover probability   pc (0 <pc <1), mutation probability pm (0 <pm <1); the original measurements of MEMS gyroscope **Output**: optimized fading factor

1:	t←0 ;
2:	Initialize population P(t) ;
3:	Call AKFA algorithm to calculate the fitness value of each individual in P(t) ;
4:	Choose the best individual from P(t) and assign it to the variable X ;
5:	While the termination condition is not satisfied, do
6:	Generate the intermediate population $P_c(t)$ by using real arithmetic crossover based on P(t) and pc ;
7:	Generate the intermediate population $P_m(t)$ by using mutation operator based on $P_c(t)$ and pm ;
8:	Call AKFA algorithm to calculate the fitness value of each individual in $P_m(t)$;
9:	Select n individuals from $P_m(t)$ and P(t) by using the roulette selection with maintaining elite , and generate the next generation P(t+1) ;
10:	Identify the best individual from P(t+1) and assign it to the variable X ;
11:	t←t+1 ;
12:	end while ;
13:	Output the best individual X as the optimal fading factor.

4   Experimental Analysis

Next, we compare EAKFA algorithm of this paper with GAKFA algorithm in order to verify the validity of the method proposed in this paper. Firstly, the experimental environment and data are given, and then provide the experimental parameters. Finally, give the experimental results and analysis.

4.1   Experimental Environment and Data

Hardware Environment: Intel core i3-2100 CPU, Samsung Galaxy Nexus; Software Environment: Win7 OS, eclipse Kepler.

Put the Samsung Galaxy Nexus smartphone flat on the ground, and remain still, shaft angle rate information of the output data of MEMS gyroscope inside smartphone is used as original data. The sampling frequency is 100 Hz, sample length is 6000.

Simulate the oscillating test by superimposing a sinusoidal signal on the basis of the collected static data. The amplitudes of the sinusoidal signal are 5°, 15°, 50°and 150° respectively, and the period is 10 s.

4.2   Experimental Parameters

4.2.1   Experimental Parameters of GAKFA Algorithm

In GAKFA algorithm, the fading factor needs to be determined based on a priori knowledge and simulation observation before the experiment. Specifically, the filtering effect is observed to choose the optimal value α by changing the value of α. The mean and standard deviation of the error before and after Kalman filtering when $\alpha = 0.9$, 0.8, 0.7, 0.6 are shown in Tables 3 and 4 respectively.

Table 3. Mean value of angular rate error in the oscillating test

Amplitude	α			
	0.9	0.8	0.7	0.6
5°	0.0392	0.0373	0.0360	0.0373
15°	0.1151	0.1093	0.1046	0.1074
50°	0.3815	0.3619	0.3458	0.3542
150°	1.1433	1.0846	1.0362	1.0606

Table 4. Standard deviation of angular rate error in the oscillating test

Amplitude	α			
	0.9	0.8	0.7	0.6
5°	0.0348	0.0247	0.0171	0.0309
15°	0.1025	0.0700	0.0396	0.0787
50°	0.3409	0.2316	0.1268	0.2546
150°	1.0226	0.6943	0.3790	0.7600

From Tables 3 and 4, we can see that both the mean value and the standard deviation of angular rate error all reach minimum value when $\alpha = 0.7$ no matter how the amplitude changes. Therefore, the fading factor of GAKFA algorithm is determined to be 0.7.

4.2.2 Experimental Parameters of EAKFA Algorithm

In this paper, the parameter α of EAKFA algorithm does not depend on a priori knowledge, which can be automatically determined during the execution of the algorithm. The chromosome length, population size, mutation probability, crossover probability and evolutional generation of EAKFA algorithm are set to 1, 30, 0.4, 0.7 and 50 respectively.

4.3 Experimental Results

To evaluate the algorithm fairly, we run the EAKFA algorithm ten times independently and compare the average with GAKFA algorithm. The results of the two algorithms are shown as Tables 5 and 6.

Table 5. Mean value of angular rate error in the oscillating test

Time	5°		15°		50°		150°	
	GAKFA	EAKFA	GAKFA	EAKFA	GAKFA	EAKFA	GAKFA	EAKFA
1	0.03597	0.03545	0.10463	0.10230	0.34583	0.33724	1.03618	1.00996
2	0.03597	0.03545	0.10463	0.10231	0.34583	0.33728	1.03618	1.01005
3	0.03597	0.03545	0.10463	0.10230	0.34583	0.33722	1.03618	1.00989
4	0.03597	0.03545	0.10463	0.10231	0.34583	0.33730	1.03618	1.01013
5	0.03597	0.03545	0.10463	0.10231	0.34583	0.33727	1.03618	1.01003
6	0.03597	0.03545	0.10463	0.10231	0.34583	0.33727	1.03618	1.01002
7	0.03597	0.03545	0.10463	0.10230	0.34583	0.33725	1.03618	1.00997
8	0.03597	0.03545	0.10463	0.10231	0.34583	0.33727	1.03618	1.01005
9	0.03597	0.03545	0.10463	0.10230	0.34583	0.33726	1.03618	1.01001
10	0.03597	0.03545	0.10463	0.10230	0.34583	0.33723	1.03618	1.00992
Average	0.03597	0.03545	0.10463	0.10230	0.34583	0.33726	1.03618	1.01000

Table 6. Standard deviation of angular rate error in the oscillating test

Time	5°		15°		50°		150°	
	GAKFA	EAKFA	GAKFA	EAKFA	GAKFA	EAKFA	GAKFA	EAKFA
1	0.01708	0.01596	0.03959	0.02208	0.12680	0.05601	0.37900	0.16258
2	0.01708	0.01595	0.03959	0.02214	0.12680	0.05630	0.37900	0.16349
3	0.01708	0.01597	0.03959	0.02205	0.12680	0.05582	0.37900	0.16196
4	0.01708	0.01595	0.03959	0.02218	0.12680	0.05654	0.37900	0.16424
5	0.01708	0.01595	0.03959	0.02213	0.12680	0.05625	0.37900	0.16332
6	0.01708	0.01595	0.03959	0.02212	0.12680	0.05622	0.37900	0.16324
7	0.01708	0.01596	0.03959	0.02209	0.12680	0.05607	0.37900	0.16275
8	0.01708	0.01595	0.03959	0.02213	0.12680	0.05629	0.37900	0.16345
9	0.01708	0.01596	0.03959	0.02211	0.12680	0.05616	0.37900	0.16306
10	0.01708	0.01597	0.03959	0.02206	0.12680	0.05590	0.37900	0.16221
Average	0.01708	0.01596	0.03959	0.02211	0.12680	0.05615	0.37900	0.16303

From Tables 5 and 6, we can see that whether the mean value or the standard deviation of the error with EAKFA algorithm is less than that of GAKFA algorithm. It indicates that using EAKFA algorithm to filter out the random noise of MEMS gyroscope is better than GAKFA algorithm in terms of the mean value and standard deviation of the error. For example, compared with GAKFA algorithm, the error mean and the standard deviation of the MEMS gyroscope are reduced by 2.5 % and 55.7 % respectively after filtered by EAKFA algorithm when the amplitude is 50°. Experimental results show that the method in this paper can effectively improve the accuracy of MEMS gyroscope in a dynamic state.

In other states, the EAKFA algorithm is equally effective. Tables 7 and 8 show the experimental results of the static test and rate test. In this paper, we simulate the rate test by superimposing a constant angular velocity on the basis of the collected static data, and the angular rate is set to 10°/s. The results show that the EAKFA algorithm is still applicable in the cases of static state and constant angular rate.

Table 7. Mean value of angular rate error in the static test and rate test

Time	Static test		Rate test	
	AKFA	EAKFA	AKFA	EAKFA
1	0.00228	0.00127	0.00228	0.00140
2	0.00228	0.00135	0.00228	0.00130
3	0.00228	0.00150	0.00228	0.00146
4	0.00228	0.00122	0.00228	0.00127
5	0.00228	0.00149	0.00228	0.00132
6	0.00228	0.00128	0.00228	0.00125
7	0.00228	0.00130	0.00228	0.00128
8	0.00228	0.00123	0.00228	0.00155
9	0.00228	0.00133	0.00228	0.00140
10	0.00228	0.00132	0.00228	0.00124
Average	0.00228	0.00133	0.00228	0.00135

Table 8. Standard deviation of angular rate error in the static test and rate test

Time	Static test		Rate test	
	AKFA	EAKFA	AKFA	EAKFA
1	0.00582	0.00248	0.00582	0.00287
2	0.00582	0.00270	0.00582	0.00257
3	0.00582	0.00317	0.00582	0.00305
4	0.00582	0.00235	0.00582	0.00248
5	0.00582	0.00313	0.00582	0.00263
6	0.00582	0.00250	0.00582	0.00241
7	0.00582	0.00258	0.00582	0.00251
8	0.00582	0.00250	0.00582	0.00333
9	0.00582	0.00237	0.00582	0.00288
10	0.00582	0.00266	0.00582	0.00238
Average	0.00582	0.00264	0.00582	0.00271

5 Conclusion

In this paper, a noise reduction method for MEMS gyroscope based on EAKFA is proposed. The method is based on AR (1) model, and combines adaptive Kalman filtering and evolutionary algorithm. Experimental results show that the proposed method can effectively improve the filtering quality of MEMS gyroscope random noise in a dynamic state, and the method is still valid in the cases of static state and constant angular rate. In the future, we will focus on improving the accuracy of the model of MEMS gyroscope random noise. The gene expression programming (GEP) algorithm will be used to model the random error of MEMS gyroscope.

Acknowledgments. This work is supported by the National Natural Science Foundation of China (No. 61305079), the open fund of State Key Laboratory of Software Engineering (No. SKLSE 2014-10-02), the Natural Science Foundation of Fujian Province of China under Grant (No. 2015J01235), the JK class project of Education Department of Fujian Province (JK2015006).

References

1. Zhang, Y.L., Zhu, T., Fu, J.: Error analysis for MEMS gyroscope based on allan variance (in Chinese). Autom. Instrum. **3**, 157–158 (2013)
2. Wang, K.D., Xiong, S.F.: An ARMA modeling method and its application in Kalman filtering (in Chinese). J. Astronaut. **33**(8), 1048–1055 (2012)
3. Gao, W.G., Chen, G.C.: Integrated GNSS/INS navigation algorithms combining adaptive filter with neural network (in Chinese). Geomatics Inf. Sci. Wuhan Univ. **11**, 1323–1328 (2014)
4. Song, H.B., Yang, P., Xu, L.B.: Analysis and processing on stochastic error of MEMS sensor (in Chinese). Chinese J. Sens. Actuators **26**(12), 1719–1723 (2013)
5. Yang, P.P., Li, Q.: Kalman filtering of MEMS gyro based on time-series model. In: 9th International Conference on Electronic Measurement & Instruments, ICEMI 2009, pp. 367–370. IEEE Press, Beijing (2009)
6. Ruan, X.G., Yu, M.M.: Modeling research of MEMS gyro drift based on kalman filter. In: Control and Decision Conference (2014 CCDC), pp. 2949–2952. IEEE Press, Beijing (2014)
7. Chen, M.M., Gao, G.W.: Research on MEMS gyroscope random error compensation algorithm based on ARMA model. J. Appl. Mech. Mater. **602**, 891–894 (2014)
8. Lu, Z.Y., Wen, H., Long, Y.Q.: Design of filtering algorithm for MEMS gyroscope (in Chinese). Transducer Microsyst. Technol. **32**(10), 83–84 (2013)
9. Li, J., Zhang, W.D., Liu, J.: Research on the application of the time-serial analysis based kalman filter in MEMS gyroscope random drift compensation (in Chinese). Chinese J. Sens. Actuators **19**(05B), 2215–2219 (2006)
10. Jin, G.M., Zhang, G.L., Chen, L.P.: Research on filter method and model of MEMS gyro static drift (in Chinese). Transducer Microsyst. Technol. **26**(11), 48–50 (2007)
11. Xu, K.: MEMS Gyroscopes Error Compensation Algorithm Research (in Chinese). Shenyang Ligong University (2012)

12. Xin, Z.F., Su, Z., Wang, X.D.: Study of fuzzy adaptive Kalman filter in MEMS gyro (in Chinese). J. Beijing Inf. Sci. Technol. Univ. **25**(1), 46–48 (2010)
13. Qiao, H.M.: The Research of MEMS Inertial Sensors Parameter Identification and Error Compensation Technology (in Chinese). Shenyang Ligong University (2013)
14. Ji, X.S., Wang, S.R., Xu, Y.S.: Application of the adaptive Kalman filter in the MEMS gyro signal processing (in Chinese). Transducer Microsyst. Technol. **25**(9), 79–81 (2006)
15. Chen, D.S., Shao, Z.H., Lei, X.S.: Multiscale fyzzy-adaptive Kalman filtering methods for MEMS gyros random drift (in Chinese). J. Beijing Univ. Aeronaut. Astronaut. **35**(2), 246–250 (2009)
16. Zamani, M., Felsenstein, E., Anderson, B.D.: Mixed frequency structured AR model identification. In: Control Conference (ECC), pp. 1928–1933. IEEE Press, European (2013)

High-Performance Embedded Synthetic Aperture Medical Ultrasound Imaging System

Junying Chen[⊠], Diqin Li, and Huaqing Min

Guangzhou Key Laboratory of Robotics and Intelligent Software,
School of Software Engineering, South China University of Technology,
Guangzhou, Guangdong, China
jychense@scut.edu.cn

Abstract. Medical ultrasound imaging technology has a large scale practical applications in medical diagnostics. In medical ultrasonic synthetic aperture imaging, an array of sensors receive ultrasound echoes and process the echoes to gain low-resolution images which are further processed to obtain high-resolution images. Currently the most common processing algorithm to obtain low-resolution images is delay-and-sum method. This paper mainly focuses on implementing synthetic aperture algorithm in high-performance embedded platform and evaluating its performance. In the estimation of the ultrasonic synthetic aperture algorithm, Field II simulator was used to generate the needed digital ultrasound transducer data. The high-performance embedded computing platform with a graphics processing unit was used to build the synthetic aperture solution and gained an 85 × speedup as compared to its single-core embedded processor implementation. Furthermore, the embedded implementation framework we have built can be easily used to build other high-definition medical ultrasound imaging algorithms.

Keywords: High-performance embedded computing · Medical ultrasound imaging · Synthetic aperture · Graphics processing unit · Parallelization

1 Introduction

Medical ultrasound imaging technology has been widely used and has been rapidly developed. This is because of its advantages of real-time imaging capability, low cost and high safety. In a variety of ultrasound imaging techniques, synthetic aperture imaging technology is one of the high-definition imaging technology. By using this technology, the ultrasound scanner can effectively improve imaging precision to obtain high-resolution ultrasound images. Ultrasonic synthetic aperture technique origins from synthetic aperture radar technology. Synthetic aperture radar [1–3] imaging technique is obtained by processing the reception data to make the relative motion of the small aperture radar and the object become a relatively larger synthesized aperture. In medical ultrasound imaging, synthetic aperture imaging technique [4, 5] processes the received echoes from the sensor array to obtain a low-resolution image, thereby repeatedly superimposing the low-resolution images to form a high-resolution image. Currently the most widely used low-resolution image processing algorithm is delay-and-sum algorithm.

© Springer Science+Business Media Singapore 2015
X. Zhang et al. (Eds.): ESTC 2015, CCIS 572, pp. 13–22, 2015.
DOI: 10.1007/978-981-10-0421-6_2

High-performance embedded platforms integrated with graphics processing units [6] possess the characteristics of targeted functionality, high computing performance, relatively lower expense, small footprint, and low energy consumption. Such characteristics make the high-performance embedded computing platforms suitable for mobile and portable functional solutions [7]. Therefore, implementing ultrasonic synthetic aperture imaging algorithm on the high-performance embedded computing platform, can help to effectively reduce the cost of building high-definition medical ultrasound imaging systems, and can help to facilitate future development of portable medical ultrasound imaging systems.

2　Medical Ultrasonic Synthetic Aperture Algorithm

Based on the research of medical ultrasonic synthetic aperture algorithm [8–10], this section will describe the details of the algorithm which is closely related to the subsequent design and implementation in the next section.

2.1　Low-Resolution Image Acquirement

The most commonly used algorithm for low-resolution image acquirement is delay-and-sum algorithm. Before the delay apodization is applied, the ultrasound receive channel data is first manipulated with Hilbert transform. The Hilbert-transformed ultrasound data sample is calculated by the following convolution output:

$$conv_{a,b}(i) = \sum_{j=1}^{i+T-1} h(j)d_{a,b}(j) \tag{1}$$

In Eq. (1), a represents for the ath ultrasound receive channel, b represents for the bth transmit firing, and i represents for the ith ultrasound imaging depth sample, thus $d_{a,b}(j)$ is the jth data sample of ath ultrasound receive channel for bth transmit firing. Furthermore, $h(j)$ denotes the Hilbert transform coefficient which is expressed as:

$$h(j) = \begin{cases} 0 & \text{for even } j \\ \frac{2}{\pi j} & \text{for odd } j \end{cases} \tag{2}$$

Hilbert transform function is similar to a finite-impulse response (FIR) filter with T number of taps, as shown in Eq. (1), where T is usually set as 51. The Hilbert transform process is shown in Fig. 1.

Delay-and-sum beamforming method is applied on the Hilbert transformed data to obtain a low-resolution image for the b th transmit firing. Use $L_b(p)$ to represent the value of pixel p in the low-resolution image of b th transmit firing, according to delay-and-sum algorithm, $L_b(p)$ can be expressed as:

$$L_b(p) = \sum_{a=1}^{N} w_a \cdot x_{a,b}(p) \tag{3}$$

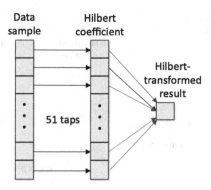

Fig. 1. Hilbert transform process

In Eq. (3), w_a is the apodization weight for the a th ultrasound receive channel which adopts Hanning window function, and $a_{max} = N$. $x_{a,b}(p)$ is the interpolated channel data sample which can be obtained by:

$$x_{a,b}(p) = \gamma \cdot conv_{a,b}(\beta) + (1 - \gamma) \cdot conv_{a,b}(\beta + 1) \tag{4}$$

$conv_{a,b}(\beta)$ and $conv_{a,b}(\beta + 1)$ are the two adjacent Hilbert-transformed data samples corresponding the most closely with the pixel's focusing delay in the a th channel. β is the imaging depth sample index corresponding to the focusing delay $\delta_{a,b}(p)$, as shown in Fig. 2(a), and γ is the interpolation weight (between 0 and 1). For a given sampling rate f_s, β and $\delta_{a,b}(p)$ can be found as:

$$\beta = \text{floor}(f_s \cdot \delta_{a,b}(p)) \tag{5}$$

$$\gamma = 1 + \beta - f_s \cdot \delta_{a,b}(p) \tag{6}$$

In Eq. (5), floor operation outputs the largest integer which is not greater than $(f_s \cdot \delta_{a,b}(p))$. $\delta_{a,b}(p)$ is calculated by:

$$\delta_{a,b}(p) = (D_t(p) + D_r(p)) \div c \tag{7}$$

In Eq. (7), $D_t(p)$ and $D_r(p)$ denote the transmit propagation distance and the receive propagation distance respectively, as shown in Fig. 2(b). c is the ultrasound propagation speed.

2.2   High-Resolution Image Recursive Synthesis

High-resolution image is obtained by recursively synthesize a series of low-resolution images. For kth high-resolution image with a frame size of M, its value of pixel p is calculated as:

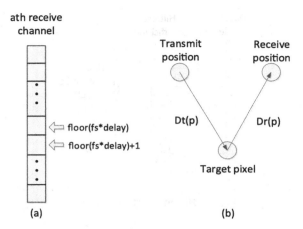

Fig. 2. (a) $\beta = \text{floor}(f_s \cdot \delta_{a,b}(p))$ for the a th ultrasound receive channel, where $\delta_{a,b}(p)$ is the focusing delay; (b) transmit propagation distance and the receive propagation distance.

$$H_k(p) = \sum_{i=k-M+1}^{k} L_i(p) \tag{8}$$

$L_i(p)$ is the corresponding pixel value from the ith low-resolution image. Equation (8) can be rewritten as:

$$H_k(p) = H_{k-1}(p) + L_k(p) - L_{k-M}(p) \tag{9}$$

In Eq. (9), $H_{k-1}(p)$, $L_k(p)$ and $L_{k-M}(p)$ are the corresponding pixel value for previous high-resolution image, the latest low-resolution image and the earliest low-resolution image.

3   High-Performance Embedded Platform and Algorithm Implementation

3.1   High-Performance Embedded Computing Platform with GPU

Figure 3 demonstrates the hardware architecture of the high-performance embedded computing platform with graphics processing unit. The simulated ultrasound channel data was first transmitted to the random-access memory (RAM) on the embedded computing platform. The synthetic aperture algorithm was performed in the embedded GPU. After the imaging process data was ready for final display, OpenCV library functions were used to display the images on the connected monitor. Finally, the imaging processed data was stored in the storage unit.

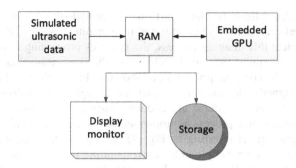

Fig. 3. Architecture of high-performance embedded computing platform

3.2   Implementation of Medical Ultrasound Synthetic Aperture Imaging

This section will describe the implementation methodology of medical ultrasound synthetic aperture imaging on high-performance embedded computing platform. The implementation procedures were conducted based on the algorithm details elaborated in Sect. 2.

Hilbert Transform Implementation. Athread block in the graphics processing unit was assigned to compute one ultrasound receive channel pre-process data. Within the thread block, each computing thread was used to execute one Hilbert transform operation to derive the Hilbert-transformed data samples for an array of consecutive imaging data samples in the receive channel. The processing data sample array was updated time by time to refresh the computing input data sources. This method was used to keep the run-time data storage at an appropriate size, so as to realize a high-efficient parallelization. The Hilbert transform implementation parallelization is shown in Fig. 4.

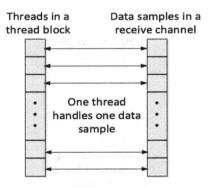

Fig. 4. GPU parallelization for Hilbert transform implementation. A thread block processes one column of 256 data samples at a time, and then repeats.

Delay-and-Sum Algorithm Implementation. Delay-and-sum processing block processes the Hilbert-transformed data samples to generate a series of low-resolution images. To complete this imaging process, the graphics processing unit assigns every thread block to compute the pixel values of the low-resolution images on a two-dimensional GPU compute grid basis, as shown in Fig. 5. Within the thread block, each thread is designed independently to calculate a single low-resolution image pixel value. The computation procedures are deduced from Eqs. (3), (4), (5), (6) and (7). Basically, the computation process is implemented by first calculating the focusing delay of the targeted pixel referring to Eq. (7). Based on the focusing delay value, calculate the imaging depth sample index corresponding to the focusing delay and the interpolation weight, according to Eqs. (5) and (6). Then, compute for the interpolated channel data sample using Eq. (4). Finally, obtain the targeted pixel value of the low-resolution image by applying apodization weights to the interpolated channel data sample as illustrated in Eq. (3).

High-Resolution Image Recursive Calculation. When low-resolution images are produced, they are transmitted to high-resolution processing block to compute for the high-resolution image. As the high-resolution image calculation process is recursive but the calculation of each high-resolution image pixel value is independent with each other, each computing thread in the graphics processing unit can be used to perform one high-resolution image pixel value, and multiple threads conduct the calculation process simultaneously.

Memory Access and Management. Memory utilization is an important part of building such a high-performance embedded medical ultrasound imaging platform. The memory access speed in the high-performance embedded computing platform is register files > local memory > global memory, but the memory capacity distribution is register files < local memory < global memory. As a result, the register files are so precious that only current processing data and results are stored in them. Local memory is usually used for intermediate calculation results, and global memory is used to store initial data and final results.

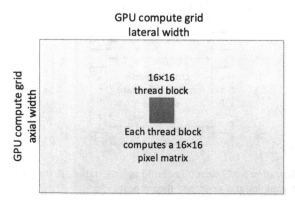

Fig. 5. GPU computing scheme for delay-and-sum algorithm implementation.

4   Experimental Design and Results

4.1   Experimental Environment and Lab Scenario Design

The experiments adopted Field II simulator [11, 12] to simulate the ultrasound channel data samples. The simulation parameters are shown in Table 1.

Table 1.   Field II simulation parameters.

Parameter	Value
Ultrasonic speed propagated in human tissue	1540 m/s
Number of transducer elements	128
Element pitch	0.3048 mm
Pulse repetition rate	5 kHz
Sampling rate	40 MHz

The experimental high-performance embedded computing platform is Nvidia Jetson TK1 embedded evaluation platform. The computing resources of this platform are a 4-plus-1 Cortex-A15 ARM processor and an Nvidia Kepler GPU with 192 CUDA computing cores. Such computing core can afford required computing power for the experiments. The architecture details of Jetson embedded computing platform is shown in Table 2.

Table 2.   Nvidia Jetson TK1 embedded platform computing parameters.

Parameter	Value
ARM processor clock rate	2.3 GHz
DDR3 memory size	2 GB
GPU processor clock rate	0.85 GHz
Global memory size	1746 MB
L2 cache size	128 KB
Constant memory	64 KB
Shared memory size per block	48 KB
Register files size per block	32768

In the Hilbert transform stage, one thread block take charge of a whole receive channel's data sample processing, and each thread inside the thread block handles the Hilbert transform for each data sample. The size of the thread block is 256, thus if the total size of the receive channel data samples is larger than 256, the computing process repeats. In delay-and-sum processing stage, every thread block calculates the low-resolution image pixel values for a two-dimensional block of 16×16 pixels. Besides, the compute grid of the thread blocks is also two-dimensional, with the lateral

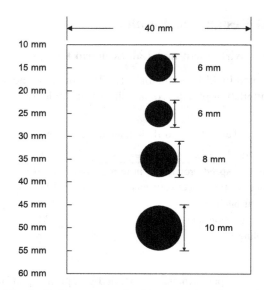

Fig. 6. Performance evaluation experimental scenario

size as one-sixteenth of the image lateral pixel size, and the axial size as one-sixteenth of the image axial pixel size.

Figure 6 illustrates the experimental scenario to evaluate the performance of the imaging algorithm implementation.

4.2   Experimental Results and Discussions

Figure 7 shows the experimental imaging output of the simulated scenario. As shown in Fig. 7, the high-definition quality of the medical ultrasonic synthetic aperture imaging was maintained by this high-performance embedded computing solution.

The computing performance improvement is shown in Table 3. As seen from Table 3, using the 4-core multi-core ARM processor can accelerate the medical ultrasonic synthetic aperture imaging algorithm by nearly 4 × speedup, and using the 192-core GPU can accelerate the imaging algorithm by around 85 × speedup, both compared to the single-core ARM processor's execution timing result.

As a result, accelerating the compute-intensive medical ultrasound synthetic aperture without distortion using high-performance parallel computing technique is a feasible. Thus, such platform can be used to facilitate other high-definition medical ultrasound imaging algorithms' acceleration and the future development of portable medical ultrasound imaging systems.

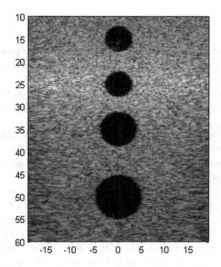

Fig. 7. Experimental output image of simulated scenario

Table 3. Imaging performance for various computing resources (number of operations = 28923002880 Ops).

Computing resource	Execution time (ms)	Throughput (Gflop/s)
Single-core ARM processor	192160.000	0.15
Multi-core ARM processor	51649.500	0.56
GPU processing cores	2282.035	12.68

5 Conclusions

We investigated the acceleration feasibility of compute-intensive medical ultrasound synthetic aperture imaging algorithm on high-performance embedded computing platform with graphics processing unit in this paper. As the data independency of the synthetic aperture imaging algorithm and the high parallelization of the GPU processing units on the embedded computing platform, the embedded GPU cores' computational acceleration is 85 × as compared to the single-core ARM processor. Furthermore, the embedded implementation framework we have built can be easily used to build other high-definition medical ultrasound imaging algorithms, which will be done in our subsequent research.

Acknowledgements. This work is supported by "Guangzhou Science and Technology Program" (Key Laboratory Project, No. 15180007) and "the Fundamental Research Funds for the Central Universities (No. 2015ZM081)".

References

1. Ossowska, A., Junghyo, K., Wiesbeck, W.: A simulation for synthetic aperture radar with digital beam-forming in elevation. In: IEEE International Conference on Geoscience and Remote Sensing Symposium (IGARSS), pp. 1407–1410 (2006)
2. Krieger, G., Gebert, N., Younis, M., Moreira, A.: Advanced synthetic aperture radar based on digital beamforming and waveform diversity. In: IEEE Radar Conference (RADAR), pp. 1–6 (2008)
3. Rincon, R.F., Fatoyinbo, T., Ranson, J., Sun, G., Perrine, M., Bonds, Q., Valett, S., Seufert, S.: Digital beamforming synthetic aperture radar (DBSAR) polarimetric operation during the Eco3D flight campaign. In: IEEE International Conference on Geoscience and Remote Sensing Symposium (IGARSS), pp. 1549–1552 (2012)
4. Ylitalo, J.T., Ermert, H.: Ultrasound synthetic aperture imaging: monostatic approach. IEEE Trans. Ultrason. Ferroelectr. Freq. Contr. 4(3), 333–339 (1994)
5. Nikolov, S.I., Jensen, J.A., Tomov, B.G.: Fast parametric beamformer for synthetic aperture imaging. IEEE Trans. Ultrason. Ferroelectr. Freq. Contr. 55(8), 1755–1767 (2008)
6. NVIDIA Tegra K1: A new era in mobile computing. Nvidia, Corp., White Paper (2014)
7. Wolf, M.: High-Performance Embedded Computing: Applications in Cyber-physical Systems and Mobile Computing. Newnes, Amsterdam (2014)
8. Jong-Ho, P., Changhan, Y., Jin-ho, C., Yangmo, Y., Tai-Kyung, S.: A real-time synthetic aperture beamformer for medical ultrasound imaging. In: IEEE Ultrasonics Symposium (IUS), pp. 1992–1995 (2010)
9. Yiu Billy, Y.S., Tsang Ivan, K.H., Yu Alfred, C.H.: GPU-based beamformer: fast realization of plane wave compounding and synthetic aperture imaging. IEEE Trans. Ultrason. Ferroelectr. Freq. Contr. 58(8), 1698–1705 (2011)
10. Choye, K., Changhan, Y., Jong-Ho, P., Yuhwa, L., Hwa, K.W., Min, C.J., Ihn, C.B., Tai-Kyong, S., Yang-Mo, Y.: Evaluation of ultrasound synthetic aperture imaging using bidirectional pixel-based focusing: preliminary phantom and in-vivo breast study. IEEE Trans. Biomed. Eng. 60(10), 2716–2724 (2013)
11. Jensen, J.A.: Field: a program for simulating ultrasound systems. In: Paper presented at the 10th Nordic-Baltic Conference on Biomedical Imaging Published in Medical & Biological Engineering & Computing, vol. 34, pp. 351–353, Supplement 1, Part 1 (1996)
12. Jensen, J.A., Svendsen, N.B.: Calculation of pressure fields from arbitrarily shaped, apodized, and excited ultrasound transducers. IEEE Trans. Ultrason. Ferroelectr. Freq. Contr. 39, 262–267 (1992)

An Improved Hierarchical Motion Estimation Algorithm

Jian Cao[1(✉)], Di Zhang[1], May Huang[2], Karl Wang[2],
Zhonghai Wu[1], and Xing Zhang[1]

[1] School of Software and Microelectronics,
Peking University, Beijing 102600, China
caojian@ss.pku.edu.cn
[2] Department of Electrical and Computer Engineering,
International Technological University, San Jose, CA 95113, USA

Abstract. High Efficiency Video Coding (HEVC) is the new generation video coding standard which provides equivalent subjective quality with 50 % bit rate reduction compared with the previous video coding standard H.264/AVC. However, to improve compression efficiency, HEVC introduces new technology and greatly increases the encoding complexity. Therefore, in order to solve the problem of high complexity of HEVC, this paper gives an improved hierarchical motion estimation search algorithm. The algorithm layers the images into four layers and uses different search template to do motion estimation. Experimental results show that the given improved hierarchical motion estimation search algorithm can reduce the encoding time up to 21.73 % on average compared with the TZ-Search algorithm. Therefore, the computational complexity can be reduced.

Keywords: HEVC · High resolution · Motion estimation · Search algorithm

1 Introduction

In recent years, because of the rapid development of network technology, video monitoring, digital TV, and mobile communications, video plays a more and more important role in human life. According to the forecast of Cisco white paper [1], the proportion of video traffic in the individual traffic will reach 80 %–90 % to 2018. Therefore, the technology of processing and transmission of video information in the network has become a focus of current global research, and HD ultra-high-definition video has become a mainstream. However, the original H.264/AVC video compression standard has been unable to meet the current market requirement for high resolution video compression [2]. In order to provide better video compression efficiency the ITU-T and ISO/IEC formally promulgated a new generation of video compression standard HEVC [3] at the beginning of 2013. This standard can save up to 50 % reduction in the bit-rate compared to previous standards without any video quality degradation. Although HEVC still adopts the hybrid video coding framework, it introduces a lot of new technology, such as flexible tree partition types [4], multiple directional intra-picture prediction [5], new motion merge mode, advanced motion

© Springer Science+Business Media Singapore 2015
X. Zhang et al. (Eds.): ESTC 2015, CCIS 572, pp. 23–29, 2015.
DOI: 10.1007/978-981-10-0421-6_3

vector prediction, DST transform mode [6], sample adaptive offset filter [7], advanced parallel processing technology and so on. Not only does the introduction of new technology improve compression efficiency, but also greatly increases the complexity and computation of video compression. And the motion estimation module is an important part of video compression [8], which has a great effect on video compression efficiency and complexity. Consequently, HEVC motion estimation algorithm has great significance for the promotion of HEVC in practice.

2   The Inter-picture Prediction Technology

The purpose of inter-picture prediction is to eliminate time correlation in the video sequence which is composed of multiple static images. Because the movement of objects in the neighboring images is small, even the background is almost the same, there is a lot of relevance. Compared with intra-picture prediction, the contribution of inter-picture prediction technology of video compression efficiency is greater.

2.1   Merge Mode

As the same as the previous video compression standard h.264 inter-picture prediction, each prediction unit has a motion vector, reference picture index in HEVC. HEVC adopts flexible data partition method, the size of the smallest piece is 4 × 4. If every piece transmits motion parameters alone, the motion information will take up a lot of bandwidth, and influence the efficiency of coding. To solve this problem, HEVC proposes a new inter-picture prediction technology, merge mode [9]. This technology uses the motion parameters of reference frame index and motion vector in the time-space domain encoded neighboring prediction unit. The process of merge mode is mainly to select the minimum cost of motion parameters from the candidate block which is composed of four neighboring block in prediction unit, and transmit the index of minimum cost block. The four type candidate blocks are: airspace candidate, the time domain candidate, the bi-directional prediction motion vector and zero motion vector. The total number of motion vector is defined at the beginning of slice, Merge process needs to delete the repeated and add new candidate. Motion merge technology can be used in skip mode of prediction units and inter-picture mode. This technology only need to transmit the unit tags, the merge index and residual signal which improves the coding efficiency.

2.2   Advanced Motion Vector Prediction

HEVC not only adopts the merge mode, but also cites the advanced motion vector prediction techniques [10]. When prediction units do not get motion parameters information through merge mode, it gets from the motion vector prediction technology. Due to the high correlation of the time and space, we only transmit the difference value between the current and predict motion vectors to save cost. The improvement of motion vector predict technology in HEVC is mainly that it adds two MV candidates from airspace and time domain neighboring blocks, but the decoding end needs to transport the corresponding index of the prediction motion vector finally. The establishment method of candidate list is same as the merge mode which chooses the available blocks from space and time neighboring prediction units, build temporal and spatial motion vector candidate list, remove the redundant candidate blocks, and add zero vector to make the length of candidate list constant. Finally, we select the best motion vector candidate block from the candidate list, and pass the index of the best motion vector candidate.

3 An Improved Motion Estimation Search Algorithm

The basic idea of hierarchical motion estimation search algorithm is to search the best block in the down-sample frame. The progress includes searching from the low resolution picture to the high resolution picture, and finally searching the original picture. Down-sampling the original image frames into multiple layer images, resolution decreases progressively from low-level to high-level. The motion search begins at the highest level, gradually to the lower level, in order to improve search precision, which uses the information obtained from the upper layer to search the next layer, and we uses all the information to search the original image in the end. The principle of hierarchical search method is that finding the best matching blocks in the highest layer image firstly, and then beginning the next layer motion search at the best matching point of upper layer. Therefore, this algorithm can effectively avoid motion estimation into local optimum, and improve the accuracy of motion estimation.

3.1 Image Layering

Method to realize the image slices is that initializing each frame image and layering the luma space of the original image to generate low resolution images which diminish one by one. We store the structure of each layer data in the frame structure, and the original picture can be sampled at most four times. If the original image resolution is 1080p and we down-sample it 3 times, the sampling process is shown in Fig. 1. The goal of image layering is mainly to search in low resolution image which absolute motion range smaller, additionally the computation and the search range is square growth. So the computation decreases.

Fig. 1. Image layering

3.2   The Starting Point Prediction

(1) First to search the highest level image the steps are as follows:

a. Partition the image into blocks whose size is 8 × 8, and store the information of each block.

b. Establish a candidate set of search center, including the motion vector obtained from the motion vector of the left, the up, the upper left and the upper right position in the corresponding macro-block of the reference frame, the motion vector at (0,0) position.

c. Set the search window, if the highest level is n (1 to 4), calculating the position of the search window according to the original search range and the position of the coding block.

d. According to the rule of sad, select the point which has the smallest matching error in the candidate set as the search center.

e. Search the up, down, left and right point around the center point, and save smallest matching error point as the new search center. Set early termination threshold to 125 according to UMHexagonS, if the matching error is less than this value, we argues that this is the best matching blocks, and early terminate search.

If not terminate, run the diamond search with its different stride length X in turn at the obtained search center using the search template shown in Fig. 2. X is 1, 2, 4, 8, 16, 32 or 64. Reset the smallest matching error point so far as the new search center.

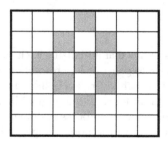

Fig. 2. Diamond template of 8 points

If the minimum cost is not less than the threshold value, run the diamond search using the template shown in Fig. 3. Save smallest matching error point to the corresponding data structure and update the search center.

Here we get the best motion vector value for this block in the highest level image. In order to get all the motion vector information of this layer, cycle above steps.

(2) Repeat the following steps from next layer image, in order to realize the motion vector iterative search.

a. Establish a candidate set of search center, including the motion vector obtained from the motion vector of the left, the up, the upper left and the upper right position in the corresponding macro-block of the reference frame, the motion vector get from the upper layer image.

b. Set the search window based on the search scope and the location of the block to be encoded.
c. Select the smallest matching error point as the search center of this layer from the candidate set.
d. Run the diamond search using the template shown in the Fig. 3, if the smallest matching error point is the search center, then stop the search, or reset the search center and repeat this step 4 times.

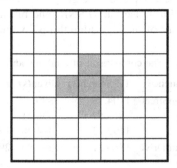

Fig. 3. Small diamond template

3.3 Original Image Searching

Due to the previous search in the lowest resolution images on a wide range, we get the rough position of optimal matching block. And on other layered image we iterate motion vector. After motion estimation of the layered image, the motion vector obtained from the lowest layer is very close to the best matching location of the original image. Therefore, in the original image, we just search the points around the motion vector obtained from layered images in order to get the best matching block. So we can save search time, find the best matching block quickly, and improve the search speed.

Here we add the best motion vector obtained from the lowest level image to the starting point candidate set of the original image, from which we select the smallest matching points as the search center. And then we run the diamond search using the template shown in Fig. 3, if the smallest matching error point is the search center, stop the search, this point is the final best matching point, or reset the search center and repeat the search. The following process is like x265. So far the improved hierarchical motion estimation search algorithm is finished.

4 Experimental Results and Analysis

Now we compare the given hierarchical motion estimation search algorithm with the TZ-Search algorithm in x265. In order to measure the performance of the algorithm, we choose 4 standard high resolution video test sequences as the input of encoder. The 2560×1600 resolution video sequence is PeopleOnStreet, and the 1920×1080

resolution video sequence is Kimono, Cactus, BasketballDrive. The experiments are performed on a server with Intel Core i5 processor of speed 2.40 GHz and 2.00 GB RAM.

In PeopleOnStreet, the background is simple but texture complicated, there are a lot of objects, and the movement of object is slow. In Kimono, the complexity of texture is high, the range of movement is large. In Cactus, background is static, the movement direction of the object is more, especially local motion. In BasketballDrive, the object moves violently. We use the TZ-Search algorithm and the given algorithm to test the seven sequences, respectively, and the test result is shown in Tables 1, 2, and 3. By encoding the standard video test sequence, we get performance data of video, including encoding time T, peak signal to noise ratio(PSNR) and bit rate. In the Table 1, we use ΔT to measure the complexity of the algorithm,the ΔT value is computed as:

Table 1. The comparison of total encoding time

Test sequence	TZ-Search(s)	Given(s)	ΔT(%)
PeopleOnStreet	1104.13	890.76	19.32
Kimono	815.52	636.21	21.99
Cactus	1192.33	994.28	16.61
BasketballDrive	1780.31	1263.86	29.01
Average	–	–	21.73

Table 2. The comparison of PSNR

Test sequence	TZ-Search(db)	Given(db)
PeopleOnStreet	36.679	36.672
Kimono	39.800	39.800
Cactus	35.980	35.978
BasketballDrive	36.858	36.864

Table 3. The comparison of bitrate

Test sequence	TZ-Search(kbps)	Given(kbps)
PeopleOnStreet	12245.35	12166.46
Kimono	1987.72	1982.74
Cactus	3207.80	3200.11
BasketballDrive	3696.74	3680.07

$$\Delta T = (Tstar - Tnew)/Tstar \times 100\% \qquad (1)$$

In the type, Tstar refers to the total encoding time of TZ-Search algorithm, and Tnew stands for the total encoding time of the given algorithm in this paper. Obviously, ΔT shows the percentage of the saved time for the given algorithm.

It is observed from Tables 1, 2, and 3 that the given algorithm decreases 21.73 % of the total encoding time on average, with the similar image quality and bit rate.

Compared with the TZ-Search algorithm, as the searching starting point can be accurately positioned to the location of the best matching block in the given algorithm, the total number of search points can effectively be reduced. Consequently, the efficiency of searching and the performance of the motion estimation search algorithm is improved.

5 Conclusions

This paper introduces an improved hierarchical motion estimation algorithm. The implementation of this algorithm is accomplished by layering images and using different search templates, which can reduce the amount of computation and achieve high search accuracy. The experimental results demonstrate that the given improved hierarchical motion estimation search algorithm improves the HEVC encoder encoding speed, reduces the encoding complexity, enhances the real-time property, and has important contributions to the popularization of the encoder.

References

1. Cisco, Visual Networking Index: 2013–2018 Forecast and Methodology (2014). http://www.cisco.com
2. Wang, J., Dong, L., Zhang, J.: A fast intra CU size decision algorithm based on spatial correlation in HEVC. J. Comput. Inf. Syst. **11**(7), 2605–2614 (2015)
3. Sullivan, G.J., Ohm, J.-R., Han, W.-J., Wiegand, T.: Overview of the high efficiency video coding (HEVC) standard. IEEE Trans. Circuits Syst. Video Technol. **22**(12), 1649–1668 (2012)
4. Yan, C., Zhang, Y., Xu, J., Dai, F., Li, L., Dai, Q., Wu, F.: A highly parallel framework for HEVC coding unit partitioning tree decision on many-core processors. IEEE Sig. Process. Lett. **21**(5), 573–576 (2014)
5. Wang, J., Wang, R., Li, W., Xu, D., Huang, M.: A high-capacity information hiding algorithm for HEVC based on intra prediction mode. J. Comput. Inform. Syst. **10**(20), 8933–8943 (2014)
6. Saxena, A., Fernandes, F.C.: DCT/DST-Based transform coding for intra prediction in image/video coding. IEEE Trans. Image Process. **22**(10), 3974–3981 (2013)
7. Subramanya, P.N., Adireddy, R., Anand, D.: SAO in CTU decoding loop for HEVC video decoder. In: 2013 International Conference on Signal Processing and Communication (ICSC) (2013)
8. Chen, H., Chen, P., Ciou, J.: A low complexity bit-transform based sorting scheme on partial distortion search for fast optimal motion estimation. J. Comput. Inf. Syst. **8**(2), 665–674 (2012)
9. JCT-VC: HEVC test model 8 (HM 8) encoder description. In: JCTVC-J1002, JCT-VC Meeting, Stockholm, July 2012
10. McCann, K., Han, W., Kim, I.: Samsung'Response to the call for proposals on video compression technology. In: ITU-T SG16 WP3 and ISO/IEC JTC1/SC29/WG11, JCTVC-A124, 1st Meeting: Dresden, DE, April 2010

Distributed Design and Implementation of SVD++ Algorithm for E-commerce Personalized Recommender System

Jian Cao[1(✉)], Hengkui Hu[1], Tianyan Luo[2], Jia Wang[2], May Huang[2], Karl Wang[2], Zhonghai Wu[1], and Xing Zhang[1]

[1] School of Software and Microelectronics,
Peking University, Beijing 102600, China
caojian@ss.pku.edu.cn
[2] Department of Electrical and Computer Engineering,
International Technological University, San Jose, CA 95113, USA

Abstract. Recommender systems can facilitate people to get effective information from the massive data, and it is the hot research currently in data mining. SVD++ is a kind of effective single model recommendation algorithm, which is based on the matrix decomposition combined with the neighborhood model. On the Spark, using the Stochastic Gradient Descent, this paper realized the distributed SVD++ algorithm through the Scala, deployed and applied the algorithm into an actual recommendation product for testing. The testing results represent that the distributed SVD++ algorithm succeeded in solving problems of terabytes of data processing in the e-commerce recommendation and the sparse data of user-item matrix, enhancing the quality in personalized commodity recommendation.

Keywords: Recommender system · Matrix decomposition · SVD++ · Distributed computation · E-commerce

1 Introduction

The basic task of recommender system is to contact users and items, to solve the problem of information overload. Recommender systems provide users with personalized suggestions about products or services to help customers easily find their favorite commodity in the tens of thousands of items [1, 2]. Now recommender system refers to the personalized recommendation system [3], which depends on the user's behavior data, generally existed in the website as an application. In nowadays e-commerce sites, the amount of data is very large, their user item matrixes has significant data sparseness problem, that is only a few users have history behavior or hit rating on a few commodities [4]. Score matrix's sparse problems will seriously affect the performance of the recommendation algorithm. The matrix decomposition method can be used to do dimension reduction to user items matrixes, for the original matrix, finding the best low dimensional approximation which can solve the problem of data sparsity in a certain sense [5].

© Springer Science+Business Media Singapore 2015
X. Zhang et al. (Eds.): ESTC 2015, CCIS 572, pp. 30–44, 2015.
DOI: 10.1007/978-981-10-0421-6_4

This paper has studied using SVD++ algorithm to improve recommendation quality of the personalized items in the recommender system, namely recalling the potential interested items to customers as much as possible, and impressed to the users in a reasonable order. SVD++ algorithm, proposed by Yehuda Koren, a matrix decomposition algorithm combined with neighborhood model [3], is an effective single recommendation algorithm. It can at the same time use the explicit and implicit user feedback data, through machine learning method, convert matrix decomposition problem to the optimization of machine learning problem, thus solving it more effectively. Todays in large e-commerce companies the amount of data has been achieved the level of TB, even PB. In order to apply SVD++ algorithm to recommendation problems of large-scale data sets, this paper tries to realize the distributed computing of the SVD++ algorithm.

2   SVD++ Algorithm and Evaluation Method

2.1   SVD++ Algorithm

SVD++ Algorithm adds history score item to the Latent Factor Model. Bias Latent Factor Model's formula is as follows [6]:

$$\hat{r}_{ui} = \mu + b_u + b_i + p_u^T \cdot q_i \tag{1}$$

In the formula $\hat{r}_{ui}$ represents the prediction score of user u's interest in item i, the greater score means the better effect; μ represents the global average; bu and bi, respectively represent user bias and item bias; pu and qi represent user matrix and commodity matrix respectively.

Item-based Collaborative Filtering can be rewritten as follows:

$$\hat{r}_{ui} = \frac{1}{\sqrt{|N(u)|}} \sum_{j \in N(u)} w_{ij} \tag{2}$$

In the formula, wij is no longer a similarity matrix of the item, but a learning parameters to complete, N(u) represents a collection of items that users like.

So SVD++ Algorithm's formula can be represent as:

$$\hat{r}_{ui} = \mu + b_u + b_i + p_u^T \cdot q_i + \frac{1}{\sqrt{|N(u)|}} x_i^T \sum_{j \in N(u)} y_j \tag{3}$$

xi and yj are two dimensional vectors of F. Here to substitute wij with xiTyj.

Koren puts forward that in order not to increase too much parameter that cause over-fitting, x = q can be made, and eventually SVD++ model is obtained [7]:

$$\hat{r}_{ui} = \mu + b_u + b_i + q_i(p_u^T + \frac{1}{\sqrt{|N(u)|}} x_i^T \sum_{j \in N(u)} y_j) \tag{4}$$

The above parameters are with the following meaning:

(1) μ The global average of all the records of score in the training set. This represents the influence of site itself to user ratings.
(2) bu The user bias. This represents the attribute factors part of the coring habit that only has the relationship with user.
(3) bi Item bias. This one represents that part of the scores of items that only has the relationship with items.

By computing the partial derivative of the loss function according to various parameters, the iterative formula can also be deduced. it is needed to optimize parameters as follows [8]:

The optimized parameters used in this article are characteristic dimensions - rank, Number of Iterations - numIter, step length - gamma1, step length - gamma2, regular terms - lambda1, regular terms - lambda2, learning rate - slowRate.

2.2   Algorithm Evaluation Method

There are mainly two kinds of experimental methods to evaluate the recommendation system, respectively are offline evaluating and online evaluation. This paper has used the online experiment method, specifically the A/B testing [7].

A/B testing is a commonly used experimental method of online evaluation algorithm [9]. First of all, by certain rules, users are separated into several groups randomly, and are applied to different algorithms to different groups of users. Through counting different evaluating indicators of different groups of users to compare different algorithms, such as counting user hits of different groups, compare the performance of the algorithm by the degree of the relative size of hits. Figure 1 is a simple diagram of the A/B testing system [7].

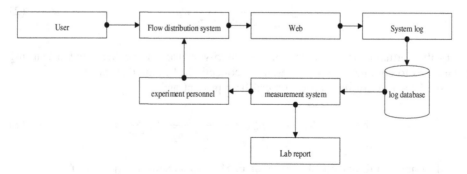

Fig. 1. A/B-test system

3   SVD++'s Distributed Design and Implementation on Spark

3.1   Spark Distributed Computing Platform

The Spark is a scalable data analysis platform based on In - Memory Computing, which has more performance advantages than Hadoop cluster storage method [10]. Spark uses the Scala language and provides a single data processing environment. Spark's features are showed on Resilient Distributed Datasets. It is a fault-tolerant, parallel data structure, which allows users to explicitly store the data into disk and memory, and to control the data partition. Spark GraphX is a distributed figure processing framework. Based on Spark platform, it provides concise, easy-to-use and colorful interfaces for graph calculation and graph mining, bringing great convenience to user demands for distributed figure processing [11].

3.2   Stochastic Gradient Descent Optimization Method

Gradient Descent is a common method of risk-minimizing function and loss function [12]. Stochastic Gradient Descent (SGD) is an iterative solution. Stochastic gradient descent is iteratively updated one time by every sample. In a large sample size such as hundreds of thousands of cases, it may only need tens of thousands or only thousands of samples to iterate the parameter to the optimal solution [13]. For the batch gradient descent, an iteration need to use tens of thousands of training samples, and an iteration may not the best, the 10-time iteration will need to traverse the training sample 10 times [14]. SGD, however, has a problem with it - the noise, which makes the SGD is not in the direction of the overall optimization on each iteration [15].

In this paper, the stochastic gradient descent method is to separate the user and commodity, fix one, update another individually. Because of the large training data set used in this article, which takes up more memory, separately update, can only put half of the data in the memory to do iteration every time, so as to reduce the computational complexity of each iteration. Tests represent that this will cause that the parameter update convergence speed is higher than the convergence speed of putting all the data of user and items into memory at the same time.

3.3   Distributed Design and Implementation Process of the SVD++ Algorithm

In this paper, Spark GraphX graph computing framework of the Spark platform is used to carry out distributed design and implementation of the SVD++ algorithm.

The key of distributed design is how to divide the data into different blocks, so that each block can be independent, and then different data blocks are distributed to different computing nodes. Variables can be divided into two categories, one is related to the user, one is related to the item, and SGD is used to update the two kinds of variables. User ratings according to the user and the item were divided into blocks, each block must have the required scores to updated the corresponding variables, while the users and the items is sent to different pieces of the calculation, and thus effectively complete distributed computing of the SVD++ algorithm.

To sum up, distributed implementation of the SVD++ algorithm is to assign the users and the items of a latent factor model to a cluster of hundreds of machines, and then use user ratings to optimize the model.

The realization of the algorithm steps are as follows:

Step 1: read the log file data, complete the digitalizing of user's and commodity's name, initialize vector at the same time.

Step 2: calculate the mean global miu: through the whole data set, add the score matrix and calculate the number of scoring at the same time; the former value can be divided by the latter to obtain miu.

Step 3: construct the graph model.

Step 4: calculate parameter values.

Calculate the mean score of each user and each commodity, namely each user's bias and commodity bias.

The history of the user behavior (i.e., read or add to cart or buy items), in order to calculate $1/|N|$.

Step 5: training model.

Training user node function, is used in fixing commodity factor and training the user factor;

Training commodity node function is used in fixing user factor and training commodity factor.

Step 6: the specific training process.

Fix q, update p, namely fix commodity factor, and update user factor and bias.

First, calculate $Pu + |N(u)| \wedge (0.5) * sum (y)$ of each user;

And then update the user factor and bias.

Fix p, update q, namely fix user factor, update commodity factor, neighborhood grade y and commodity bias.

(1) First, calculate $Pu + |N(u)| \wedge (0.5) * sum (y)$ of each user;
(2) And then update the commodity factor, the neighborhood grade y and commodity bias.
(3) Remember to update step size after every training session.

4   Experimental Design and Test Analysis

4.1   Experimental Design and Application Deployment

The recommendation strategy this article used is to transfer recommend problems into score predict problems, then using SVD++ algorithm to predict ratings for items, and according to the grading sorting to make recommendation for users. Figure 2 is the flow chart of SVD++ algorithm applied for e-commerce recommender system.

Data Pre-processing. Data sources contain four parts of users' behavior, namely, the user's browsing data, attention or collection data, data added to cart and the purchase order. After logging out the original data from the website, the preliminary filter treatment has been carried on: to filter out enterprise users, and only preserve personal

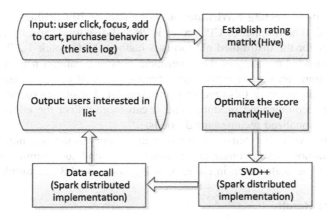

Fig. 2. SVD++ algorithm applied for e-commerce recommender system flow chart

user data; to filter out pates, failure Stock Keeping Unit (SKU) or invalid SKU caused by other reason; Due to the Standard Product Unit (SPU) granularity is more in line with the recommended logical meaning and more relevant to the user's interest model, so commodities SKU has been transferred into the SPU.

Design and Optimization of Score Matrix. The data needed by SVD++ algorithm is the user's commodity score matrix. The data which extracted from web, although has done some business processing, but still need to annotate them in the right way and build up the score matrix, so the algorithm can be used normally. The following is the elaboration to the electronic commerce recommender system's grading design rules of the matrix and its optimization method.

The user feedback data for items usually have five typical types: browse, search, click, attention/collect and add to cart, buy, and explicit feedbacks such as rating or review. These behavior data reflects that the weight of user's interest in the items is different and substantially increased in turn. From SVD++ algorithm is derived from the hidden factor model, it can be known that the main mining target of SVD++ algorithm is the user's potential interest. It mainly uses implicit feedback behavior of users, and the actual users' explicit feedback behavior for items usually is very limited, for example, the majority of users have not the habit of marking comment for the items. So this paper mainly adopts the four kinds of user's recessive feedback behavior to items, including browse, attention, add to cart and buy.

Considering the differences of the weight of user's interest from the different feedback behavior from users for items, this paper takes a 5-point system: the user views within 3 times (containing) is 2.6 points, browses more than five times (not included) or browses the 3 to 4 times at the same time and there is concern or collection behavior is 3.0 points, the add to cart behavior is 3.5 points, an order behavior is 4.5 points, more than twice (containing) order is 5.0 points.

The time factor for further optimization can also be considered.

The Deployment of Testing Environment. For a total of 70 machines, each machine memory is 56 G. The number of CPU cores is 28 and disk total capacity is 2 PB. The version number for the distributed platforms is hadoop-2.2.0, spark-1.2.0.

The recommended products of the experiment choose a column named "guess you like". The column can utmost reflects the characteristics of personalized recommendation, because the scene of this product is the weakest. Therefore experiments will be located on the recommended products, and it can more reflect the effect of SVD++ algorithm in personalized recommended goods.

Experiments involve the items which cover all category of the site, number of users is on tens-of-millions level, commodity number is on hundreds-of-millions level, and the data need to be dealt with in the experiment is on the TB magnitude.

4.2   The Test Results

This section uses A/B testing method for doing a synchronous contrast experiment on line testing to SVD++ algorithm. The online benchmark experiment is based on the Item-based CF recommendation algorithm. Online recommendation report usually adopts evaluation index to measure the effect of the various experimental methods of different recommender system, which mainly include request, display, click, orders and price. Request quantity represents the user traffic to your website, and display quantity is the amount of website commodity exposure under the user request. Hits is the user's clicks on items, quantity of orders is the items' amount users bought, and the price is unit price for the item.

The main parameters in this article are Request Conversion Rate (RCVR), Conversion Rate refers to the order quantity divided by the amount of requests, Gross Merchandise Volume (GMV) is the product of sales price and sales quantity.

Coverage:

$$\text{Coverage} = \text{Display Quantity/Request Quantity}. \tag{5}$$

Click Through Rate (CTR):

$$\text{CTR} = \text{Hits/Display Quantity}. \tag{6}$$

Click Conversion Rate (CCVR):

$$\text{CCVR} = \text{Order Quantity/Hits}. \tag{7}$$

Impression Conversion Rate (ICVR):

$$\text{Display Conversion Rate} = \text{Order Quantity/Display Quantity}. \tag{8}$$

Request Conversion Rate (RCVR):

$$RCVR = \text{Order Quantity/Request Quantity.} \tag{9}$$

Gross Merchandise Volume (GMV):

$$\text{Sales Revenue} = \text{Sale Price} * \text{Sales Quantity.} \tag{10}$$

Statistics Indicators of Test Evaluation. The Following are a statistics chart extracted from online A/B testing experiment. The time interval of experiment statistical data is from February 19, 2015 to March 1, 2015, totals 11 days. In the 11 days, the request, display, click, order and average data of this benchmark model Item-based CF and test model SVD++ are shown in Table 1.

Table 1. Business statistics of benchmark model Item-based CF and test model SVD++

A total of 11 days	Item-based collaborative filtering	SVD++
Request	62233152	24021521
Display	2790711	2136821
Click	32080	44755
Order	45	53
Average price	1647.08	3429.95

Table 2. Coverage

Date	Item-based CF	SVD++
20150219	0.04541036	0.09699144
20150220	0.04577684	0.09653428
20150221	0.04637238	0.09396935
20150222	0.04695301	0.09125606
20150223	0.04749833	0.09165352
20150224	0.04562790	0.08823611
20150225	0.04374205	0.08386233
20150226	0.04204751	0.08046467
20150227	0.04374723	0.08492822
20150228	0.04293864	0.08343252
20150301	0.04287641	0.08304753

Figure 3 is a graph based on the data from Table 2. The horizontal axis represents time, and the vertical axis represents the coverage of the two different methods.

Based on the data of Fig. 3, Coverage's formula is:

Sum(CF) = 0.49299065, Sum(SVD++) = 0.97437603.

Ratio = Sum(SVD++)/Sum(CF) * 100 % = 198 %.

SVD++ is 1.98 times than the benchmark model CF for Coverage.

Figure 4 is a graph based on the data from Table 3. The horizontal axis represents time, and the vertical axis represents the click through rate of the two methods.

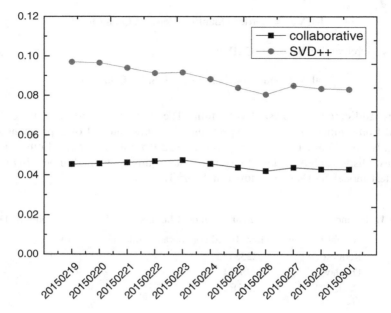

Fig. 3. Coverage

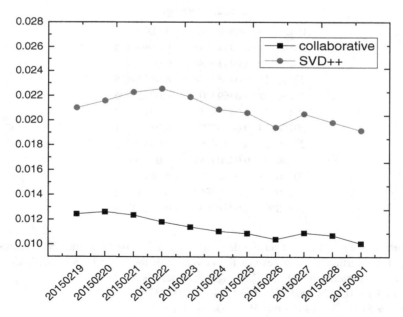

Fig. 4. CTR

Table 3. CTR

Date	Item-based CF	SVD++
20150219	0.01244407	0.02102437
20150220	0.01260828	0.02158315
20150221	0.01236271	0.02227533
20150222	0.01181024	0.02255305
20150223	0.01139838	0.02188653
20150224	0.01105066	0.02088070
20150225	0.01088227	0.02061793
20150226	0.01041635	0.01941242
20150227	0.01092723	0.02053252
20150228	0.01072970	0.01981970
20150301	0.01007968	0.01916598

Based on the data of Figure *******4.33, CTR's formula is:
Sum(CF) = 0.12470957, Sum(SVD++) = 0.22975168.
Ratio = Sum(SVD++)/Sum(CF) * 100 % = 184 %.
SVD++ is 1.84 times than the benchmark model CF for CTR.
Figure 5 is a graph based on the data from Table 4. The horizontal axis represents time, and the vertical axis represents the Click Conversion Rate.
Based on the data of Fig. 4, CCVR's formula is:
Sum(CF) = 0.01519496, Sum(SVD++) = 0.01328705.
Ratio = Sum(SVD++)/Sum(CF) * 100 % = 87 %.
SVD++ is 0.87 times than the benchmark model CF for CCVR.

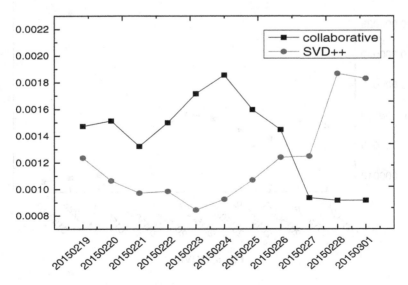

Fig. 5. CCVR

Table 4. CCVR

Date	Item-based CF	SVD++
20150219	0.00147275	0.00123653
20150220	0.00151384	0.00106496
20150221	0.00132205	0.00097182
20150222	0.00149981	0.00098522
20150223	0.00171674	0.00084412
20150224	0.00185615	0.00092535
20150225	0.00159744	0.00106980
20150226	0.00144665	0.00124069
20150227	0.00093633	0.00124961
20150228	0.00091617	0.00186800
20150301	0.00091701	0.00183094

Figure 6 is a graph based on the data from Table 5. The horizontal axis represents time, and the vertical axis represents the Impress Conversion Rate.

Based on the data of Fig. 6, ICVR's formula is:

Sum(CF) = 0.00017331, Sum(SVD++) = 0.00027456.

Ratio = Sum(SVD++)/Sum(CF) * 100 % = 158 %.

SVD++ is 1.58 times than the benchmark model CF for ICVR.

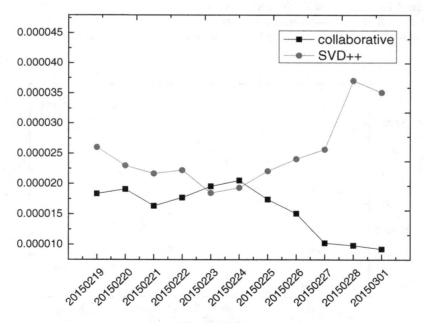

Fig. 6. ICVR

Table 5. ICVR (Order Line/Display).

Date	Item-based CF	SVD++
20150219	0.00001833	0.00002600
20150220	0.00001909	0.00002299
20150221	0.00001634	0.00002165
20150222	0.00001771	0.00002222
20150223	0.00001957	0.00001847
20150224	0.00002051	0.00001932
20150225	0.00001738	0.00002206
20150226	0.00001507	0.00002408
20150227	0.00001023	0.00002566
20150228	0.00000983	0.00003702
20150301	0.00000924	0.00003509

Figure 7 is a graph based on the data from Table 6. The horizontal axis represents time, and the vertical axis represents the Request Conversion Rate.

Based on the data of Fig. 7, RCVR's formula is:

Sum(CF) = 0.00000782, Sum(SVD++) = 0.00002417.

Ratio = Sum(SVD++)/Sum(CF) * 100 % = 309 %.

SVD++ is 3.09 times than the benchmark model CF for RCVR.

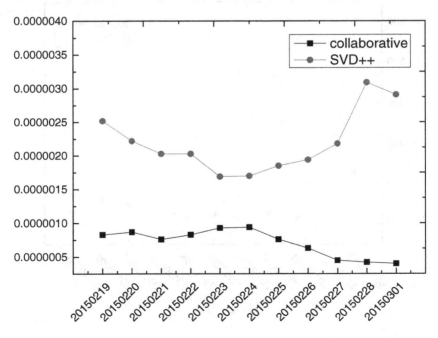

Fig. 7. RCVR

Table 6. RCVR

Date	Item-based CF	SVD++
20150219	0.00000083	0.00000252
20150220	0.00000087	0.00000222
20150221	0.00000076	0.00000203
20150222	0.00000083	0.00000203
20150223	0.00000093	0.00000169
20150224	0.00000094	0.00000170
20150225	0.00000076	0.00000185
20150226	0.00000063	0.00000194
20150227	0.00000045	0.00000218
20150228	0.00000042	0.00000309
20150301	0.00000040	0.00000291

Figure 8 is a graph based on the data from Table 7. The horizontal axis represents time, and the vertical axis represents the Gross Merchandise Volume.

Based on the data of Fig. 8, GMV's formula is:

Sum(CF) = 7245.23, Sum(SVD++) = 17683.91.

Ratio = Sum(SVD++)/Sum(CF) * 100 % = 244 %.

SVD++ is 2.44 times than the benchmark model CF for GMV.

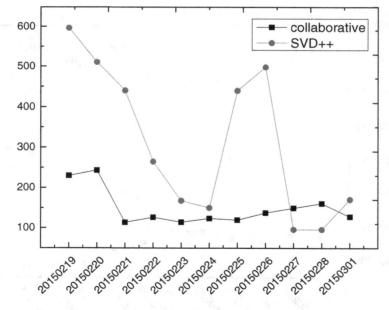

Fig. 8. GMV

Table 7. GMV (Unit: Yuan).

Date	Item-based CF	SVD++
20150219	229.96	596.32
20150220	243.28	510.56
20150221	113.68	440.41
20150222	126.42	264.85
20150223	114.34	167.49
20150224	123.79	149.91
20150225	119.73	439.89
20150226	137.64	497.86
20150227	149.50	96.07
20150228	160.75	96.07
20150301	128.00	170.52

4.3 Analysis of Test Result

The above online statistic results represent that SVD++ algorithm's dimension effects in the above statistics is better than the benchmark index Item-based CF algorithm. Except CCVR, Coverage increased 98 %, CTR increased 84 %, ICVR increased 58 %, RCVR increased 209 %, and GMV increased 144 %. the advantage is obvious, and CCVR of SVD++ was slightly lower than that of the Item-based CF, that is mainly because SVD++ hits is more than the Item-based CF, which leads to a big denominator.

5 Conclusion

In this paper, based on the current e-commerce needs and the current situation of the development of personalized recommender system, how to use SVD++ algorithm to improve the recommendation of personalized items quality problem has been studied. This paper has carried on the design and implementation of a distributed SVD++ algorithm, and applied the algorithm implementation in the actual test in the recommended products. In the process of application, this article is based on the electronic commerce recommendation background to confirm the optimization goal of SVD++, and the original data set also be optimized according to the business needs. The final test results represent that this paper successfully solved the problem of mass data processing in e-commerce personalized recommender systems, the size of its data upped to TB level, and it solved the problem of sparse matrix to a certain extent, and significantly improved the quality of the personalized product recommendation, the evaluation indicator, Coverage increased 98 %, CTR increased 84 %, ICVR increased 58 %, RCVR increased 209 %, and GMV increased 144 %.

References

1. Jia, Y., Zhang, C., Lu, Q., Wang, P.: Users' brands preference based on SVD++ in recommender systems. In: 2014 IEEE Workshop on Advanced Research and Technology in Industry Applications (WARTIA), pp. 1175–1178. IEEE Press, Ottawa (2014)
2. Hu., Y.F., Koren, Y., Volinsky, C.: Collaborative filtering for implicit feedback datasets. In: Proceedings of the IEEE International Conference on Data Mining (ICDM 2008), pp. 263–272. IEEE CS Press (2008)
3. Zhang C.Y.: A LBS-based mobile personalized recommendation system. Sci. Technol. Eng. **30**, 7439–7442, 7447 (2011)
4. Zhang, X., Niu, B., Zhao, J.: A novel data mining model based on SOAP in E-commerce. In: Ninth International Conference on Hybrid Intelligent Systems (HIS 2009), pp. 404–407. IEEE, Shenyang (2009)
5. Ren, F., Zhang, C., Liu, L., Xu, W., Owall, V., Markovic, D.: A square-root-free matrix decomposition method for energy-efficient least square computation on embedded systems. Embedded Syst. Lett. **6**, 73–76 (2014). IEEE
6. Funk, S.: Netflix Update: Try This at Home. http://sifter.org/~simon/journal/20061211.html
7. Liang, X.: Recommendation System Practice, pp. 179–193. People's Posts and Telecommunications Press, Beijing (2012)
8. Koren ,Y.: Factorization meets the neighborhood: a multifaceted collaborative filtering model. In: Proceedings of the 14th ACM SIGKDD Conference, pp. 426–434 (2008)
9. Hynninen, P., Kauppinen, M.: A/B testing: A promising tool for customer value evaluation. In: Requirements Engineering and Testing (RET), pp. 16–17. IEEE, Karlskrona (2014)
10. Lin, X., Wang, P., Wu, B.: Log analysis in cloud computing environment with Hadoop and Spark. In: Broadband Network & Multimedia Technology (IC-BNMT), pp. 273–276. IEEE, Guilin (2013)
11. IBM Corperation: Spark, an alternative for fast data analytics. http://www.ibm.com/developerworks/library/os-spark
12. Hanna, A.I., Yates, I., Mandic, D.P.: Analysis of the class of complex-valued error adaptive normalised nonlinear gradient descent algorithms. In: Proceedings of the 2003 IEEE International Conference on Acoustics, Speech, and Signal Processing (ICASSP 2003), vol. 2, pp. II–705–708. IEEE (2003)
13. Malago, L., Matteo. M., Pistone, G.: Stochastic Natural Gradient Descent by estimation of empirical covariances. In: 2011 IEEE Congress Evolutionary Computation (CEC), pp. 949–956. IEEE, New Orleans (2011)
14. Boukis, C.G., Papoulis, E.V.: A normalised adaptive amplitude nonlinear gradient descent algorithm for system identification. In: Proceedings of the 2003 10th IEEE International Conference on Electronics, Circuits and Systems (ICECS 2003), vol. 3, pp. 1042–1045. IEEE (2003)

Static Analysis Refinement on Defect Path Segment

Tianshuang Wu[1], Junwen Zhang[1(⊠)], Dalin Zhang[2], and Dahai Jin[3]

[1] School of Computer and Technology, Beijing Jiaotong University,
Beijing, China
{13120435,zjw}@bjtu.edu.cn
[2] National Research Center of Railway Safety Assessment,
Beijing Jiaotong University, Beijing, China
dalin@bjtu.edu.cn
[3] State Key Laboratory of Networking and Switching Technology,
Beijing University of Posts and Telecommunications, Beijing, China
jindh@bupt.edu.cn

Abstract. In this paper, we present a refinement method of static analysis based on path segment. The dataflow analysis generates the initial defect detection results and the defect path. Then the path constraints that might cause the defect are searched for on the defect path for a reported defect. Finally, all the path constraints are solved by a constraint solver. If no solution is found, the defect is a false positive, otherwise not. The comparative experiment on an embedded software of certain key field and the comparisons with similar tool PC-Lint show that our method has better analytical accuracy and efficiency.

Keywords: Static analysis · Path segment · Constraint solving · Embedded software

1 Introduction

Embedded software is widely applied in various safety-critical fields. These embedded systems' failure will bring great impact on people's work and life, and even cause significant economic losses and casualties. Software testing is an important way to improve the credibility of embedded software.

Software testing can be divided into dynamic testing and static testing. Compared with dynamic testing, static testing analyzes syntax and semantics of program statically rather than run them to detect defects, and it can find defects early in the software development process. Therefore, static testing is an important safeguard measure for embedded systems' credibility. False Negative Rate and False Positive Rate are two important indicators to measure the static defect detection. A false negative refers to the situation that a defect exists in the program while the static analysis did not report it. A false positive refers to the situation that the static analysis reported a defect while in fact it does not exist in the program. If the analysis results contain a large number of false

Supported by Foundation for Talents of Beijing Jiaotong University (Grant No. O14RC00010).

X. Zhang et al. (Eds.): ESTC 2015, CCIS 572, pp. 45–57, 2015.
DOI: 10.1007/978-981-10-0421-6_5

positives, identifying the real defects still requires a lot of manual labor and time. Therefore, in order to improve the accuracy of static analysis, how to reduce false positives is essential.

From this perspective, we propose a refinement method to eliminate false positives by searching path constraints and deciding their satisfiability. After dataflow analysis generates the initial defect detection result and the defect path, we forward search for the path constraints that might cause the defect on the defect path. Then, we post all the queried path constraints to a constraint solver. Finding no solution means that the defect is a false positive and furthermore the accuracy of static defect detection is improved. The process of searching for path constraints is along the defect path, and the defect path is obtained from the dataflow analysis. We implemented our method on DTS (Defect Testing System) [1–4]. The analysis results of an embedded software from a certain key field and the comparison experiment on our method and similar tool PC-Lint show that our refinement method can eliminate some false positives and has better analytical accuracy and efficiency.

The remainder of the paper is organized as follows. In Sect. 2, we illustrate our research motivation by an example and provide the research progress of this field. Section 3 firstly introduces the dataflow analysis, and then describes the thought and algorithm of our method in detail. In Sect. 4, we present the experimental results, followed by the conclusions in Sect. 5.

2   Motivation and Research Progress

Static analysis can be divided into path-sensitive analysis and path-insensitive analysis from the angle of abstraction and approximation of path. Path-sensitive detection method takes the combination relations between branches into account, so it can record the information of different paths on control flow graph, effectively reducing false positives. Compared with the path-sensitive analysis, path-insensitive analysis will generate more false positives due to the fact that dataflow information on different paths is merged at the confluence node of control flow graph or dataflow information is transferred on infeasible paths.

In order to achieve the balance between accuracy and efficiency, the dataflow analysis in DTS merges the symbolic dataflow information at the confluence node of control flow graph, implementing path-insensitive analysis. This means that it loses some path information, which will lead to the generation of false positives. Quote an example from reference [5], which is shown below.

```
1: int array [10];
2: if (x>0)
3:     f=1;
4: else
5:     f=0;
6: y=x;
7: if (f>0)
8:     array[y] =5; //OOB: y< 0
```

After a symbolic interval analysis, in line 2, the symbolic value of x is X (symbolic values of variables in this paper are expressed in capital letters), and its interval is $(0, INF]$; in line 4, the symbolic value of x is still X, but its interval is $[-INF, 0]$; in line 6, symbolic dataflow information is merged, and the symbolic value of x is X and its interval is $[-INF, INF]$. Since the dataflow analysis misses the implied path information "$x > 0 \&\& f == 1$" and the interval of y in line 6 is $[-INF, INF]$ (in line 6, y is assigned of x), DTS will report an OOB (out of boundary) defect in line 8.

In response to this false positive, reference [5] combines the forward dataflow analysis and backward constraint query techniques. It uses the conservative results of forward dataflow analysis to iterative defect status, getting an initial defect detection result. Then, by querying the potential constraints that might cause defects, the satisfiability of the initial defects could be determined by the collection of queried constraints, which refines the initial detection results. The constraints that the method mainly extracts are the direct and indirect path conditions of the program statement where the static analysis reported a defect. In the program fragment, the statement where the defect occurs is $array[y] = 5$ and its path condition is $f > 0$ (direct path condition). The defect is directly related to the variable y (y may be less than 0), and the variable which impact the defect's occurring is f and the variable which impact y's value is x. For f, there are two path conditions (indirect path conditions) of its definition statement: $x > 0$ and $x <= 0$. By comparing the obtained dataflow value (in this example, is $f > 0$) with $f = 0$ and $f = 1$, the choice between the true branch and the false branch is determined. But this process depends on accurate dataflow analysis results, so the choice between the true and false branch under path-insensitive dataflow analysis is difficult.

Wei et al. [6] propose a method based on segmented symbolic analysis, combining static analysis and dynamic execution. The method, which is mainly used to deal with the library function calls and loops that traditional symbolic analysis cannot analyze, partitions program on demand, dynamically executes the selected program segment, and applies regression analysis to the execution's input and output to generate symbol replacement rules. Xiao et al. [1, 2] use variables' value information to express the path state of program, so as to achieve the path-sensitive analysis. Zhou et al. [7], extending the original DTS symbolic interval field, propose interval abstract domain based on filed-sensitive point-to analysis and improve the detection accuracy of pointer related defects.

Based on the above analysis, our refinement method preserves the path information during the iteration of defect state machine instance. If static analysis reports a defect, the path constraints on the obtained defect path are extracted. The obtained defect path is a complete path, so there is no trade-offs between true and false branches. In addition, a constraint solver can handle complex constraint expressions and has high precision, so we can accurately determine if the reported defect is a true defect or not according to the solving results a constraint solver.

3 Research on Static Analysis Refinement

This section first introduces what is the dataflow analysis, and then describes the main thought and algorithm of our method in detail.

3.1 Basis of Dataflow Analysis

Abstract domain portrays the value information of the program variables and their relationships. The essential reason of defect detection imprecise is lack of dynamic execution information, and the most important dynamic execution information is the value of variables in the program. Calculating the abstract value of every variable on every program point is the basis of static defect detection based on abstract interpretation, which usually implemented by traversing programs' control flow graph and calling the corresponding operation of the abstract domain on control flow graph nodes. From the above, we can see that defect detection based on state machine is essentially a dataflow problem.

Definition 1 Control Flow Graph (CFG): $G = (N, E, entry, exit)$ is a control flow graph, where: N is the set of nodes, E is the set of edges, *entry* is the entry node, and *exit* is the exit node.

Data flow analysis framework $< D, S, \wedge, G, F >$ is the basis of DTS defect detection:

- D stands for the analysis direction, which can be forward direction or backward direction. The two directions of analysis are both useful.
- S stands for the status of program, namely the value set of variables at a certain moment. In particular, S_{entry} represents the initial state of program, and S_{exit} represents the terminal state.
- $\wedge$ is the aggregation operation on S.
- As shown in Definition 1, G represents the control flow graph of program.
- F is the state transfer function, and $F = 2^s$.

We can see that the solution of dataflow framework depends on the definition of aggregation operation $\wedge$. For an example of forward dataflow, there are three typical dataflow solutions.

The three typical solutions include: *Ideal (IDEAL)* solution, *Meet Over all Paths (MOP)* solution and *Maximal/Minimal Fixed Point (MFP)* solution. Supposing the dataflow problem discussed here is a forward dataflow problem and considering seeking the dataflow information at a program point n, the meaning of the mentioned three solutions is given below.

1. IDEAL

The *IDEAL* solution, the most accurate solution, is the actual execution information of program. *IDEAL* solution to the dataflow calculation can be expressed as:

$$\text{IDEAL}[n] = \bigwedge_{p \text{ is a feasible path from entry to } n} f_p(l_{\text{entry}})$$

Where: p is a feasible path from *entry* to n, and f is the transfer function.

The key is to determine the feasible path, but this is an NP problem.

2. MOP

The *IDEAL* solution is not available. So if unfeasible paths of program are ignored and all paths are treated as feasible path, then we can get the *MOP* solution which can be expressed as:

$$\text{MOP}[n] = \bigwedge_{p \text{ is a feasible path from entry to } n} f_p(l_{\text{entry}})$$

3. MFP

MFP solution is obtained by continuously iterating the dataflow equation on the control flow graph nodes to get a final convergence solution. The forward dataflow equation is shown below:

$$\text{IN}[n] = \bigwedge_{n' \, \varepsilon \, \text{pred}(n)} \text{OUT}(n')$$

$$\text{OUT}[n] = f_n(\text{IN}[n])$$

A further illustration of the three typical solutions is in Fig. 1. There are two paths on the control flow graph theoretically, but the upside path is an unfeasible path. *IDEAL* solution only calculates exit status on feasible a path, namely $\text{OUT}_{\text{IDEAL}} = f(y)$; *MOP* solution analyzes all paths, aggregating at the end of all paths, namely $\text{MOP} = f(x) \wedge f(y)$; *MFP* solution aggregates dataflow information at the confluence node of control flow graph, namely $\text{MFP} = f(x \wedge y)$. In the program fragment shown

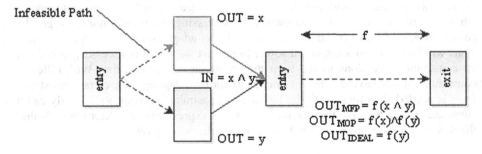

Fig. 1. Different solutions of dataflow

in Sect. 1, aggregation operation is done at the confluence node after line 5, giving an *MFP* solution, which leads to accuracy loss.

3.2 Constraints Solving on Defect Path Segment

Firstly, we give the concepts of Inspection Point and Defect Path.

Definition 2 Inspection Point (IP): The program statement where a defect occurs is called Inspection Point.

Definition 3 Defect Path (DP): Sequence of nodes on the control flow graph from the entry node to the node related to IP, namely DP = {VNode$_1$, VNode$_2$, VNode$_3$, ..., VNode$_n$}.

DP tracks a complete path when defect state machine instance iterates along the control flow graph.

Definition 4 Path Constraint (PC): At every branch on DP, the limited condition statement of true or false branch is the path constraint of the statements under the branch.

Our static analysis refinement method preserves the *DP* that the defect state machine instance iterates along. Once a defect is reported, the progress of searching for *PCs* on the obtained *DP* begins, which is followed by all path constraints and dataflow value of *IP* being posted to a constraint solver to determine the satisfiability of the defect. If the result of constraint solving is no solution, the corresponding defect is a false positive.

The whole procedure includes four steps. The first step is to extract the control flow graph nodes associated with the constraints that we want to get. According to the preserved defect path and the location of the defect, we search for every branch node on control flow graph from the entry node, and according to the true/false branch information stored in the edge of the control flow graph to determine to extract the conditional expression or its reverse. The second step is to extract the constraint expressions. On the abstract syntax tree of program, the conditional expression node contains a number of child nodes, some of which describe the constraint relationship, such as greater-than, less-than and equals sign, some of which describe the operators of the expression, such as addition, subtraction, multiplication and division, and some of which describe the variables or constants. By traversing every child node, we get the constraint expressions. The third step is constrains adaptation. All constraint expressions will be posted to a constraint solver in the last step, so it is necessary to convert all constraint expressions to the form the constraint solver specifies. With different constraint solvers having different constraint forms, adapting to a certain constraint form is needed. The fourth and the last step is constraints solving. We directly call a constraint solver to solve the obtained constraint expressions and determine whether the defect is a false positive or not according to the solving results.

This algorithm is as follows:

```
//Input:IP and DP; Output: YES/NO
Step1.
for (each vexNode in DP){
    if (vexNode is branchNode)
        {
            simpleNode=GetSimpleNode(vexNode);
            b=GetTrueOrFalse(vexNode);
            List.add(hashtable<simpleNode,b>);
        }
}
Step2.
for (each hashtable in List){
    pc=GetPC(simpleNode);
    domain=GetVarDomain(vexNode,PC);
    CovertToSolverVar(PC,domain);
    rc=CovertTSolverConstrainT(Pc);
    ConstraintList.add(rc);
}
Step3.
ConstraintList.post(solver);
solver.Solve();
Step4.
if (solver.hasSolution())
    return YES;
else return NO;
```

A description of the above algorithm:

- *GetSimpleNode(vexNode)*: Get the abstract syntax tree node corresponding to the control flow graph node *vexNode*;
- *GetTrueOrFalse(vexNode)*: Get the true/false information from the out-edge stored on control flow graph node *vexNode*;
- *GetPC(simpleNode)*: Get the constraint expression from the abstract syntax tree node *simpleNode*;
- *GetVarDomain(vexNode, PC)*: Get the interval information for all variables that appear in the constraint expression *PC* from the control flow graph node *vexNode*;
- *CovertToSolverVar(PC)*: Convert all variables that appear in constraint expression *PC* to the form the constraint solver specifies;
- *CovertTSolverConstraint(PC)*: Convert the constraint expression *PC* to the form the constraint solver specifies;
- *ConstraintList.post(solver)*: Post all the constraints to a constraint solver instance;
- *Solve()*: Call the constraint solver to solve all the constraints that posted to it;
- *hasSolution()*: Get a solution from the constraint solver.

Our goal is to determine whether the reported IP is a real defect by determining whether the preserved defect path is a feasible path, so we preserve all the control flow graph nodes on the path that the state machine iterates along. The sequence of these nodes comprises the defect path, and the true or false branch on this defect path determines the direction of the path. By extracting and solving the conditional expressions on these branch nodes, we can know whether the defect path is an infeasible path, and if so the defect must be a false positive.

The method is path-sensitive because of the iteration process of defect state machine instance is path-sensitive. The corresponding path information is preserved during the iteration process, and more important, every node on the path stores all variables that appear on the node and their interval information. The interval information is obtained by a path-sensitive analysis, which ensures the accuracy of the constraint solving result that we use to determine whether the defect is a false positive.

4 Experimental Results

We implement our method on DTS. DTS, defect-pattern-oriented, is a static defect detection tool, using the state machine to describe the defect pattern and checking if the target program violates the defect pattern within a framework of abstract semantic. The static analysis algorithm of DTS combines abstract interpretation, dataflow analysis, symbolic analysis, model checking, function summary and other technologies, It can statically detects source codes with context-sensitive and partial path-sensitive analysis. The overall analysis process of DTS is shown in Fig. 2, and the process can be summarized as five aspects [8]:

1. **Input**. This part collects the source files that can be compiled, and reads the defect patterns according to the defect pattern configuration files. For C/C ++ programs, the source files include all files in the project (.c/cpp,.h/.hpp files) and external libraries. For Java programs, the source files include the.*java* files in the project and external libraries (jar package).
2. **Basic process**. This part first generates the abstract syntax tree of source codes under test by a parser, and traverses the abstract syntax tree to generate symbol table, which contains the type, scope and other information of every lexical unit; then generates the control flow graph of every function and does *def-use* chain analysis with the help of control flow graph; finally, analyzes the function call relations to determine the detection order of functions.
3. **Semantic computation**. The results of abstract semantic analysis of program directly affect the accuracy of defect detection, so DTS respectively achieved partial path-sensitive innerprocedual analysis and context-sensitive interprocedural analysis based on function summary model.
4. **Automated testing and optimization**. Defect detection module iterates automat state in each function according to the reverse order of topology of function call relations. The state machine instance iterates along the control flow graph from the entry node. If the defect state transfers to *Error* state, it means that a certain type of defects is found; or it transfers to *End* state, it means that no defect is found and the state machine instance will be automatically destroy. Automated testing optimization uses the information obtained during the static analysis or the analysis results to

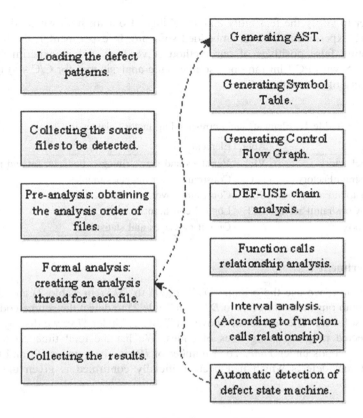

Fig. 2. Analysis process of DTS

optimize the accuracy of static analysis, so that the final defect detection results are more accurate and the confirmation of alarms is more efficient.

5. **Test results output**. The final test results and auxiliary alarm information is presented to users through the UI system for further analysis and confirmation.

We use Choco, a Java class library that can be used to solve the satisfiability problem of constraints, as the constraint solver in this paper. A constraint problem has three elements: variables, the domain of these variables and the constraint relationship on these variables. Choco uses *Factory Pattern* to describe constraints, providing corresponding factory class for each element, as shown in Table 1. The process of constraint solving includes the following steps:

- Create a Solver: *Solver solver = new Solver()*;
- Create variables by using the variable factories and initialize their domain;
- Create constraints by using constraint factories and post them to a solver instance;
- Launch the resolution process;
- Print search statistics.

In order to verify the feasibility and scalability of our method, we conducted two comparative experiments with an embedded software. In experiment 1, the feasibility of eliminating false positives of our method is verified; and in experiment 2, we compare DTS with PC-Lint (an open source static analysis tool for C/C ++) to verify the scalability of our method.

Table 1. Elements and corresponding factory classes in Choco

Factory	Abbr.	Element
VariableFactory	VF	Variables and views (integer, boolean, set and real)
IntConstraintFactory	ICF	Constraints over integer variables
SetConstraintFactory	SCF	Constraints over set variables
LogicalConstraintFactory	LCF	Logical constraints
Chatterbox	/	Output messages and statistics

4.1   Experiment 1

In experiment 1, we use the original DTS (refers to *DTS1* in Table 2) and the DTS optimized with our method (refers to *DTS2* in Table 2) to detect the source codes of an embedded software. The results are shown in Table 2. Under *Size*, we display the size of the detected program using lines of codes. We list the total time used for two methods in seconds under *Time*. Total number of *IPs* is given under *IPs* and the total number of real defects which had been artificially confirmed is given under *Real Defects*.

Table 2. Results of comparison experiment 1

Method	Size(Loc)	Time(s)	IPs	Real defects
DTS1	10898	342	48	23
DTS2	10898	481	39	23

As it can be seen from the experimental results, *DTS1*'s false positive rate is 52.8 % while *DTS2*'s is 41.1 %, which indicates that the proposed method can reduce false positives and improve the accuracy of static analysis. Our method improves the accuracy of static analysis from two aspects. Firstly, with the help of path-sensitive analysis, interval information of variables is more accurate, such that the extracted path constraints are more effective. Secondly, the constraint solver can deal with complex math operations that dataflow analysis cannot handle, which also eliminates some false positives to some extent.

The limitation is that our method cannot deal with some program variables of some types, such as structure, string, etc., resulting in a lot of condition expressions cannot being converted to constraints. In addition, the use of path-sensitive analysis makes detecting time greatly increased.

4.2   Experiment 2

Experiment 2 mainly compares the optimized DTS and PC-Lint to verify the scalability of the proposed method. The comparison result is given in Table 3.

We can conclude that DTS can find more semantic defects and potential riskiest than PC-Lint. Detection results of DTS include 39 *FAULTs*, of which the actual riskiest are 26; 2319 *RULEs*, of which the actual riskiest are 500 (using the *GOTO* statement results in some false positives); 587 *QUESTIONs*, of which the actual riskiest are 300. PC-Lint reports 5536 warning messages (it uses the standard *UNIX* encoding mode to check *OPENVMS*, generating many false positives that related with compilers and system selection and thus can be ignored) mainly for recurring of unused header files, duplicate macro references, casts, unused variables and other defects. As can be seen, DTS is more convenient and can detect more problems in semantics.

Table 3. Results of comparison experiment 2

Defect type	Defect description	PC-Lint	DTS
FAULT	Buffer overflow		✓
	Macro definition is wrong	✓	
	Casts	✓	✓
	Pointers may be empty	✓	✓
	Variables are not used	✓	✓
	Variables are uninitialized		✓
QUESTION	Header files are not used	✓	
	Duplicate macro references	✓	
	Functions must be defined before using	✓	
	Goto statement destructs program structure		✓
	External variables are treated as boundary in the cycle		✓
	Files including functions of static type must be called		✓
	Variables of type *void* can't be passed as a parameter		✓

In addition, we compare DTS with PC-Lint in terms of detection mode, detection strength, flexibility and so on, as follows:

1. Detection mode
   PC-Lint directly analyzes the source codes with complete deployment file structure and appropriate compiler options according to the system and hardware, so that the configuration management personnel must be familiar with setting up environment of PC-Lint.
   DTS uses intermediate files (.i files) which are compiled by a compiler to check source codes, saving more time to focus on the code checking.
2. Detection strength
   PC-Lint only checks grammars and simple semantics. DTS supports more semantic detection modes and checks context, such as the initialization of structure, unused variables and so on.

3. Flexibility

PC-Lint is an open source software that provides more parameters, compilers, and hardware selection parameters. It is more flexible, but requires more professional persons to provide technical support.

DTS only needs to be provided with compiled intermediate files and source codes files. It can analyze codes without a complete software compiling environment, and the checking rules can be configured according to the demand.

4. Detection time

PC-Lint is a detection tool that based on static codes without checking semantics. Detection time of a single file is about 30 s.

DTS checks codes according to the detection rules. More semantic rules, more time will be spend. For example, detection time for *Fault* rules is more than 2 h and for others is approximately 30 min. DTS can adjust the detection rules to satisfy the demand of time management for different software security levels.

5. Usage mode

The two tools are both used under Windows. PC-Lint provides command line mode only while DTS provides both interface and command line mode.

6. Detection Report

PC-Lint generates detection report in a fixed or a custom form; while DTS generates PDF report for different classifications, which includes defect samples.

5   Conclusion and Future Work

We present a static analysis refinement method on defect path segment. The dataflow analysis generates the initial defect detection results and the defect path. Once a defect is reported, the progress of searching for path constraints on the defect path begins. Then, all path constraints and dataflow value of inspect point are posted to a constraint solver to determine the satisfiability of the defect. If no solution is found, the defect is a false positive, otherwise not. The detection results of an embedded software show that our method can eliminate some false positives and improve the accuracy of static analysis. However, our method adopts path-sensitive analysis, making analysis time increases; and since the data type that can be dealt with is limited, part of extracted constraints cannot be solved. Therefore, how to improve refinement efficiency and how to deal with different data types are our future work.

References

1. Xiao, Q., Gong, Y.Z., Yang, C.H., Jin, D.H., Wang, Y.W.: Path sensitive static defect detecting method. J. Softw. **21**(2), 209–217 (2010)
2. Xiao, Q.: Research on Key Technologies of Improving the Accuracy of Static Defect Detecting. Beijing University of Posts and Telecommunications, Beijing (2011)
3. Zhao, Y.S.: Research on Symbolic Analysis Based Static Defect Detection Technique. Beijing University of Posts and Telecommunications, Beijing (2012)

4. Wang, Y.W.: Research on Software Testing Technology Based on Defect Pattern. Beijing University of Posts and Telecommunications, Beijing (2009)

5. Zhao, Y.S., Gong, Y.Z., Zhou, A., Wang, Q., Zhou, H.B.: False positive elimination in static defect detection. J. Comput. Res. Develop. **49**(9), 1822–1831 (2012)

6. Wei, L.: Segmented symbolic analysis. In: Proceedings of ICSE 2013, pp. 212–221. IEEE Press, San Francisco (2013)

7. Zhou, H.B., Wang, Q., Jin, D.H., Gong, Y.Z.: A static detecting model for invalid arithmetic operation based on alias analysis. In: Proceedings of the 2012 IEEE 23rd International Symposium on Software Reliability Engineering Workshops (ISSREW), pp. 183–188. IEEE Press, New York (2012)

8. Zhang, D.L., Jin, D.H., Gong, Y.Z., Wang, Q., Dong, Y.K., Zhang, H.L.: Optimizing static analysis based on defect correlations. J. Softw. **25**(2), 386–399 (2014)

3D Localization Algorithm for Wireless Sensor Networks Based on DCP and VRT

Guozhi Song$^{(\boxtimes)}$, Dayuan Tam, Dongyang Liao, Qianshen Lee,
and Rundong Lee

School of Computer Science and Software Engineering,
Tianjin Polytechnic University, Tianjin 300387, China
{guozhi.song,dayuan.tam,dongyang.liao,
qianshen.lee,rundong.lee}@gmail.com

Abstract. Localization is an important part of Wireless Sensor Networks technology, and the 3D location technology is more appropriate for real applications. We propose a novel 3D localization algorithm based on DCP (Degree of Coplanarity) and VRT (Volume Ratio of Tetrahedron). Simulation results indicate that the average location accuracy of the improved localization algorithm is much better than classical 3D DV-hop algorithm and Centroid algorithm. Moreover the stability of the new algorithm is better than others'.

Keywords: Wireless sensor network · 3D localization · Degree of coplanarity · Volume ratio of tetrahedron

1 Introduction

Wireless Sensor Network (WSN) is a rapid developing technique used to get information from real world and deal with it for humans. It has many characteristics including self-organization, robust, cheap and low-power. It has been applied in the fields of military affairs, industry and agriculture, medical treatment, smart home, etc. [1]. Localization, as a significant technology, plays an increasingly important role in Wireless Sensor Networks. Nowadays, position information is regarded as the fundamental information for a lot of applications, so the development of better localization techniques is much in demand [2].

The localization algorithms can be divided into two categories: Range-Based localization algorithms and Range-free localization algorithms [3].

Range-Based localization uses absolute point-to-point distance or angular information to get the locations. There are lots of common Range-Based Algorithms such as Received Signal Strength indication (RSSI) [4], Time Difference of Arrival (TDOA) [5], Angle of Arrival (AOA) [6], etc.

Range-free localization is usually employed to estimate the position of a node based on its connectivity with other nodes. There are some typical Range-free localization algorithms such as Distance Vector-hop (DV-hop) [7, 8], Centroid [9], Approximate Point in Triangulation (APIT) [10], etc. Compared with Range-free localization algorithms, Range-Based localization might have high hardware constraints and energy

© Springer Science+Business Media Singapore 2015
X. Zhang et al. (Eds.): ESTC 2015, CCIS 572, pp. 58–67, 2015.
DOI: 10.1007/978-981-10-0421-6_6

cost, with additional equipment requirements. So in this paper we focus on Range-Free localization rather than Range-Based localization.

In real applications, the nodes can be deployed anywhere, from underwater to high mountains. That means, they are deployed in a three dimensional (3-D) environment. Therefore 2D localization will not be able to meet the demands in the real world. It is necessary to develop the 3D localization technique.

With the development of localization technique, many outstanding and unique algorithms were proposed for many various problems and special areas. [11] proposed an improved 2D weighted Centroid algorithm and extended it to adapt to the 3D environment; [12] also extended their algorithm from 2D DV-hop to 3D DV-hop, meanwhile considering the coplanarity and projection.

On the other hand, unlike algorithms introduced above, [13] proposed a Constrain 3-D algorithm, calculating the position through the traditional triangular function. [14] constructs tetrahedron and use Centroid algorithm to calculate the unknown nodes' positions with the help of vector and matrix. [15] introduces the position estimation deviation into the Weighted Centroid algorithm based on other 3D localization algorithms.

In the paper, we propose a novel 3D localization algorithm, which based on the Degree of Coplanarity and Volume Ratio of Tetrahedron, to reduce the positioning error. The rest of the paper is organized as follows. Section 2 will introduce the background of the theory, and then the new algorithm is put forward in Sect. 3, and we also provide the procedure of the new algorithm and result analysis of thresholds; In Sect. 4, simulation results are reported. Finally conclusions are given in Sect. 5.

2 Theoretical Background

Before we introduce the new 3D localization algorithm based on DCP (Degree of Coplanarity) and VRT (Volume Ratio of Tetrahedron), the theoretical background of the proposed algorithm will be introduced in this section.

2.1 Novel Centroid Algorithm

A Novel Centroid algorithm is proposed in [16], it solves the three-dimensional localization problem by taking the centroid of tetrahedron as the unknown nodes' position. The tetrahedron is structured by four of the beacon nodes around the unknown node. The formula for the position of unknown nodes, according to [16], is:

$$Z_{c1} = (G_c^T G_c)^{-1} G_c^T h_{c1} \tag{1}$$

Where Z_{c1} means the unknown node's coordinates, G_c and h_{c1} are two parameters which can be calculated with the tetrahedron's four vertexes' coordinates. The detailed derivation process can be found in [16].

2.2 Degree of Coplanarity

DCP (Degree of Coplanarity) is used in the study of shape in tetrahedron in [17] and it is first used for WSN localization in [18], According to [17], we have:

$$\rho = \frac{216v^2}{\sum_{i=0}^{3} s_i \sqrt{(a+b+c)(a+b-c)(a+c-b)(b+c-a)}} \tag{2}$$

$$\text{DCP} = \begin{cases} 0 & , Coplanarity \\ \rho & , others \end{cases} \tag{3}$$

Where a, b, c are the products of the lengths of the opposite edges of tetrahedrons, v is the volume of the tetrahedron, the S_i is the summed area of the four faces of tetrahedron. The range of values of DCP is (0,1], while approaching 1 means the shape of tetrahedron is approaching the normal tetrahedron. Conversely, approaching 0 means the coordinates of vertexes of tetrahedron are approaching being coplanar.

2.3 Volume Ratio of Tetrahedron

We have introduced the Novel Centroid algorithm proposed in [16]. However, there is a high potential situation which will leading to a terrible localization error has not been discussed in [16] that it is possible that unknown node is located outside the constructed tetrahedron. So making sure the tetrahedron can encase the unknown node is essential. In order to ensure the unknown node exists inside the constructed tetrahedron, we set a threshold named VRT:

$$VRT = \frac{V_{MA_2A_3A_4} + V_{A_1MA_3A_4} + V_{A_1A_2MA_4} + V_{A_1A_2A_3M}}{V_{A_1A_2A_3A_4}} \tag{4}$$

As what has been showed in Fig. 1, M is the unknown node, the tetrahedron $A_1A_2A_3A_4$ is divided into four sub-tetrahedrons, $MA_2A_3A_4$, $A_1MA_3A_4$, $A_1A_2MA_4$, $A_1A_2A_3M$. We use their volumes to calculate the value of VRT. The VRT will equal to 1

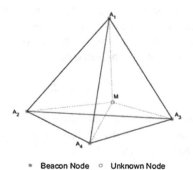

■ Beacon Node   ○ Unknown Node

Fig. 1. Division of a Tetrahedron into Sub-Tetrahedrons

when unknown node exists within the constructed tetrahedron. However, it is a pity that the coordinates of unknown node M is a measured values in real applications, that means the VRT may not be exactly 1. So it is necessary to discuss the relationship between the value of *VRT* and whether the unknown node exists inside the tetrahedron or not. Finally we will talk about the threshold of VRT in the next section.

3   3D Localization Algorithm Based on DCP and VRT

In this section, we will propose our 3D localization algorithm Based on DCP (Degree of Coplanarity) and VRT (Volume Ratio of Tetrahedron), for Wireless Sensor Networks Localization. We also analyze the thresholds of DCP and VRT after introducing the procedure detail of our proposed algorithm.

3.1   Procedure Detail of Our Proposed Algorithm

The procedure of our proposed algorithm can be summarized in five steps, which are as follows.

Step 1: All beacon nodes broadcast their positions within their transmission range. Each unknown node collects all the nodes ID, signals and calculates the distance between node and node.

Step 2: Each unknown node rearrange nodes ID they have been selected order by the distance between them and unknown node, then select four beacon nodes once (in the order of node number) to construct a tetrahedron.

Step 3: Make a decision based on the value of DCP of tetrahedron constructed in step 3, if it is less than the DCP threshold, continue to the next step. Else, go back to step 2 and construct next tetrahedron.

Step 4: Make a decision based on the value of VRT of tetrahedrons which have satisfied the condition in step 3, if is less than VRT threshold, continue to the next step. Else, go back to step 2 and construct next tetrahedron.

Step 5: Calculate the position of eligible tetrahedrons using Novel Centroid Algorithm which has been introduced in Sect. 2.1, then set the average of the series coordinates as the final coordinates of unknown nodes.

Two thresholds have been designed in our proposed algorithm in order to ensure the localization error low and stability high. In the next section, we analyze the most appropriate values of the thresholds of DCP and VRT, and we choose MATLAB as our analysis platform.

3.2   Degree of Coplanarity

Herein, we analyze the influence of the values of DCP on the localization error, by changing different parameters once a time, for example, the node number, beacon nodes ratio and communication range, which makes experiments more representative.

Considering logical integrity, Volume Ratio of Tetrahedron will not be included in our algorithm at this stage. Related experiment parameters are showed in Table 1. All series of experiments has been conducted 100 times and set the average of those results as the final result under corresponding situation.

Table 1. Parameters used in experiments about the impact of DCP

Figure No.	Figure 2(a)	Figure 2(b)	Figure 2(c)
Space	100 m*100 m*100 m	100 m*100 m*100 m	100 m*100 m*100 m
Number of Nodes	200	200	200
Beacon Node Ratio	15 %	30 %	15 %
Communication Range	50 m	50 m	70 m
DCP(ρ)	0.1–0.9	0.1–0.9	0.1–0.9

Figure 2 shows the location errors of our proposed algorithm in different DCP values from 0.1 to 0.9. We can observe that the location accuracy improves as the DCP increases. Meanwhile we also have experimented with the DCP which are above 0.9 but it turned out to be not stable enough. Finally we choose 0.9 as the best value of DCP threshold for it can balance the stability and localization accuracy.

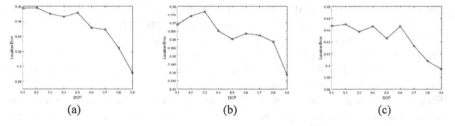

Fig. 2. (a) Impact of DCP upon Localization Errors; (b) Impact of DCP upon Localization Errors with different Beacon Node Ratio; (c) Impact of DCP upon Localization Errors with different Communication Range

3.3 Volume Ratio of Tetrahedron

In this Section, we will investigate the impact of VRT (Volume Ratio of Tetrahedron) on localization error, by conducting a series of experiments with different values of VRT from 0.7 to 5. The DCP threshold is set as 0.9 considering the conclusion we have got in Sect. 3.2. The results of experiments are shown in the Fig. 3. All series of experiments has been conducted 100 times and set the average of those results as the final result under corresponding situation.

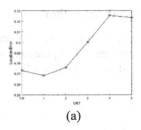
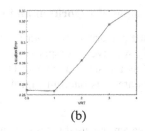
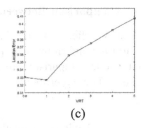

(a)   (b)   (c)

Fig. 3. (a) Impact of VRT upon Localization Errors; (b). Impact of VRT upon Localization Errors with different Beacon Node Ratio; (c). Impact of VRT upon Localization Errors with different Communication Range

All of the parameters are listed in Table 2.

Table 2. Simulation parameters used in experiments about the impact of VRT

Figure No.	Figure 3(a)	Figure 3(b)	Figure 3(c)
Space	100 m*100 m*100 m	100 m*100 m*100 m	100 m*100 m*100 m
Number of Nodes	200	200	200
Beacon Node Ratio	15 %	30 %	15 %
Communication Range	50 m	50 m	70 m
DCP(ρ)	0.9	0.9	0.9
VRT	0.9–5	0.9–5	0.9–5

It is obvious that increasing VRT values lead to the rise of location errors. In general, we are willing to make the VRT as smaller as possible to achieve a better performance. However, through the analysis we found that while VRT is decreasing, it result in a more and more unstable performance. Due to the uncertainty of estimation of distance between beacon node and unknown node, there will be localization errors less than 1 as we have found out in our simulations. Since the localization errors decrease slowly when the VRT is smaller than 1 and continue decreasing, we set 1 as the most appropriate value of VRT threshold for balancing the algorithm performance and stability.

4 Simulations Results and Analysis

We have introduced the original algorithm from [16] in Sect. 2 and described our proposed algorithm in Sect. 3. Then in this section, we will use proposed algorithm to do some simulations, comparing with original algorithm in Sect. 4.1 and some typical localization algorithms in Sect. 4.2. MATLAB was chosen as our simulation platform as before. All series of experiments have been conducted 100 times and the average of those results is treated as the final result under corresponding situation.

4.1   Comparison Between Proposed Algorithm and Original Algorithm

As stated earlier, to verify that the performance of our proposed algorithm is better than the original algorithm from [16], we give a comparison between them. The parameters used in our comparison are set as the same as that in [16], and all of them are list in Table 3. The experiment results are illustrated in Fig. 4.

Table 3. Simulation parameters used in tests upon localization errors

Figure No.	Figure 4(a)	Figure 4(b)
Space	100 m*100 m*100 m	100 m*100 m*100 m
Number of Nodes	100	200
Beacon node	10–20	20
Communication Range	40 m	30 m–70 m
DCP(ρ)	0.6	0.6
VRT	1	1

It can be observed from Fig. 4(b) that when communication radius is less than or equals 50, the algorithm proposed in this paper is obviously superior to the original algorithm, but when the radius is more than 50 the original algorithm becomes superior to the algorithm proposed by us. We can observe from Fig. 4(a) that the performance of proposed algorithm is always better than the original algorithm. In general, the stability of our proposed algorithm is always superior to the original algorithm.

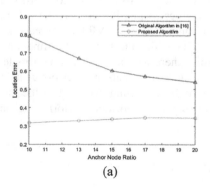
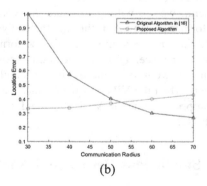

(a)   (b)

Fig. 4. (a). Comparison of Impact of Beacon Node Ratio upon Localization Errors between the Original Centroid Algorithm and Our Proposed Algorithm; (b). Comparison of Impact of Communication Radius upon Localization Errors between the Original Centroid Algorithm and Our Proposed Algorithm

4.2   Comparison with Some Typical Localization Algorithms

Next we will compare our proposed algorithm with some typical localization algorithms, which are traditional 3D DV-hop algorithm [15], classic Centroid Algorithm [16]. The comparison will be made in three different aspects.

It can be observed from above three Figures that Asterisked lines have the lowest location errors among the three algorithms. That means, compare with original 3D DV-hop Algorithm and classic Centroid Algorithm, with different Beacon Node Ratio in Fig. 5(a), different Communication range in Fig. 5(b), different Node Number in Fig. 5(c), the proposed algorithm always have the best performance, meanwhile maintaining a excellent stability (Table 4).

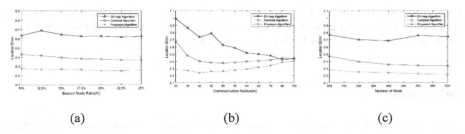

(a)   (b)   (c)

Fig. 5. (a). Comparison of Impact of Different Beacon Node Ratio upon Location Error; (b). Comparison of Impact of Different Communication Range upon Location Error; (c). Comparison of Impact of Different Node Number upon Location Error

In short, after comparing with the original 3D DV-hop Algorithm and classical Centroid Algorithm above, we can prove that our proposed 3D localization algorithm based on DCP and VRT has a great improvement in reducing location error. Moreover it has a better stability than others.

Table 4. Simulation parameters used in experiments about comparison with three algorithms

Figures No.	Figure 5(a) Comparison with different Beacon Node Ratio	Figure 5(b) Comparison with different Communication Range	Figure 5(c) Comparison with different Number of Nodes
Space	100 m*100 m*100 m	100 m*100 m*100 m	100 m*100 m*100 m
Number of Nodes	200	200	200–600
Beacon Node Ratio	10 %–25 %	20 %	15 %
Communication Range	50 m	30 m–100 m	50 m
DCP(ρ)	0.9	0.9	0.9
VRT	1	1	1

5 Conclusions

In this paper, we proposed a 3D Localization Algorithm Based on DCP and VRT for Wireless Sensor Networks localization, and we also have done lots of simulations and final results showed that the proposed algorithm can effectively reduce location errors and maintain stability than the two traditional localization algorithms. In addition our proposed algorithm is built in 3D environment, this means compared to current 2D localization algorithms, our proposed algorithm will be more appropriate for real applications. Thirdly we make full use of tetrahedrons to make algorithm easy. In the future, we will continue to improve and optimize the algorithm to get the balance of localization accuracy and complexity.

Acknowledgements. This work is supported by Tianjin Higher Education Fund for Science and Technology Development under Grant No. 20110808 and National Training Program of Innovation and Entrepreneurship for Undergraduates (201510058140)

References

1. Akyildiz, I.F., Su, W., Sankarasubramaniam, Y., Cayirci, E.: Wireless sensor networks: a survey. Comput. Netw. **38**(4), 393–422 (2002)
2. Mao, G., Fidan, B., Anderson, B.D.: Wireless sensor network localization techniques. Comput. Netw. **51**(10), 2529–2553 (2007)
3. Zhang, J., Yang, R., Li, J.: An enhanced DV-Hop localization algorithm using RSSI. Int. J. Future Gener. Commun. Netw. **6**(6), 91–98 (2013)
4. Rappaport, T.S.: Wireless Communications: Principles and Practice, vol. 2. Prentice Hall PTR, Upper Saddle River (1996)
5. Cheng, X., Thaeler, A., Xue, G., Chen, D.: TPS: a time-based positioning scheme for outdoor wireless sensor networks. In: Twenty-Third Annual Joint Conference of the IEEE Computer and Communications Societies, INFOCOM 2004, vol. 4, pp. 2685–2696. IEEE, March 2004
6. Torrieri, D.J.: Statistical Theory of Passive Location Systems (No. CM/CCM-83-1). Army Materiel Development and Readiness Command Adelphi Md Countermeasures/Counter-Countermeasures Office (1983)
7. Niculescu, D., Nath, B.: Ad hoc positioning system (APS). In: Global Telecommunications Conference, GLOBECOM 2001, vol. 5, pp. 2926–2931. IEEE (2001)
8. Niculescu, D., Nath, B.: DV based positioning in ad hoc networks. Telecommun. Syst. **22** (1–4), 267–280 (2003)
9. Bulusu, N., Heidemann, J., Estrin, D.: GPS-less low-cost outdoor localization for very small devices. IEEE Pers. Commun. **7**(5), 28–34 (2000)
10. He, T., Huang, C., Blum, B.M., Stankovic, J.A., Abdelzaher, T.: Range-free localization schemes for large scale sensor networks. In: Proceedings of the 9th Annual International Conference on Mobile Computing and Networking, pp. 81–95. ACM, September 2003
11. Xu, L., Wang, K., Jiang, Y., Yang, F., Du, Y., Li, Q.: A study on 2D and 3D weighted centroid localization algorithm in wireless sensor networks. In: 3rd International Conference on Advanced Computer Control (ICACC 2011), pp. 155–159. IEEE, January 2011

12. Wenxiu, C.Q.M.K.H., Ben, Z.X.S.: 3D localization algorithm based on degree of coplanarity and layered structure for wireless sensor networks. J. Electron. Meas. Instrum. **8**, 003 (2012)
13. Liang, J., Shao, J., Xu, Y., Tan, J., Davis, B.T., Bergstrom, P.L.: Sensor network localization in constrained 3-d spaces. In: Proceedings of the 2006 IEEE International Conference on Mechatronics and Automation, pp. 49–54. IEEE, June 2006
14. Li, H., Xiong, S.W., Duan, P.F.: Novel three-dimensional localization algorithm in wireless sensor networks. Comput. Sci. **39**(7), 54–55 (2012)
15. Jiang, Y., Feng, Y., Guan, F., Li, P.: Range-free three-dimensional node location algorithm for the wireless sensor network. J. Xidian Univ. **5**, 023 (2012)
16. Chen, H., et al.: Novel centroid localization algorithm for three-dimensional wireless sensor networks. In: 4th International Conference on Networking and Mobile Computing, WiCOM 2008, pp. 1–4. IEEE (2008)
17. Liu, A., Joe, B.: Relationship between tetrahedron shape measures. BIT Numer. Math. **34**(2), 268–287 (1994)
18. He, W., Chen, L., Mao, K., Shao, B., Chen, Q.: 3D localization algorithm base on degree of coplanarity for WSN. J. Inf. Comput. Sci. **10**(18), 5911–5918 (2013)

SEDOSN: A Secure Decentralized Online Social Networking Framework

Yuejian Fang[(⊠)], Zilong Wen, Qingni Shen,
Yahui Yang, and Zhonghai Wu

School of Software and Microelectronics, Peking University, Beijing, China
{fangyj,qingnishen,yhyang}@ss.pku.edu.cn,
{zlwen,wuzh}@pku.edu.cn

Abstract. Today's online social networking services (OSN) such as Facebook, Twitter are centralized. Users' information may be leaked by these service providers, which results in potential privacy problems. Decentralized online social networking (DOSN) is provided to solve the problems. This paper presents a secure decentralized online social networking framework named SEDOSN. A peer-to-peer (p2p) online networking system is designed, and attribute-based encryption (ABE) technique is used. Different to existing ABE schemes which relies on a single authority or several authorities to authorize users and generating decryption keys for uses, we firstly proposed an ABE scheme with discretionary authorization. In our system, each user can authorize his friend, and generate decryption keys for his friend based on his friend's attributes. We give our implementation and experiment results in the paper.

Keywords: DOSN · P2P · Attribute-Based Encryption · Discretionary authorization

1 Introduction

Today, online social networking sites such as Facebook, Twitter have millions of users using theirs services every day. These sites are centralized and present two problems: Firstly, the service provider of the online social networking site can secretly gather any user's private information without agreement from the user. Secondly, since data content are often stored in unencrypted form, they are in high risk.

Decentralized online social networking (DOSN) is provided to solve the problems [9]. In DOSN system, such as a peer-to-peer OSN system, users can store data on their local devices, disseminate information according to their preferences and friendship relations. Users can decide who to show the information to and what restriction there is on the data, thus privacy of the users can be ensued.

Furthermore, Data can be encrypted to enhance security. Attribute-based encryption [3] was introduced by Sahai and Waters and is regarded as one of the most suitable techniques for secure data access control. According to access policy, ABE can be classified as key-policy ABE (KP-ABE) and ciphertext-policy ABE (CP-ABE). In KP-ABE, ciphertexts are associated with sets of attributes, and user's keys are associated with access structure. While in CP-ABE, ciphertexts are created with an access

© Springer Science+Business Media Singapore 2015
X. Zhang et al. (Eds.): ESTC 2015, CCIS 572, pp. 68–74, 2015.
DOI: 10.1007/978-981-10-0421-6_7

structure, which specifies the encryption policy, and there is an authority to generate secret keys to the users according to their attributes. A user can decrypt the ciphertext if his attributes in the private key satisfy the access structure specified in the ciphertext. Many ABE algorithms have been proposed in recent years [4, 5, 15–20].

There have been many research works for secure OSN to protect users' privacy [1, 2, 7–12]. Some of the works [7, 8] use attribute-based encryption to secure the OSN. However, these works mainly focus on securing centralized online social network. When ABE is used for securing centralized OSN in these works, the common characteristic is that it relies on a single authority or several authorities to authorize users and generating decryption keys for uses. However, this would result in severe privacy risk. Since in an centralized OSN system which uses a single ABE authority, the authority can generating all the users' decryption keys, it may deliberately generating decrypting keys for its own purpose that harm users' privacy. For OSN system with several ABE authorities, there is still privacy risk for the authorities may collude to harm users' privacy.

In this paper, we propose a secure decentralized online social networking framework named SEDOSN. A peer-to-peer (p2p) online networking system is designed, and attribute-based encryption (ABE) technique is used. Different to existing ABE schemes which relies on a single authority or several authorities to authorize users and generating decryption keys for uses, we firstly proposed an ABE scheme with discretionary authorization. In our system, each user can authorize his friend, and generate decryption keys for his friend based on his friend's attributes. So each user has full control of his personal data. Information can be securely disseminated according to users' preferences and friendship relations. The rest of the paper is organized as follows: In Sect. 2, we present the related works. In Sect. 3, the system model, software architecture, and stages of our system. In Sect. 4, we present the experiment results of our prototype. In the last section, we conclude our work.

2   Related Work

There have been many research works for securing online social networking. Locker [1] used access control list based on the relationship between two users. Luo et al. [2] proposed an architecture named FaceCloak to protect users' privacy. In their system, users' sensitive data are encrypted and stored on a separate server. Pirretti et al. [7] proposed an online social framework using attribute-based encryption that only reveals information about a user if his attributes match another user's defined access policy. Their system relies on a single authority to distribute all decryption keys. Baden et al. [8] used attributed-based encryption technique to protect users' privacy in the centralized online social networking services. Beyond using encryption techniques to protect users' privacy, some works [9–12] solved this problem by adopting a decentralized approach to online social networks. In these systems, users can choose where to store their data and have more control over the data.

For attribute-based encryption research, Sahai and Waters introduced the first ABE scheme [3]. Since then, many CP-ABE algorithms were proposed in recent years. Some research works were focused on the structure of attributes, such as [4, 5]. Some research works were related with other issues in ABE, such as multi-authority ABE [15–17], User Revocation [18, 19], user accountability [20], etc. Recently, Rouselakis and Waters [6] proposed a large universe attribute-based encryption method. An ABE system can be classified to "small universe" and "Large Universe" constructions. In the "small universe" construction, the attributes are fixed at system setup and the size of attributes is polynomially bounded and furthermore the size of public parameters grows linearly with number of attributes. While in the "Large Universe" construction, the attributes need not be specified at system setup and the size of attribute universe is unbounded. The large universe ABE encryption method can provide more flexibility, so it is more suitable for online social networking applications.

3 Proposed Framework

3.1 System Model

In our system, as shown in Fig. 1, peers are connected on a P2P network. Each peer manages its resources respectively. The system allows users to create "groups" and adds users to these groups. A group associates with an access structure. A user can encrypt a message with ABE technique.

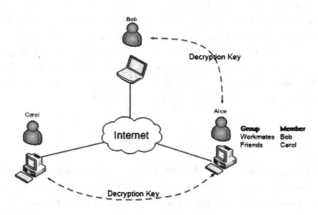

Fig. 1. System model

Different to existing ABE schemes which relies on a single authority or several authorities to authorize users and generating decryption keys for uses with the authority's master key, in our system, each user holds a unique master key, and each user uses his own master key to encrypt a message and generate decryption keys for his friends.

3.2 Software Architecture

In each user's device, the software consists of three layers: overlay network layer, function layer and user interface layer as shown in Fig. 2.

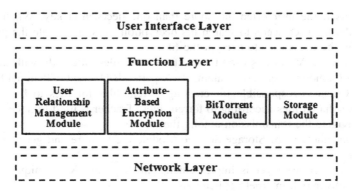

Fig. 2. Software architecture

In the network layer, an open source DHT library named TomP2P is used in the software module, and a peer to peer (P2P) network in built upon physical network to make the peers independent from the physical network.

In the function layer, four modules are contained: User Relationship Management Module, Attribute-Based Encryption Module, BitTorrent Module and Storage Service Module.

The User Relationship Management Module is used to manage users' relationship with other users. In this module, Sqlite, which is a light weight database, is used to manage the metadata of the relationships of the users.

The Attribute-Based Encryption Module is used to achieve fine-grained access control on users' data. It consists of four sub-modules: Initialization, Key Generation, Encryption and Decryption. The Initialization sub-module is designed to run the setup algorithm of ABE, and obtains his public key and his secret master key. The Key Generation sub-module is designed to generate secret key for users' friends. If a user u_1 sends a request to be a friend of user u_2, after u_2 receives the request, he generates the decryption key for u_1 according to $u_1's$ attributes using his master key. Encryption sub-module is designed to encrypt message with access policy. The Decryption sub-module is used for decrypting ciphertexts. Anytime a user obtains a ciphertext from one of his friend, he needs to uses his decryption key generated by the friend. If his attributes satisfies the ciphertext's access policy, he will decrypt the ciphertext successfully; otherwise, an error message occurs. We use RW's attribute-based encryption algorithms [6] for the Attribute-Based Encryption Module.

There are two characteristics with our design: Firstly, for existing centralized ABE schemes, the key generation sub-module is contained only on a single authority or several authorities, and the encryption sub-module and decryption sub-module are contained in the users' devices, but in our design, each user's device software consists of all these sub-modules. So each user can act as all the roles: authorizer who authorizes his friends and generating decryption keys for his friends, content owner who encrypt his data using his master key and content consumer who gets decryption key to decrypt data. Secondly, for existing centralized ABE schemes, a user only has a decryption key; but in our system, since every friend of a user can send a decryption key to the user, the user often has more than one decryption key. When trying to decrypt a file, the user needs to search his decryption keys and locate the proper key generated by the file owner to decrypt the file.

The BitTorrent Module is used to transfer shared files efficiently with the BitTorrent protocol among users. It contains two parts: BitTorrent Client and Tracker. BitTorrent Client is responsible for creating torrent files for files to be shared and downloading shared files according to torrent files. Tracker is used to trace the torrent files and navigate the transmission among the users.

The main functions of Storage Service Module are to store and get objects in the P2P network.

The User Interface layer is implemented with the JavaFX technique which can create and deliver rich internet applications.

3.3 Stages

There are four stages including SystemInit, EstablishFriendRelationship, CreateSharingData and ObtainSharingData in our system.

SystemInit: In this stage, a user's email needs to be inputted which is used to generate the Global ID gid. After obtaining the gid, the user's peer needs to bootstrap to a known peer in p2p network. At the same time, each user obtains key pairs (PK, MSK) by running the *Setup* algorithm of the RW-ABE scheme. The public key PK is distributed to the user's friends and the master key MSK should be kept secret to generate decryption keys for friends.

EstablishFriendRelationship: A user adds his friend to a group. The User generates a decryption key for his friend and sends the decryption key to his friend.

CreateSharingData: This stage is done by a user who wants to share a file F to his friends. Firstly, the user should make an access policy $\ominus$ of the shared file. And then, the shared file is encrypted by the encryption algorithm of the RW-ABE scheme [6]. For file encryption, at first a symmetric key is generated to encrypt the file F with Advanced Encryption Standard (AES) algorithm to produce an encrypted file Encf; then the symmetric key is encrypted with an access structure to produce a ciphertext C. In our implementation, the ciphertext C is inserted to the head of the encrypted file Encf. Next, a torrent file is generated according to the encrypted file $Encf$. At last, the torrent file is published to the p2p network.

ObtainSharingData: A user downloads the encrypted file $Encf$ using the BitTorrent Protocol. After the file is downloaded, the user search his decryption keys to get the proper decryption key generated by the file owner, and then if the attributes included in the decryption key satisfies the access structure of the ciphertext C, the decryption algorithm first decrypts the ciphertext C to get the symmetric key, and then uses the symmetric key to decrypted the file $Encf$. At last the user successfully obtains the shared file F.

4 Implementation

We have implemented our prototype system on laptop with Windows 8 operating system, 1.66 GHz CPU and 2G memory, with the JPBC [14] (Java Pairing-Based Cryptography) library. We implemented the RW-ABE algorithm [6] and used an open source DHT library named TomP2P [13]. We integrated BitTorrent protocol to transfer files among users. The interface of our prototype is shown in Fig. 3. The functions of the software modules, the stages of the system flow have been successfully tested and verified.

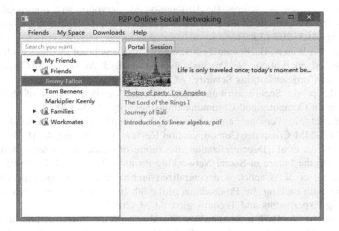

Fig. 3. Interface of our protype system

5 Conclusion

In this paper, we have proposed a secure decentralized social networking framework to protect users' privacy. We firstly proposed an ABE scheme with discretionary authorization. Our system allows each user to authorize his friends and generate decryption keys for his friends and define flexible access policy to achieve secure fine-grained access control.

We plan to transplant our work to mobile platform and further improve our work in the future.

Acknowledgments. This work is supported by the National High Technology Research and Development Program ("863" Program) of China under Grant No. 2015AA016009, the National Natural Science Foundation of China under Grant No. 61232005, and the Science and Technology Program of Shen Zhen, China under Grant No. JSGG20140516162852628.

References

1. Tootoonchian, et al.: Locker: social access control for web 2.0. In: WOSN (2008)
2. Luo, W., Xie, Q., Hengartner, U.: Facecloak: an architecture for user privacy on social networking sites. In: International Conference on Computational Science and Engineering, CSE 2009, vol. 3. IEEE (2009)
3. Sahai, A., Waters, B.: Fuzzy identity-based encryption. In: Cramer, R. (ed.) EUROCRYPT 2005. LNCS, vol. 3494, pp. 457–473. Springer, Heidelberg (2005)
4. Bethencourt, J., Sahai, A., Waters, B.: Ciphertext-policy attribute-based encryption. In: IEEE Symposium on Security and Privacy, SP 2007. IEEE (2007)
5. Ostrovsky, R., Sahai, A., Waters, B.: Attribute-based encryption with non-monotonic access structures. In: Proceedings of the 14th ACM Conference on Computer and Communications Security, pp. 195−203 (2007)
6. Rouselakis, Y., Waters, B.: Practical constructions and new proof methods for large universe attribute-based encryption. In: Proceedings of the 2013 ACM SIGSAC Conference on Computer & Communications Security. ACM (2013)
7. Pirretti, M., et al.: Secure attribute-based systems. In: Proceedings of the 13th ACM Conference on Computer and Communications Security. ACM (2006)
8. Baden, R., et al.: Persona: an online social network with user-defined privacy. In: ACM SIGCOMM Computer Communication Review, vol. 39., no. 4. ACM (2009)
9. Yeung, C.M.A., et al.: Decentralization: the future of online social networking. In: W3C Workshop on the Future of Social Networking Position Papers, vol. 2 (2009)
10. Nilizadeh, S., et al.: Cachet: a decentralized architecture for privacy preserving social networking with caching. In: Proceedings of the 8th International Conference on Emerging Networking Experiments and Technologies. ACM (2012)
11. Seong, S.-W., et al.: PrPl: a decentralized social networking infrastructure. In: Proceedings of the 1st ACM Workshop on Mobile Cloud Computing & Services: Social Networks and Beyond. ACM (2010)
12. Buchegger, S., et al.: PeerSoN: P2P social networking: early experiences and insights. In: Proceedings of the Second ACM EuroSys Workshop on Social Network Systems. ACM (2009)
13. Bocek, T.: TomP2P-A Distributed Multi Map (2009)
14. De Caro, A., Lovino, V.: jPBC: Java pairing based cryptography. In: 2011 IEEE Symposium on Computers and Communications, (ISCC). IEEE (2011)
15. Müller, S., Katzenbeisser, S., Eckert, C.: Distributed attribute-based encryption. In: Information Security and Cryptology, pp. 20−36 (2009)
16. Chase, M., Chow, S.: Improving privacy and security in multi-authority attribute-based encryption. In: Proceedings of the 16th ACM Conference on Computer and Communications security, pp. 121−130 (2009)
17. Lewko, A., Waters, B.: Decentralizing attribute-based encryption. In: Advances in Cryptology, CEUROCRYPT 2011, pp. 568−588 (2011)
18. Jahid, S., Mittal, P., Borisov, N.: EASiER: encryption-based access control in social networks with efficient revocation. In: Proceedings of 6th ACM Symposium on Information, Computer and Communication Security, pp. 411–415 (2011)
19. Cheng, Y., Wang, Z.Y., Ma, J., Wu, J.J., Mei, S.Z., Ren, J.C.: Ciphertext-policy attribute-based encryption with efficient revocation. J. Zhejiang Univ. SCIENCE C **14**(2), 85–97 (2013)
20. Ren, K., Zhu, B., Li, J., Wan, Z.: Privacy-aware attribute-based encryption with user accountability. In: Samarati, P., Yung, M., Martinelli, F., Ardagna, C.A. (eds.) ISC 2009. LNCS, vol. 5735, pp. 347–362. Springer, Heidelberg (2009)

Smart Hardware

Agricultural Data Acquisition and Communication Embedded System Based on MSP430

Hua-Jie Cao[1(✉)], Hao-Dong Liu[2], and Ming Liu[3]

[1] School of Information Technology, Southwest Jioatong University,
Chengdu 611756, Sichuan, China
yishuishui@foxmail.com
[2] School of Electrical Engineering, Southwest Jioatong University,
Chengdu 611756, Sichuan, China
1025793698@qq.com
[3] School of Information Science and Mathematics, Changzhou University,
Changzhou 213164, Jiangsu, China
2226508261@qq.com

Abstract. Under the background of big data and cloud computing, in order to design a kind of agricultural data collection and communication system, MSP430 is taken as core controller and processor. DS18B20 as temperature acquisition, DHT11 sensor as humidity data acquisition, BH1750FV1 as light sensor. The collected data will be transmitted through the wireless communication module, and communication with the host computer. The design of the system is divided into hardware design and software design. This system can extend to join the ZigBee or BeiDou communication module, which can be applied to the large-scale intelligent agricultural control.

Keywords: Agricultural data acquisition · MSP430 · Temperature and humidity sensor · Wireless communication

1 Introduction

At present, China's agricultural production efficiency is not high mechanization and information technology is also not high. Due to various reasons, farmland is not easy to management directly [1]. With the development of the Internet of things (IoT), the IoT technology will quickly penetrate into every link of agriculture. Temperature, humidity, light intensity and other data are important environmental parameters in agricultural production, especially in greenhouse cultivation, aquaculture and other precision agriculture. They are essential for agricultural production, these parameter will directly affect the quality of agricultural production and agricultural production, especially in the environment changes, if not check and control timely, agricultural production will cause serious damage [2]. In many agricultural and even industrial applications, the measurement of process, production and environmental parameters is still a real time monitoring. The purpose of this design is to study the distributed node control and

© Springer Science+Business Media Singapore 2015
X. Zhang et al. (Eds.): ESTC 2015, CCIS 572, pp. 77–86, 2015.
DOI: 10.1007/978-981-10-0421-6_8

communication program, to further promote, it can be suitable for large-scale information agriculture.

2 Overall System Architecture

The wireless data acquisition and communication system including three parts, the first part is the universal application of DS18B20 as the core of the temperature measurement module, the digital sensor DHT11 as the core of the humidity measurement. BH1750FV1 is used for light intensity. In this system, NRF24L01 is selected for the wireless transceiver module. The microcontroller is MSP430, it is mainly responsible for real-time data display, and it can communicate with PC through the USB interface, which can achieve real-time monitoring of temperature, light intensity, humidity and record the results of the measurement.

The architecture diagram of this system is shown in Fig. 1.

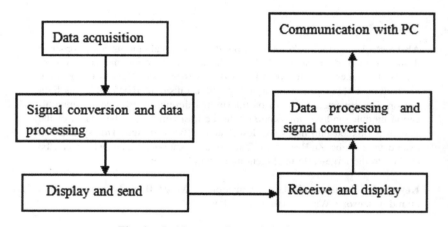

Fig. 1. Architecture diagram of this system

3 Hardware Design of This System

The hardware part is composed of MSP430F149 microcontroller, temperature sensor DS18B20 module, humidity sensor DHT11 module, light intensity sensor BH1750FV1 module, NRF24L01 wireless transceiver module and 1602 LCD module. The sender is to complete the measurement of three parameters which is temperature, humidity, light intensity, and send them to the LCD for real-time display in the premise of high accuracy. The measurement data will be also send to the receiver. On the receiver, the received data will also display in the PC terminal for real-time monitoring and saving.

The following will highlights the DS18B20 sensor, DHT11 humidity sensor and BH1750FV1 light intensity sensor and other modules.

3.1 Design of Temperature Sensor Circuit

Temperature controller has been widely used in metallurgy, textile, chemical, medical and many other fields. In this design, the temperature sensor uses DS18B20, which uses the three wire interface, which is a signal bus type device. It has the advantages of miniaturization, low power consumption, strong anti-interference ability, simple interface, high performance and so on, which can be directly converted to digital signal

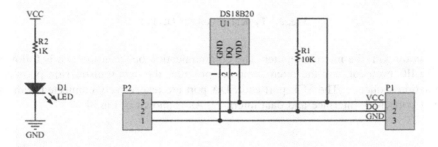

Fig. 2. Temperature sensor circuit

processing. Composed with the traditional method of thermocouple temperature measurement, DS18B20 can greatly improve the accuracy of temperature measurement, and its three-wire connection is very convenient. DS18B20 pins are power pin GND, data signal pin DQ and power supply pin VDD. Its application circuit is shown in Fig. 2.

3.2 Design of Humidity Sensor Circuit

DHT11 digital humidity sensor is a kind of serial bidirectional interface, which has the advantages of fast response, strong anti-interference ability and high cost performance ratio. As shown in Fig. 3, a typical application circuit for the DHT11, if the signal between master and slave length of less than 20 m, a pull-up resistor will be required between data side and VCC. The typical value of the resistor is 4.7 K. When the signal line is more than 20 m, the resistor should be adjusted resistance.

3.3 Design of Light Intensity Sensor Circuit

BH1750FV1 is a digital intensity sensor integrated module, using two wire serial bus interface. In comparison with the analog device, the BH1750FV1 is more stable, less power consumption, simple hardware circuit interface. In the software design, it uses IIC protocol, which has a high transmission efficiency. The sensor adapt the double-wire

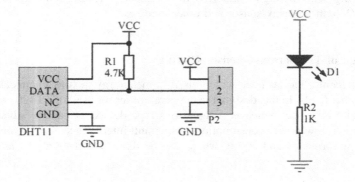

Fig. 3. Typical circuit for DHT11

connection with the microcomputer. The communication between the two is followed by the IIC protocol, and the microcomputer provides the data transmission ports and simulation sequence. The SCL port and SDA port are respectively connected with the output port clock interface and data interface. As is shown in Fig. 4.

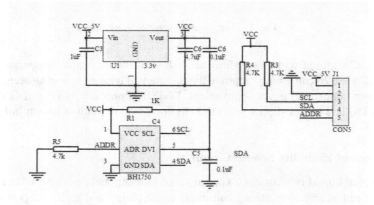

Fig. 4. Circuit of BH1750FV1

4 Software Design of This System

The software of the whole system is designed by each subroutine, which is composed of temperature measurement module, humidity measurement, light intensity data acquisition program and wireless communication program. After the initialization of the microcomputer, the data of each sub module is collected, the data is transmitted through the wireless module and the other receiver also transmit the received data to the PC terminal. The program design of each sub module are introduced respectively.

4.1 Temperature Acquisition Program

DS18B20 requires for a period of time waiting for the internal register to complete the first numerical profile. The first step is to set up the temperature register when it is in normal work, set the corresponding to $-55°$.

The temperature data is divided into high 8 bit and low 8 bit, working with 12 bit accuracy, the temperature index value is $0.0625°$. Above this paper, in the collection function of DS18B20, the data is collected of two bytes circularly, after the acquisition, the high 8 bit will multiply 256 and then add the low 8 bit. In order to overcome the fractional part, we will expand to ten times and then to display them in LCD.

4.2 Humidity Acquisition Program

The communication between MSP430 and DHT11 is based on signal bus data format, and the time of the master communicate with slave is about 4 ms. The data is 5 byte (40 bit) which is collected once. The first 2 bytes of the 5 bytes are humidity parameter, then the two bytes are temperature parameter. The actual temperature is consists of the integer part and the fractional part. Humidity parameter is also the same. The last byte of the 5 bytes is the check byte. When the value is equal to the sum of the first four bytes, the acquisition is not fault. In this case, the collected data can be used as measurement data.

The specific format are as follows (Table 1):

Table 1. A sample data of the DHT11

Received data	0010 0001	0000 0000	0011 0000	0000 0000	0101 0001
Data bit	High byte of humidity	Low byte of humidity	High byte of temperature	Low byte of temperature	Parity byte

Calculation and Verification: If the 0010 0001 + 0000 0000 + 0011 0000 + 0000 0000 = 0101 0001, then the receiving data is collectively. The humidity is: 0010 0001 = 21H = 33 %RH and the temperature is: 0011 0000 = 30H = 48 °C.

If the received parity does not equal to 01010001, then the acquisition or data transmission is error. The result of the acquisition should be abandoned, then to recapture. What's more, the communication protocol between DHT11 and micro-computer can refer to the datasheet. The program's running flow is shown in Fig. 5.

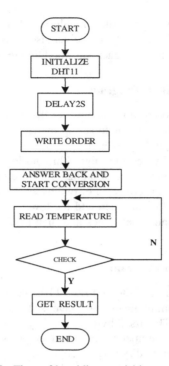

Fig. 5. Flow of humidity acquisition program

4.3 Optical Intensity Acquisition Program

The BH1750FV1 module and the MSP430 adopt the way of double line connection, the communication between them follows the IIC protocol. When initialization the BH1750FV1, first to send the local machine address to the microcomputer, then read the data from this address, then make a response to the host. At the same time, convert the data to the character and send it to the liquid crystal for display. The program design flow is shown in Fig. 6.

4.4 Wireless Communication Program

NRF24L01 module uses the SPI communication interface, and it can connect to the SPI port of the microcomputer. What's more, it can also uses the I/O port to analog the SPI communication. About the SPI protocol, designers can refer to the datasheet of NRF24L01.

The wireless receiving module needs to configure the communication channel, working mode and so on. After the completion of the initialization, the register CONFIG will come into the receive mode, and the CE is waiting for the arrival of the data packet. In the end, the LCD will display it.

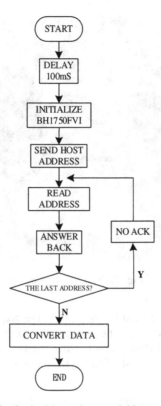

Fig. 6. Optical intensity acquisition program

5 Debug the System

After the completion of the debugging of the various modules, then come into overall debugging. The wireless transceiver module to send the data of light intensity, temperature and humidity to another receiver system. The original selection of USB was a way of direct power supply, and it has generated a problem that the power of the wireless transmission is not enough. When exchange a separate two-way power to supply the receiving module and transmitting module, this problem of the power is not stable can be solved well.

The whole system can send and receive more smoothy after changing the circuit of power supply. To complete two rounds in one second. As is shown in Fig. 7, this system is the successful implementation of the function of data acquisition and transmission. The receiving data of temperature and humidity are specially 27.7°and 42 %RH, because of the small delay of the system and the change of the environmental light, the result of the receiving data is in agreement with the reality.

The PC terminal is designed by Studio Visual 2013 that is developed by Microsoft. It is mainly to receive the data from the wireless receiver, and it also can monitor the serial port. Open the serial port and set some parameters such as baud rate, parity bit

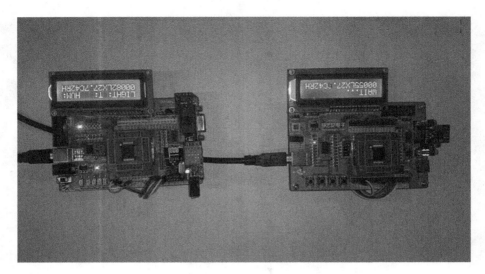

Fig. 7. Test the system

and word length. It also can be used in response to the acquisition. The PC is also can monitor the data from the receiver. The data can be saved at their own discretion or automatically. The interval of data it can be saved is one minutes.

As is shown in Fig. 8, it's a test of the system communicates with the host PC.

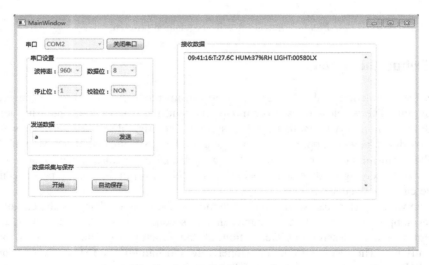

Fig. 8. A test of data transmission

6 Data Analysis

In comparison with the actual measurement of the actual temperature, humidity and light intensity, this paper collects some data, and the analysis is as follows:

From the data in Table 2 can be found that the temperature range of the system is better when the temperature is below 55°, and the error is lower than the actual temperature at 0.5°. When the temperature is above 55°, the temperature error of the system is about 1.5°. But to some extent, it can meet the needs of agricultural production.

Table 2. Comparison between the measured temperature and actual

Actual range of temperature (°C)	Thermometer indicator	System measurement
5–15	14.3	14.5
15–25	20.6	20.1
25–35	28.8	28.2
35–45	36.5	37.1
45–55	48.2	47.8
55–65	55.7	57.6
65–75	70.5	72.9
More than 75	81.3	83.2

From Table 3, the error of the data from the system and the actual is about 5 %, so the accuracy of the system can not be achieved because of the precision of humidity measurement, the humidity sensor needs to be upgraded, but to a certain extent, it can meet the demands of agricultural production (Table 4).

Table 3. Comparision of the humidity and actual under different conditions

Environment	Humidity Gauge (%RH)	System data (%RH)
Outdoor (fine)	40	44
Indoor (ventilation)	45	49
Closed dry container	37	31
Air conditioning	71	74
Sprayer action	75	81

Table 4. Light intensity under different circumstances

Environment	Test (Lx)
Outdoor (fine)	356
Indoor (overcase)	126
Outdoor (not strong light)	4652
Outdoor (strong light)	65536
LED illumination (20 cm)	4078

Through the analysis, the accuracy is very high, but it can not test strong light, it's a limitation.

7 Summary

This design can archive the information and transmit three environment factors, such as temperature, humidity and intensity, which is closely related to agricultural production and daily life. This paper mainly introduces the process of the design. The final test shows that the whole system can work correctly. In this paper, the data is also analyzed in details. The next step of this system is to add the Zigbee module which can extend to large-scale nodes. At the same time, data can also be transmitted by GPS or BeiDou satellite. In the end, this system can process and control large-scale agricultural production.

References

1. Xiang, Z., Zou, X., Liu, Z., Li, S.: Scheme of FPGA verification for scaler chip design, Huazhong Keji Daxue Xuebao (Ziran Kexue Ban)/J. Huazhong Univ. Sci. Technol. (Natural Science edn), **34**(1), pp. 90–92 (2006)
2. Viele, M., Shorey, E.E., Dase, C.G., Hoose, K.V. Light, K.H.: A novel approach to free-piston engine control using an FPGA based control system. In: Internal Combustion Engine Division Fall Technical Conference, pp. 823–825 (2011)

Embryonic Electronic Circuit Optimization Design Method Based on Genetic Algorithm

Tao Wang$^{(\boxtimes)}$, Jinyan Cai, and Yafeng Meng

Department of Electronic and Optical Engineering,
Mechanical Engineering College,
No. 97 Heping West Road, Shijiazhuang, China
wangtao920110@126.com

Abstract. With the progress of science and technology, the existing electronic system is developing to complication and miniaturization, this requires that the system has high reliability and low resource consumption. Embryonic electronic cell array (EECA) is a new kind of circuit structure based on the embryonic evolution of biology, with the feature of self-organization, self-healing and self-adaptive. Compared with traditional circuit design method of electronic system, the electronic system implemented with EECA has higher reliability, however, it also means more hardware resource consumption. In this paper, the function circuit is implemented by EECA, and it's consumption of electric cell is presented by matrix. In order to optimize the consumption of embryonic cells, the genetic algorithms (GA) is utilized, through the optimization of circuit design is optimized, the hardware resource consumption of the circuit is reduced. Through the study of the optimization design of a typical circuit, both the hardware resource consumption and the reliability of the system have improved a lot, compared with the traditional design method,which has great engineering application value.

Keywords: Embryonic electronic cell array · Genetic algorithm · Matrix · Hardware consumption

1 Introduction

With the development of science and technology, modern electronic system is developing to the direction of integration, intelligent and complicated, the traditional circuit design method can't meet the needs of existing electronic systems. EECA technology is a new circuit structure, which is based on the biology embryonic development process, the EECA has the same feature as the biological tissue, with excellent self-adaptive, self-organizing and self-healing properties [1], which can meet the requirements of modern electronic system design for high reliability.

Embryonic hardware was proposed as the field programmable gate array (FPGA) by Mange and Marchal since 1996, which was inspired by multicellular organism development. When the theory was put forward, it has attracted wide attention of scholars both at home and abroad. Thus embryonic hardware has developed rapidly in recent years, it has more powerful than the FPGA in self-detection, self-adaptive and

© Springer Science+Business Media Singapore 2015
X. Zhang et al. (Eds.): ESTC 2015, CCIS 572, pp. 87–98, 2015.
DOI: 10.1007/978-981-10-0421-6_9

self-healing. The EECA research mainly includes three aspects: structure design of EECA, the development and self-healing of embryonic cell array and the application of EECA. At present,it has obtained certain research results both in theory research and application research, such as: literature [2] introduces the basic structure of embryonic cell and embryonic cell array; literature [3] using MUX structure to achieve the embryonic cell array structure; literature [4] using LUT as a functional unit to achieve the embryonic cell array; literature [5] introduces the key technology of embryonic cell array; literature [6] realized the verification of fault-tolerant circuit structure of embryonic cell array on FPGA; literature [7, 8] study the prokaryotic cell array structure and self-healing strategy; literature [9] studies the cell array structure based on BUS and it's self-healing strategy; literature [10] studies the embryonic cell array structure with multiple connection mode; literature [11] studies the selection of self-healing strategy; literature [12] designs a new kind of high efficient self-healing system; literature [13] studies a multilayer bio-inspired self-healing hardware. In general, the study of embryonic bio-inspired hardware started earlier at abroad, theoretical knowledge is comparatively mature, and some small hardware with self-repairing based on embryonic cell array has been implemented, such as the Swiss federal institute of technology has been developed the Bio-Watch [14] and the Bio-Wall [15], the European Community has developed POE chip [16] and Ubichip [17] chips, etc. Domestic research is mainly in theory study, the related theory is not mature, and lack of practical application.

The circuit which is designed based on EECA, it can meet the needs of existing electronic systems for high reliability, however, the high hardware resources cost is one big drawback, which directly limits its large-scale application in the actual circuit design. In this paper, the characteristics of the circuit design based on EECA is researched, the structure of designed circuit is represented by matrix, the GA is carried out on the optimization of circuit structure for it's optimization property,to achieve the aim of reducing the consumption of hardware resources in circuit design, and to realize the engineering application of EECA circuit design method.

2   The Basic Theory

2.1   The Basic Theory of EECA

Multicellular organisms is formed from fertilized egg through mitosis, function differentiation. Each cell divides into two daughter cells that have the exact same DNA. In the process of function differentiation, different cells express the corresponding genes according to its position in biology embryo, different genes expressing implement specific functions, then the cell differentiation is completed. When a cell dead in biological tissue, the dead cell's gene will be delivered to free cell in the biological tissue, so the free cell will implement the dead cell's function, to ensure the normal operation of the biology [18].

A designed EECA based on the biological embryo development, as shown in Fig. 1, it's a two-dimensional array with self-organizing, self-healing and self-adaptive properties [19, 20], which is composed of the electronic cell with the same structure. Electronic cells is a basic unit of EECA, its structure as shown in Fig. 2. The electronic cell is mainly composed of the address unit, function unit, configuration memory, control unit, I/O block and BIT [21]. Address module mainly produce cell identification, through the cell identification expressing the corresponding genes; The function unit is mainly perform the logic function of cells, according to the different genes configuration implements different functions. The configuration memory is mainly store all genes of the whole circuit, different genes stand for the different function of the circuit and the connection between the cells; Control unit is mainly control the cell self-organizing and self-repairing process; I/O block is mainly realize the connections between cells and the transformation of data between the cells. BIT is mainly detect the real-time running state of the cells [22].

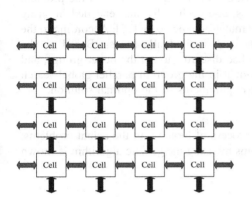

Fig. 1. Structure of embryonic array   **Fig. 2.** Structure of embryonic cell

When the circuit's functional differentiation is finished, all the configuration genes of target circuit is obtained. Different cells according to their position in the array to express specific genes, different gens determine the different connection and logic function, all cells in the array cooperate to complete the target circuit function. The essence of array self-healing is cell replacement, in the process of array operation, the self-checking unit detect the real-time running state of cells, when a failure is detected, the "fault" signal passes to control unit, start the self-healing function of circuit. Recalculate the address information for all the cells, transfer the configuration information from the fault cell to free cells, the free cells instead of the fault cell to implement the corresponding function, guarantee the normal work of the circuit, so the circuit realized the function self-healing.

As shown in Fig. 2, the structure of embryonic cell, for calculating the resource consumption of an EECA, firstly, using professional integrated circuit analysis software to realize the simulation of embryonic cells, the resource consumption of each cell is mainly the number of basic logic gates and wiring resource consumption. Then complete the whole simulation of embryonic circuit, the consumption of the total basic logic gates and routing were analyzed, so as to evaluate the resource consumption of whole EECA.

2.2 The Basic Theory of GA

2.2.1 The GA

GA is an adaptive and global probability search method, which is simulated from biological Genetic and evolutionary process. It was presented by professor Holland in the 1960s [23], and it was used for the study of natural and artificial adaptive systems. When the GA is presented, it got the wide attention of scholars both at home and abroad, and it has developed rapidly in these years. Now, the GA has been widely used in many area such as biotechnology, microelectronics, artificial intelligence, computer aided design and so on, it becomes the most powerful global optimization tool.

The core idea of GA is "evolution" [24], the GA uses the artificial evolution way to search the target space stochastically, it considers the feasible solution of the problem as an individual or a chromosome of groups, and each individual encoded in string form, to operate the selection, crossover and mutation repeatedly [25]. According to the intended target fitness function to evaluate each individual's fitness. Based on the evolution rule of "survival of the fittest and bad discard", to get the better groups, and to search the optimization of the best individual in the group in parallel global search way at the same time, in order to meet the requirements of the optimal solution.

2.2.2 The Solving Step of GA

According to the genetic and evolutionary process of biology, to the actual problems, the process to solve the optimization problems by using the genetic algorithm is shown in Fig. 3.

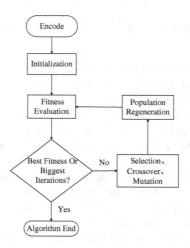

Fig. 3. The flow chart of GA

Step1. Code the problem;

Step2. Initialize the population;

Step3. Calculate the fitness value of each individual in population;

Step4. Determine whether meet the termination conditions, if not satisfied, to Step 5, if satisfied, to Step 7;

Step5. The selection, crossover and mutation operation to initial population;
Step6. Update the population, to Step 3;
Step7. Terminate the algorithm.

3   Circuit Structure Optimization Based on GA

Considering the circuit's characteristics which is implemented based on the EECA, using matrix to represent the circuit's structure. Take advantage of the optimization property of GA, to find the most suitable circuit structure, while guarantee the circuit with high reliability, and reduce the consumption of hardware resources.

3.1   The EECA with Multiple Connection Mode

In EECA with multiple connections, according to the position relationship between each other, the connection between the cells can be divided into local connection and remote connection [26]. For the adjacent cells, using wires to connect each cells, complete the intercellular signal transmission; For non-adjacent cells, adopt switch box inside each cell and wires to connect each cells, to complete the signal transmission between the cells. The EECA with multiple connection mode structure as shown in Fig. 4.

In Fig. 4, for example, the cell in the middle of the array with the surrounding eight adjacent cells S, SE, E, EN, N, NW, W and WS connected by direct connection mode, the black line shown in Fig. 4 represents for remote connection mode, the intersection in the cell is switch box, to achieve the non-adjacent cell's connection and information transmission. In this paper, based on the GA to realize the circuit's structure optimization implemented by EECA with multiple connection mode.

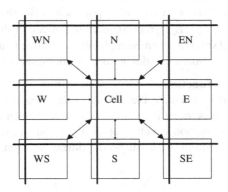

Fig. 4. The connection mode in EECA

3.2   The Array Representation Method Based on Matrix

EECA is formed by a two-dimensional cell arrays with the same structure, this structure is similar with the two-dimensional matrix. In the mathematics, the matrix is easy to operate mathematical operation. According to the structure characteristics of electronic array, using the two-dimensional matrix to represent the use of embryonic cells.

For a $m \times n$ EECA, define a matrix $E_{m \times n}$ to represent the use of embryonic cells, so the functional circuit implemented based on EECA can be expressed as a matrix:

$$E_{m \times n} = \begin{pmatrix} e_{11} & \cdots & e_{1n} \\ \vdots & \ddots & \vdots \\ e_{m1} & \cdots & e_{mn} \end{pmatrix} \tag{1}$$

In the matrix $E_{m \times n}$, e_{ij} can be 0 or 1, if $e_{ij} = 1$, means the cell in row i and column j is used, if $e_{ij} = 0$, means the cell in row i and column j is not used. When the function circuit is implemented by EECA, the matrix $E_{m \times n}$ is confirmed, the same function can be implemented by different circuit, so can get different $E_{m \times n}$.

3.3 Circuit Structure Optimization Based on GA

The two-dimensional EECA can be expressed as a two-dimensional matrix, the GA is applied to operate the two-dimensional matrix, to optimize the layout of the function circuit, when implement the same function, using the least amount of cells, to reduce the consumption of hardware resources in circuit design.

(1) Coding
The circuit implemented by EECA with multiple connection mode can use the matrix coding described in Sect. 2.2, the coded matrix keeps the original circuit structure characteristic, it's easy to operate by GA, and it's easy to decode the matrix to function circuit.

(2) Initializing the population
The same circuit function can be done by different circuit structure, the different matrices represent the same circuit function are initial population. Set the initial population as $P_s = \left\{ E_{m \times n}^1, E_{m \times n}^2, \ldots, E_{m \times n}^s \right\}$, $E_{m \times n}^i$ represents a kind of circuit structure. Using the GA To P_s, to find the optimal solution of problem, finally according to the optimization result to gets the optimal circuit structure, reducing the consumption of hardware resources.

(3) Choosing the fitness function
Fitness function is used to calculate the fitness value of each individuals during the evolutionary, and the fitness value is an important evaluating indicator of individuals. In this paper, the fitness function selection primarily based on the least electronic cells using, wiring resources used in the least. So the fitness function can be choosed as:

$$f = \min(\sum_{j=1}^{n} \sum_{i=1}^{m} (e_{ij} | e_{ij} = 1|)) \tag{2}$$

The $\sum_{j=1}^{n} \sum_{i=1}^{m} (e_{ij} | e_{ij} = 1|)$ represents the cells consumption.

(4) The GA Operation

Selection Operation. Selection operation is to calculate the fitness value of each individuals in population, through the fitness value to retain high fitness individuals in a population, eliminate the low fitness individuals in a population. Through constantly evolution, improve the adaptability of the population constantly.

Crossover Operation. Set p_c as the crossover rate between individuals, in the process of crossover operation, two matrices carry on the element exchange in corresponding row (column) position at the probability of p_c, the row (column) exchanged is randomly selected. For example, there are two matrices in the process of evolution,

$$E_{m \times n}^i = \begin{bmatrix} e_{11}^i & e_{12}^i & \cdots & e_{1n}^i \\ e_{21}^i & e_{22}^i & \cdots & e_{2n}^i \\ \cdot & \cdot & \cdots & \cdot \\ \cdot & \cdot & \cdots & \cdot \\ \cdot & \cdot & \cdots & \cdot \\ e_{m1}^i & e_{m2}^i & \cdots & e_{mn}^i \end{bmatrix} \tag{3}$$

$$E_{m \times n}^j = \begin{bmatrix} e_{11}^j & e_{12}^j & \cdots & e_{1n}^j \\ e_{21}^j & e_{22}^j & \cdots & e_{2n}^j \\ \cdot & \cdot & \cdots & \cdot \\ \cdot & \cdot & \cdots & \cdot \\ \cdot & \cdot & \cdots & \cdot \\ e_{m1}^j & e_{m2}^j & \cdots & e_{mn}^j \end{bmatrix} \tag{4}$$

After the crossover operation, $E_{m \times n}^i$ and $E_{m \times n}^j$ respectively to:

$$E_{m \times n}^i = \begin{bmatrix} e_{11}^i & e_{12}^j & \cdots & e_{1n}^i \\ e_{21}^i & e_{22}^j & \cdots & e_{2n}^i \\ \cdot & \cdot & \cdots & \cdot \\ \cdot & \cdot & \cdots & \cdot \\ \cdot & \cdot & \cdots & \cdot \\ e_{m1}^i & e_{m2}^j & \cdots & e_{mn}^i \end{bmatrix} \tag{5}$$

$$E_{m \times n}^j = \begin{bmatrix} e_{11}^j & e_{12}^i & \cdots & e_{1n}^j \\ e_{21}^j & e_{22}^i & \cdots & e_{2n}^j \\ \cdot & \cdot & \cdots & \cdot \\ \cdot & \cdot & \cdots & \cdot \\ \cdot & \cdot & \cdots & \cdot \\ e_{m1}^j & e_{m2}^i & \cdots & e_{mn}^j \end{bmatrix} \tag{6}$$

Mutation Operation. Set p_m as the single point mutation rate for individual, in the process of mutation, the certain element in matrix mutates to another value, the mutation position is randomly selected. For example, to a certain individual matrix

$$
E_{m \times n}^i = \begin{bmatrix} e_{11}^i & e_{12}^j & \cdots & e_{1n}^i \\ e_{21}^i & e_{22}^j & \cdots & e_{2n}^i \\ \cdot & \cdot & \cdots & \cdot \\ \cdot & \cdot & \cdots & \cdot \\ \cdot & \cdot & \cdots & \cdot \\ e_{m1}^i & e_{m2}^j & \cdots & e_{mn}^i \end{bmatrix} \tag{7}
$$

After a single point mutation operation $E_{m \times n}^i$ becomes:

$$
E_{m \times n}^i = \begin{bmatrix} e_{11}^i & e_{12}^j & \cdots & e_{1n}^i \\ e_{21}^i & a & \cdots & e_{2n}^i \\ \cdot & \cdot & \cdots & \cdot \\ \cdot & \cdot & \cdots & \cdot \\ \cdot & \cdot & \cdots & \cdot \\ e_{m1}^i & e_{m2}^j & \cdots & e_{mn}^i \end{bmatrix} \tag{8}
$$

While a is the mutated element value according to certain rules.

4   Experimental Verification

To verify the above method,he example in literature [27] is selected as the verification object,the digital circuit can be described as:

$$
F = A\bar{C} + ABC + AC\bar{D} + CD \tag{9}
$$

The corresponding truth table shown in Table 1. The verification steps as follows:

(1) The EECA structure obtained by the traditional circuit differentiation method as shown in Fig. 5a;
(2) Encode the array structure, shown as 10a;
(3) Set the initial population N = 20, the crossover rate p_c = 0.8, the mutation rate p_m = 0.15, the iteration n = 200;
(4) Randomly initialize the population P_s;
(5) Start the GA operation;
(6) After the GA operation,the matrix shown as 10b, decode the matrix to EECA structure as shown in Fig. 5b.

Table 1. The truth table of verification circuit

Input				Output
A	B	C	D	F
0	0	0	0	0
0	0	0	1	0
0	0	1	0	0
0	0	1	1	1
0	1	0	0	0
0	1	0	1	0
0	1	1	0	0
0	1	1	1	1
1	0	0	0	1
1	0	0	1	1
1	0	1	0	1
1	0	1	1	1
1	1	0	0	1
1	1	0	1	1
1	1	1	0	1
1	1	1	1	1

$$\begin{bmatrix} 1 & 0 & 0 & 0 & 0 \\ 1 & 1 & 0 & 0 & 0 \\ 1 & 1 & 1 & 0 & 0 \\ 1 & 1 & 1 & 0 & 0 \\ 1 & 1 & 0 & 0 & 0 \end{bmatrix} \tag{10a}$$

$$\begin{bmatrix} 1 & 0 & 0 & 0 & 0 \\ 1 & 1 & 0 & 0 & 0 \\ 1 & 0 & 0 & 0 & 0 \\ 1 & 1 & 0 & 0 & 0 \\ 1 & 0 & 0 & 0 & 0 \end{bmatrix} \tag{10b}$$

Analysis of Figs. 5a and 5b shows that achieve the same function circuit, the consumption of traditional binary decision diagram method in EECA is 11 cells, using the GA to the optimization design of the same circuit, the consumption are 7 cells, which reduces the consumption of hardware resources. This method's advantage is not obvious in small scale circuit, when it was used in large scale or very large scale embryonic array, the overall resource consumption is larger. Using the GA to the realization of the same circuit to find the optimal embryonic circuit structure, which is of great significance to reduce resource consumption. For the same circuit function with

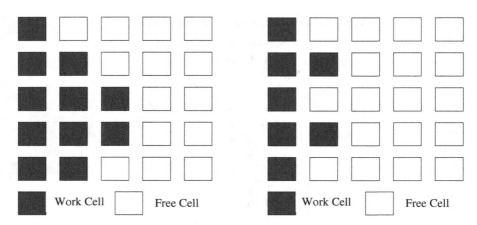

Fig. 5a. The original circuit array   **Fig. 5b.** The optimized circuit array

the same array size, the latter implementation circuit has more free cells, which can realize more self-repairing operations, so the reliability is higher compared with the traditional method of circuit design. But embryonic circuit optimization design is based on the existing circuit realization, so more time is needed compared with traditional circuit design.

For embryonic circuits based on GA optimization design method mainly for large scale circuit design, when the circuit units is less, the evolution design can also completed based on the principle of the chapter 2.3, but the result may be consistent with the traditional method, and may consume more design time, so the advantage is not obvious. Embryonic circuit optimization design based on GA can reduce the embryonic hardware resource consumption of the circuit, and improve the reliability of embryonic circuit at the same time

5   Conclusion

At present, the electronic system is require for high reliability and miniaturization, the circuit implemented by EECA has high reliability, but the hardware resource consumption is a big disadvantage, at the same time the circuit's characteristics which is based on the EECA is analyzed. In this paper,proposes to use matrix represent the circuit implemented by EECA. Based on these work,the same function circuit can be implemented by different circuit structure,different circuit means different hardware resource consumption. The GA is a good global optimization algorithms, and it can be used to optimize the function circuit structure, to find the circuit with the minimal resource consumption.

Through a typical circuit to verify the proposed theory, the verification results shows that it is feasible to use the matrix to represent the circuit implemented based on EECA, and based on the GA to optimize the circuit implementation. Through this method can effectively reduce the consumption of hardware resources for circuit implementation, it's helpful to put the EECA used for the actual large-scale circuit design, which has practical engineering value.

References

1. Wang, Y.R., Cui, J., You, X.: Theory and technology development of bio-inspired hardware. Chin. Space Sci. Technol. **2004**(6), 32–42 (2004)
2. Ortega, C., Tyrrell, A.: Biologically inspired reconfigurable hardware for dependable applications. In: Proceedings of the 1997 IEE Colloquium on Hardware Systems for Dependable Applications, pp. 1–4 (1997)
3. Mange, D., Sanchez, E., Stauffer, A., et al.: Embryonics: a new methodology for designing field-programmable gate arrays with self-repair and self-replicationg properties. IEEE Trans Very Large Scale Integr. (VLSI) Syst. **6**(3), 387–399 (1998)
4. Canham, R.O., Tyrrell, A.M.: Hardware artificial immune system and embryonic array for fault tolerant systems. Genet. Program Evolvable Mach. **4**(4), 359–382 (2003)
5. Yao, R., Wang, Y., Yu, S.: Research on embryonic system and its key technologies. J. Luoyang Inst. Technol. **26**(3), 33–36 (2005)
6. Rong, H., Yu, C.: FPGA validation based on embryonic arrays fault-tolerant system. J. Fudan Univ. (Nat. Sci.) **45**(1), 127–130 (2006)
7. Samie, M., Dragffy, G., Popescu, A.: Prokaryotic bio-inspired system. In: Proceedings of the Forth NASA/ESA Conference on Adaptive Hardware and Systems, pp. 171–178 (2009)
8. Wang, N.: Research of Self-healing Technique Based on Prokaryotic Bio-inspired Array. National University of Defense Technology, Changsha (2011)
9. Li, T.-P.: Research on Bio-inspired Self-repairing Technology Based on Bus Structure. National University of Defense Technology, Changsha (2012)
10. Sai, Z., Jinyan, C., Yafeng, M., et al.: A novel structure of embryonics electronic cell array. WSEAS Trans. Circuits Syst. **13**(10), 224–232 (2014)
11. Zhang, Z., Wang, Y.R.: Method to self-repairing reconfiguration strategy selection of embryonic cellular array on reliability analysis. In: 2014 NASA/ESA Conference on Adaptive Hardware and Systems (AHS), pp. 225–232 (2014)
12. Micheal, G., Arunachalam, A.R.: Design of an efficient self-repairing system. Middle-East J. Sci. Res. **19**(10), 1284–1289 (2014)
13. Wang, N.T., Qian, Y.L., Li, Y.: Design method for a multi-layer bio-inspired self-healing hardware. In: Prognostics and System Health Management Conference (PHM 2014), Hunan, pp. 653–657 (2014)
14. Tempesti, G., Mange, D., Stauffer, A., et al.: The bioWall: an electronic tissue for prototyping bio-inspired systems. In: Proceedings 2002 NASA/DoD Conference on Evolvable Hardware, pp. 221–230 (2002)
15. Stauffer, A., Mange, D., Tempesti, G., Teuscher, C.: A self-repairing and self-healing electronic watch: the biowatch. In: Liu, Y., Tanaka, K., Iwata, M., Iwata, M., Higuchi, T., Yasunaga, M. (eds.) ICES 2001. LNCS, vol. 2210, pp. 112–127. Springer, Heidelberg (2001)
16. Tyrrell, A.M., Sánchez, E., Floreano, D., Tempesti, G., Mange, D., Moreno, O., Rosenberg, A.L., Villa, A.E.: POEtic tissue: an integrated architecture for bio-inspired hardware. In: Tyrrell, A.M., Haddow, P.C., Torresen, J. (eds.) ICES 2003. LNCS, vol. 2606, pp. 129–140. Springer, Heidelberg (2003)

17. Upegui, A., Thoma, Y., Satizábal, H.F., Mondada, F., Rétornaz, P., Perez-Uribe, A., Graf, Y., Sanchez, E.: Ubichip, ubidule, and marxbot: a hardware platform for the simulation of complex systems. In: Tempesti, G., Tyrrell, A.M., Miller, J.F. (eds.) ICES 2010. LNCS, vol. 6274, pp. 286–298. Springer, Heidelberg (2010)

18. Xu, J.: Research on Bio-inspired Self-adaptive Multicellular Array Architecture. National University of Defense Technology, Changsha (2012)

19. Mange, D., Sanchez, E., Stauffer, A.: Embryonics: a new methodology for designing field-programmable gate arrays with self-repair and self-replicating properties. IEEE Trans. Very Large Scale Integr. (VLSI) 6(3), 387–399 (1998)

20. Wang, N., Qian, Y., Li, Y., et al.: Study of embryonic type on-line self-healing FIR filters. Chin. J. Sci. Instrum. 33(6), 1385–1391 (2012)

21. Zhou, G., Qian, Y., Wang, N., et al.: Design and simulation of FIR filters based on embryonic bio-inspired hardware architecture. J. Electron. Meas. Instrument. 24((Suppl.)), 61–65 (2010)

22. Wang, N.: Research of Self-healing Technique Based on Prokaryotic Bio-inspired Array. National University of Defense Technology, Changsha (2011)

23. Wang, J., Zhang, Q., Liang, L.: Adaptive stochastic resonance based on genetic algorithm with applications in weak signal detection adaptive stochastic resonance based on genetic algorithm with applications in weak signal detection. J. Xi'an Jiaotong Univ. 3(44), 32–36 (2010)

24. Pan, Z., Kang, L., Chen, Y.: Evolutionary Computation. Tsinghua University Press, BeiJing (1998)

25. Solteiro Pires, E.J., Tenreiro Machado, J.A., de Moura Oliveira, P.B.: Dynamical modeling of a genetic algorithm. Sig. Process. 86(10), 2760–2770 (2006)

26. Zhu, S., Cai, J., Meng, Y., et al.: A novel structure of embryonics electronic cell array. WSEAS Trans. Circ. Syst. 13(10), 224–232 (2014)

27. Zhang, W.: Hardware evolution based on evolutionary algorithm. Nanjing University of Science and Technology, Nanjing (2008)

Isolation of Physical and Logical Views of Dark-Silicon Many-Core Systems for Reliability and Performance Co-Optimization

Lei Yang[1], Weichen Liu[1](✉), Weiwen Jiang[1], Mengquan Li[1], and Jie Wang[2]

[1] College of Computer Science, Chongqing University, Chongqing, China
{leiyang,wliu,jiang.wwen,mengquan}@cqu.edu.cn
[2] School of Software Technology, Dalian University of Technology, Dalian, China
wangjie1003@163.com

Abstract. A fraction of a many-core chip has to become powered off in order to maintain allowable power budget and safe temperature in the dark silicon era. Techniques have been developed to selectively activate cores in distributed physical locations to avoid temperature hotspot. It results in the unexpected increase of communication overhead due to longer average distance between active cores on Network-on-Chip (NoC). We propose a physical and logical isolated framework based on Folded Torus-like NoC for heterogeneous many-core systems to achieve the guaranteed temperature reliability and satisfied application performance requirement. Physically distributed cores are interconnected through folded torus-like NoC and organized in clusters to enable logically condensed intercommunications within it. Compared to traditional mesh-like systems, the proposed folded torus-like organization can achieve on average 39.44 % application performance improvement and decrease average 9.3°C of the chip.

Keywords: Many-cores · Network-on-chip · Dark silicon · Folded torus

1 Introduction

Network-on-Chip (NoC) has been developed as a promising communication architecture for Multi-Processor System-on-Chips to provide scalable communication power for interconnected multiprocessors. NoC is beneficial for inter-chip communication and on-chip computation that directly influence the overall system performance. However, as the increasing scale of the network, there are more difficulties on NoC architecture design complexity, chip reliability, energy efficiency and so on.

As the increasing integration level of the on-chip network, the increased power density would threaten the life of the chip, and further damage the chip reliability. Dark silicon [4, 11, 12] is a new trend, which powers off parts of the chip to keep the safety, also brings new challenges in many-core systems. On the dark

© Springer Science+Business Media Singapore 2015
X. Zhang et al. (Eds.): ESTC 2015, CCIS 572, pp. 99–109, 2015.
DOI 10.1007/978-981-10-0421-6_10

silicon chip, cores are selected in distributed physical locations to avoid temperature hotspot. However, it increase the unexpected increase of communication overhead due to the longer average distance between active cores, which can further affect the application performance. Thus, in real-time application mapping and scheduling, how to improve the parallel computing, and how to improve the system performance with the new challenges in the dark silicon era are the major problems in many-core architectures.

2 The Development of NoCs and the Dark Silicon

2.1 Network-on-chip Systems

Multi-processor System-on-Chip (MPSoC) has satisfied the ever-growing demands on high performance and low power consumption in embedded systems design. It is significant to effectively optimize communication for achieving maximum parallelism on MPSoC, especially on NoC-based architecture. NoC is a new generation of MPSoC architectures, which integrates complex components on the single chip, including computing and communication resources. It has advantages on high performance communicating, multi-tasks parallel, high capacity of data storage, low communication delay and expandability.

Moores Law [13], the doubling of transistors on a chip in every 18 months, has been the fundamental driver of computing advancement. Continuous technology scaling leads to a utilization wall challenge. Although we can still pack more transistors per area with technology scaling, the switching power per transistor is not scaling commensurately, hence power density has been trending upwards. Coupled with the physical limits imposed by device packaging and cooling technology on the peak power and peak power density, consequently, silicon chips cannot be fully utilized and a large portion will be *dark* or *dim* silicon, which rises the so-called Dark silicon problem. Additionally, the fraction of a silicon chip that can be powered on is dropping exponentially with generations of process technology. According to the technological data from ITRS and Intel, at 8-nm node, more than 70 % of the chip will be dark [5,6,10]. Nevertheless, there are many design challenges in manycore architectures, such as communication and performance optimization, energy saving and chip temperature control. It is a rather difficult problem to make a balance among them.

2.2 Dark Silicon: Development and the Challenges

Dark silicon refers to the constraint that a significant fraction of transistors on a chip cannot be powered on at the nominal voltage for a Thermal Design Power (TDP) budget and have to remain dark,i.e., power-gated. In case the TDP is exceeded, the chip temperature will start rise beyond the cooling capacity, resulting in either the thermal run-away or activation of dynamic thermal management (DTM) mechanism that will throttle the chip.

Dark Silicon Patterning: *Dark silicon patterning determines the temporal and spatial shutdown of on-chip resources with the goal of minimizing peak temperature without violating TDP.*

Much of the state-of-the-art works in literature addresses the dark silicon problems to decide *if* and *how* the cores can be harnesses to improve performance within a power or peak temperature constraint. Works are based on design philosophies including the use of architectural heterogeneity and specialized cores, near-threshold voltages computing, dynamic voltage and frequency scaling, power management for dark and dim silicon to enable a larger fraction of the chip to be powered on. In the dark silicon era, performance focused works addressed that maximizing performance within a power or temperature budget and optimizing energy efficiency are new challenges. To fully exploit the abundance of transistors in the dark silicon era, there are new challenges urgently need to be addressed.

(i) **On-Chip Network Design with Dark Silicon.** *For many-cores on the chip, how to effectively interconnect the large number of powered on processing cores is a design time challenge. The only portion of the powered on cores are simultaneously active and this portion changes with time. The decision on the active portion of cores and the time period for the active cores give rise to the need for a high adaptive.*

(ii) **Thermal Management for Dark Silicon Multicores.** *Dark silicon introduces new opportunities to optimize the run-time thermal profile under the thermal constraint. The run-time systems need to perform efficient thermal management and maximize performance by choosing amongst one of many available TDP modes. The goal is to reduce the peak temperature of the chip, that can increase system performance by providing more power to the chip, above and beyond the TDP.*

(iii) **Chip Variability and Reliability Exploiting.** *The many-cores architectures gives more additional transistors available for increasing reliability. While the variability of manufacturing process gives rise to the complexity of dark silicon thermal profile choosing.*

(iv) **Chip Temperature and Performance Leveraging.** *In many-cores systems, run-time on-chip temperature control and the system performance improving should be leveraged in application mapping and scheduling.*

Facing the challenges brought by dark silicon, system performance, energy efficiency and chip temperature control are interacted with each other, which increases the difficulty for system management. Real-time applications prefer to be assigned on adjacent cores to decrease communication delay, while running processor cores prefer to be surrounded by dark cores for better heat dissipation. Architecture and software optimization techniques in multiple views are necessary to take these contradictory aspects into account and co-optimize them.

On a 8 × 8 64-core mesh-based platform as shown in Fig. 3(b), we study the chip temperature and system performance in different dark silicon patterns, which refers to the pattern formed by distributing the same number of active cores in different physical locations. Four regular patterns and one random pat-

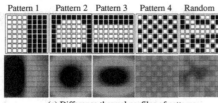
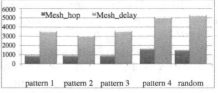

(a) Difference thermal profiles of patterns   (b) Communication delay and application performance

Fig. 1. Different dark silicon patterns have different impact on the temperature of the chip and the performance of system. (a) Pattern 4 has the lowest peak temperature with heat distribution, (b) while it results almost the worst performance.

tern result in extremely different thermal states after a period of computation. Activating a set of adjacent cores as pattern 1, 2 and 3 leads to thermal hotspots and high peak temperature (80.00°C, 82.17°C and 82.15°C, respectively), which threaten the chip temperature reliability. Active cores in pattern 4 are evenly distributed on the chip that the heat conducting effect is alleviated to the greatest extent. Apparently, the temperature of pattern 4 (72.81°C) is lower than other patterns, including the Random one (75.67°C). However, long distance for communication in pattern 4 increases network communication delay which consequently impacts system performance (37.4 % worse than pattern 3) as shown in Fig. 1(b). Dark silicon-aware management as hardware-software co-design are urgent to effectively optimize performance, energy efficiency and even chip reliability within power and thermal constraints.

In this paper, we propose a Folded Torus based NoC architecture for dark silicon chip, such that physically distributed processor cores are interconnected with reduced intercommunication cost and organized in logically condensed processor cores interconnection as shown in Fig. 2.

3   Dark Silicon Manycores

3.1   Physical Locations of Many Cores

A 2-D mesh based NoC as shown in Fig. 3(a) consists of $n \times n$ tiles. Each tile is formed of a general-purpose Processor Element (PE), a router (R) and Network Interface (NI). Generally, there is a Main Controller in network, which takes charge of all transactions. Figure 3(b) is a simplified 8×8 NoC. On the physical platform, cores are numbered from 1 to 64 for unification in the following discussion.

We theoretically determine dark silicon pattern with different darkness ratio to directly minimize the peak temperature via the consideration of conductance between two heatsink elements. Fouriers law [2] provides the definition of thermal conductivity and shows that the heat flow has an inverse relationship with the physical distance of two objects, which is the basic theory for the decision of dark silicon pattern.

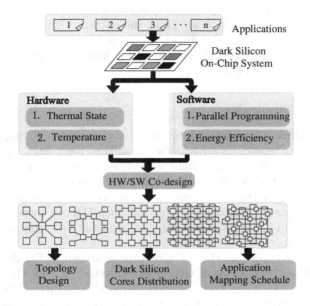

Fig. 2. The overview of hardware/software co-design.

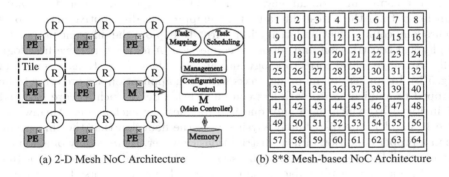

(a) 2-D Mesh NoC Architecture   (b) 8*8 Mesh-based NoC Architecture

Fig. 3. 2-D mesh based Network-on-Chip architectures.

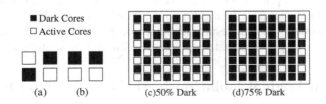

Fig. 4. The dark silicon patterns with different dark ratio.

Cores are powered on every other one as shown in Fig. 4(b) is better for heat dissipation compared with Fig. 4(a). Thus, the pattern with darkness ratio 50 % shown in Fig. 4(c) is chosen according to Fouriers law, in which active cores are denoted as white circles and dark cores are solid. We further present dark silicon pattern with 75 % in Fig. 4(d).

3.2   Network Topologies

NoC is a communication centric interconnection approach to improve system performance. Basic topologies are categorized as Bus, Ring, Star, Tree and Mesh, and more complex networks are built as hybrids of two or more of the basic topologies, such as Full Mesh, Unfolded Torus, Folded Torus, Octagon, SPIN, BFT, etc. [1]. One of the main goals is to improve network performance by providing better static topological characteristics. We are interested in Mesh, Unfolded Torus and Folded Torus topologies, which are the commonly used on-chip network connections for intensive study.

We provide a 64 cores on-chip architecture as shown in Fig. 3(b). Formally, it comprises of a 8×8 array of tiles interconnected by link channels on the physical platform. As mesh and unfolded torus are unbefitting to balance the contradiction of performance and chip temperature in the dark silicon era, we focus on the folded torus topology as shown in Fig. 5(a). On folded torus topology, application with inter-processor communication should be mapped adjacent to reduce communication latency, while the chip temperature should be maintain lower than the threshold value that mapping on distributive active cores incurs long communication latency in return. To explore the inherent properties of physical construction and topology connection of folded torus, we first logically rearrange folded torus topology into an equivalent connections as shown in Fig. 5(b). In application mapping, tasks within an application are preferred to be mapped to ambient cores with less communication delay, such as core 1, 3 and 17 in Fig. 5(b), which have only one hop for message exchanging. Meanwhile, core 1, 3 and 17 are distributed physically on the floorplan that the chip would be in a proper condition of heat distribution. However, there is only one hop for the curve linked pairs of cores, such as (1, 2), (9, 10) and (7, 8), (15, 16), (63, 64), which are physically adjacent on the chip and may lead worse temperature. Thus, we get rid all of these curve links that the logical folded torus topology, as shown in Fig. 5(c), is constituted with four clusters.

To explore the applicability of physical-logical isolation in folded torus topology in dark silicon domain. In logical connection of cores, folded torus has less communication delay, which results in better performance. In physical configuration, folded torus provides better power distribution on many-core platform.

4   Physical-Logical Isolation in the Dark Silicon Era

In this paper, we isolate the folded torus into physical and logical views to demonstrate the hardware and software co-design in the dark silicon era. On top

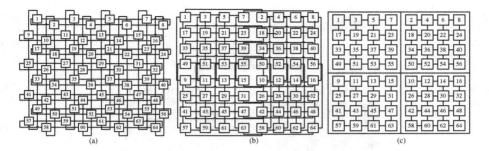

Fig. 5. Folded torus network topologies. (a) Folded torus topology. (b) Equivalent folded torus topology. (c) Modified clustered folded torus topology.

of it, we target on mapping a set of independent applications to the architecture as proposed in Fig. 5, and managing the dark silicon many-core system to achieve high performance and keep the chip temperature below the safe temperature threshold.

Given a task graph and a heterogenous folded torus, we do the application on the folded torus. Figure 6 shows an example of mapping an application to a target platform with four clusters, b (big cores with high frequency), M_1, M_2 and L (LITTLE cores with low frequency). Each cluster is composed of the same type of cores. In this example, application is mapped to cluster b with big cores. Tasks are mapped decentralized on the chip in the physical view, such as tasks t_1 and t_2 are mapped to core 1 and core 3, respectively. However, they are directly connected in the logic view. In this way, the peak temperature of the chip is kept low due to the better heat dissipation; tasks communicate with the low delay due to the logical interconnection.

5   Experiment

We consider the 64-core system presented in Fig. 3 as the platform. The experimental evaluation is on a heterogeneous clustered Folded Torus, consisting of four types of cores, Little (L), Mid (M_1, M_2) and big (b), with increasing computation power [9]. Particularly, the micro-architectural parameters of the core libraries are detailed in Table 1. We employ McPAT [8] as the power estimation engine for Alpha 21264 cores of different types in 22-nm technology. As the benchmark applications, we first randomly generate a large set of synthetic task graphs with mixed workloads using the Task Graph For Free (TGFF) suit [3]. The message sizes on the edges of the synthetic task graphs are assigned randomly in the ranges that make the communication delays in the same order of magnitude as the task execution times.

First, we compare the steady state temperature and heat distribution of Mesh-based and Folded Torus-based NoCs by running applications. The results are shown in Fig. 7. Applications are mapped for achieving minimum communication latency with heat concentrated within an area in mesh NoC, as shown

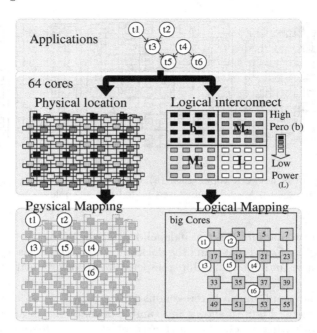

Fig. 6. Application mapping on folded torus architectural in physical and logical views.

Table 1. Core configurations

Cluster type	Freq (GHz)	Cache level	Power (W)	Area (mm^2)
L	3.0	L2	3.715	0.816
M_1	3.5	L2	6.544	1.046
M_2	4.0	L2	19.691	1.086
b	4.5	L2	28.808	1.178

in Fig. 7(a), so that the heat cannot be dissipated effectively. Though mesh can obtain similar performance as clustered folded torus NoC, the mapping on mesh topology results in thermal hotspot on the chip. The thermal gradients are reduced in folded torus, on which tasks are distributed on the chip physically. The temperature difference between mesh and folded torus could be as high as 9.3°C as observed in Fig. 8, where the thermal states are generated by HotSpot v 5.02 [7]. At the same time, minimum communication cost is achieved by application mapping in the logically condensed topology, such that the elimination of hotspot and equilibrium of temperature are achieved with better performance on folded torus. That means the isolation of folded torus-like organization is efficient for temperature control and performance improving in many-core systems with dark silicon.

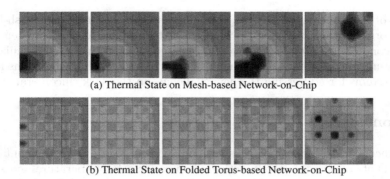

(a) Thermal State on Mesh-based Network-on-Chip

(b) Thermal State on Folded Torus-based Network-on-Chip

Fig. 7. Comparison of chip temperature and application performance on Mesh and Folded Torus.

Second, to further explore the communication overheads in the NoC, we compare the performance on mesh and folded torus NoC, in which both topologies have the same application mapping on the physical cores. Thus, the locations of active cores running the application are the same, so the chip temperature on both NoCs are expected to be similar, and we compare the difference on communication overhead. The results are summarized in Fig. 8(b), where the applications generated by TGFF are scheduled on mesh and folded torus NoC. Though applications are executed on the same set of cores according to their physical locations, the application performance in terms of schedule length on folded torus is on average 39.44 % better than that on mesh. This proves that the folded torus-like organization can greatly reduce communication overhead and in turn transform to significantly improved performance for dark silicon many-core systems, compared to traditional mesh-based architectures. Combined with the

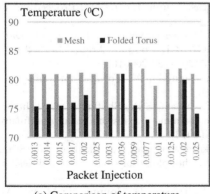

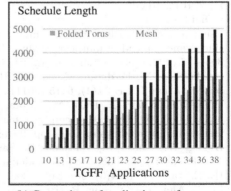

(a) Comparison of temperature

(b) Comparison of application performance

Fig. 8. Comparison of the heat distribution on Mesh and Folded Torus.

first set of experiments, we observe that different from the traditional mesh-based system organization, which could only select to optimize either chip temperature or communication performance, the isolated folded torus-based organization could result in consistent improvement in both objectives. It outperforms mesh-based systems for addressing the new challenges in the dark silicon era.

6 Conclusion

Dark silicon brings new challenges to many-core system due to the conflicting requirements on the selectively activated cores for safe temperature and short-distance communication considerations. We propose physical and logical isolated framework such that the cores within a cluster are physically distant but logically adjacent to each other for the best temperature and inter-communication performance. Performance evaluation results show significant advantages of the proposed approach compared to traditional mesh-based systems.

Acknowledgement. This work is partially supported by Natural Science Foundation Of China (NSFC) No.61402060, National 863 Program 2013AA013202 and 2015AA015304, and Chongqing High-Tech Research Program cstc2014yykfB40007, China.

References

1. Bhople, S.S., Gaikwad, M.A.: Article: A comparative study of different topologies for network-on-chip architecture. IJCA Special Issue on Recent Trends in Engineering Technology RETRET, 27–29, March 2013
2. Chantem, T., Dick, R., Hu, X.: Temperature-aware scheduling and assignment for hard real-time applications on mpsocs. In: Proceedings of DATE, pp. 288–293, March 2008
3. Dick, R.P., Rhodes, D.L., Wolf, W.: Tgff: Task graphs for free. In: Proceedings of CODES+ISSS
4. Esmaeilzadeh, H., Blem, E., St. Amant, R., Sankaralingam, K., Burger, D.: Dark silicon and the end of multicore scaling. SIGARCH Comput. Archit. News **39**(3), 365–376 (2011). http://doi.acm.org/10.1145/2024723.2000108
5. Hardavellas, N., Ferdman, M., Falsafi, B., Ailamaki, A.: Toward dark silicon in servers. Micro IEEE **31**(4), 6–15 (2011)
6. Henkel, J., Bauer, L., Dutt, N., Gupta, P., Nassif, S.R., Shafique, M., Tahoori, M.B., Wehn, N.: Reliable on-chip systems in the nano-era: lessons learnt and future trends. In: Proceedings of DAC, pp. 99–99 (2013)
7. Huang, W., Ghosh, S., Velusamy, S., Sankaranarayanan, K., Skadron, K., Stan, M.: Hotspot: a compact thermal modeling methodology for early-stage vlsi design. IEEE Tran. VLSI **14**(5), 501–513 (2006)
8. Li, S., Ahn, J.H., Strong, R., Brockman, J., Tullsen, D., Jouppi, N.: Mcpat: An integrated power, area, and timing modeling framework for multicore and manycore architectures. In: Proceedings of MICRO, pp. 469–480, December 2009

9. Pagani, S., Khdr, H., Munawar, W., Chen, J.J., Shafique, M., Li, M., Henkel, J.: Tsp: Thermal safe power: Efficient power budgeting for many-core systems in dark silicon. In: Proceedings of CODES+ISSS, pp. 10:1–10:10. ACM, New York (2014). http://doi.acm.org/10.1145/2656075.2656103

10. Shafique, M., Garg, S., Henkel, J., Marculescu, D.: The eda challenges in the dark silicon era: temperature, reliability, and variability perspectives. In: Proceedings of DAC, pp. 185:1–185:6. ACM, New York (2014). http://doi.acm.org/10.1145/2593069.2593229

11. Shafique, M., Garg, S., Mitra, T., Parameswaran, S., Henkel, J.: Dark silicon as a challenge for hardware/software co-design: Invited special session paper. In: Proceedings of CODES+ISSS, pp. 13:1–13:10. ACM, New York (2014). http://doi.acm.org/10.1145/2656075.2661645

12. Taylor, M.: Is dark silicon useful? harnessing the four horsemen of the coming dark silicon apocalypse. In: Proceedings of DAC, pp. 1131–1136, June 2012

13. Taylor, M., Kim, J., Miller, J., Wentzlaff, D., Ghodrat, F., Greenwald, B., Hoffman, H., Johnson, P., Lee, J.W., Lee, W., Ma, A., Saraf, A., Seneski, M., Shnidman, N., Strumpen, V., Frank, M., Amarasinghe, S., Agarwal, A.: The raw microprocessor: a computational fabric for software circuits and general-purpose programs. Micro IEEE **22**(2), 25–35 (2002)

Development of the Lithium Battery On-Board Charger for Electric Vehicle Based on ZCS

Tian Yan-fang$^{(\boxtimes)}$ and Mei Jian-wei

College of Electrical and Information Engineering,
Hubei University of Automotive Technology, Shiyan 442002, China
2362567039@qq.com

Abstract. The lithium battery on-board charger was developed for electric vehicles, Single phase full bridge ZCS circuit is the main loop of the power transformation, TMS320F28027 is used as the control core of supervisory control and data transmission system, a constant voltage, constant current and charging process control algorithm is developed, the hardware control circuit based on ZCS power transformation is designed. The experimental results show that the car charger well implement the charging process control, data transmission and monitoring and protection function, high reliability.

Keywords: On-board charger · ZCS · Slope compensation · Double-loop control

1 Introduction

Car charger is one of the major projects of electric vehicle, current domestic production of the few units in car charger of electric vehicle (ev) mainly has two kinds of structure, one is the traditional structure of two levels of power transformation, have the features of large volume, low efficiency, it is difficult to meet the needs of the electric car to car charger, the other is structure of single stage power conversion, power conversion unit reality the adjustment of power factor and power conversion at the same time, small volume, power density increased significantly, but also has the problem of reliability. Subject of the pure electric vehicle power vehicle charging machine adopts soft switch technology based on ZCS, small switch loss, switching stress is small, high reliability [1, 2].

2 Main Circuit Topology Structure

The main circuit is single phase full bridge inverter circuit based on zero current switch, L_{g1} and auxiliary capacitance C_1, C_2 is the input EMI filter, L_0, C_3 is low-pass filter converts, pulsating dc voltage of the rectifier output constant dc voltage, Q1, Q2, Q3, Q4, T, D9, D10, D11, D12 is power conversion circuit, L_{g2} and auxiliary capacitance C_6, C_7 is the output EMI filter, reduce the output voltage ripple [3–5] (Fig. 1).

© Springer Science+Business Media Singapore 2015
X. Zhang et al. (Eds.): ESTC 2015, CCIS 572, pp. 110–117, 2015.
DOI: 10.1007/978-981-10-0421-6_11

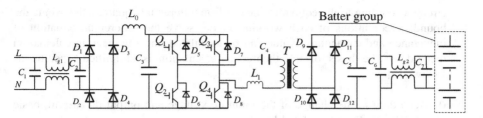

Fig. 1. Main circuit diagram of charger

3   The Hardware Circuit Design

(1) The main technical parameters

(1)   input voltage: AC 187 V ~ 253 V, output voltage: DC 120 V ~ 175 V;
(2)   Rated current: 16 A;
(3)   The efficiency: >90 %;
(4)   Working temperature: −20 0 C ~ 85 0 C;

(2) Transformer design

The working frequency of high frequency transformer of subject is 20 KHz, small loss at high frequency, core permeability capability and resist saturated ability is strong. The output is up to 400 v dc side voltage, transformer turn ratio is 1:2, so using nickel zinc EE type as magnetic core.

The secondary side power: $P_{2S} = I_O \times (V_O + 2V_d) = 20.0 \times (175 + 2) = 3540$ (VA)

The total apparent power: $P_t = P_{2S} + \frac{P_{2S}}{\eta} = 3540 + \frac{3540}{0.93} = 7346.5$ (VA)

Electromagnetic state coefficient:

$$Ke = 0.145 \times (K_f)^2 f^2 B_m^2 \times 10^{-4} = 0.145 \times 4^2 \times 20^2 \times 10^6 \times 0.2^2 \times 10^{-4}$$
$$= 3712 \ (\text{W/cm}^5)$$

Magnetic core geometry factor: $Kg = \frac{P_t}{2Ke\alpha} = \frac{5873.1}{2 \times 3712 \times 0.5} = 1.97 (\text{cm}^5)$.

The skeleton occupy core window area, the actual use of the core of the window area, just can achieve the theoretical value of 0.6, so the whole window utilization coefficient was reduced, the core geometry constants is multiplied by 1.67, so:

$$Kg = 1.67 \times 1.97 = 3.298 (\text{cm}^5)$$

We choose iron powder EE core, core models: EE75.

(3) The resonant circuit parameters design

For the theoretical calculation of the resonant circuit parameters, according to the working state of the series resonance soft switch circuit, draw the equivalent circuit, according to the equivalent circuit lists differential equation, determine the boundary conditions of each working mode, solve the differential equation of inductance and capacitance value can be calculated out. Engineering calculation method on the basis of the theoretical calculation is simplified, specific as follows [6].

(a) According to the change of the input dc voltage and output dc current, basic impedance Zb is calculated by (1)

$$Z_b = \frac{U_{imin}}{I_{omax}} \tag{1}$$

(b) According to the capacity of converter and selection of switching devices, as well as to requirements of the size, weight, reliability, and cost, choose the highest working frequency f_{max}, so as to determine the basic angular frequency w_b.

$$w_b > 2\pi f_{max} \tag{2}$$

(c) According to the following two type, we can calculate basic resonant parameters:

$$L_b = \frac{Z_b}{w_b} \quad C_b = \frac{1}{w_b \times Z_b} \tag{3}$$

(d) In order to make the converter work in discontinuous conduction mode, the parameters must be made by (4)

$$L_1 = 0.833 L_b, C_1 = 1.2 C_b \tag{4}$$

Resonant inductance L1 and resonant capacitor C1 are equivalent parameters.

$$L_1 = L_{串} + L_{漏} \tag{5}$$

The former is series inductance, $L_{漏}$ is the sum of the transformer with secondary sliding sideways feeling after conversion (secondary side).

$$C_1 = C_{串} + C_{分布} . \tag{6}$$

The former is a series capacitor, $C_{分布}$ is distributed capacitance value in a circuit.

By practical calculation: $L_1 = 0.5 mH, C_1 = 2\mu F$.

(4) Control circuit design

The main functions of the control circuit is: the inverter bridge drive and control, signal acquisition, process control and protection function. So this control system is divided into the following several parts [7, 8] (Fig. 2).

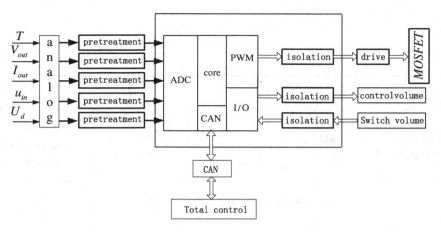

Fig. 2. Structure diagram of system control

(5) The control circuit voltage/current adjusting

In Fig. 3, U_0, I_0 is the output voltage and output current feedback, including 1 foot of U_{1A} is current the output as the reference voltage inner ring, R_3, C_1 is current loop feedback compensation link, R_{14}, C_{13} is the voltage loop feedback compensation, the output of the linear light lotus root is 5 feet of U_{14} input, the input voltage adjust the pulse width of control voltage [9].

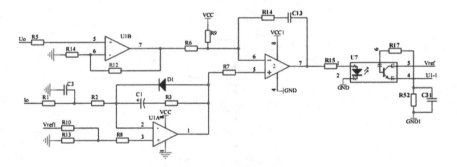

Fig. 3. Control circuit diagram of double closed loop

4 The Software Design

The main functions of the function of the software system: diagnoses before the start of charger, after conform to technical requirements, modules in the process of the promoter is controlled by the software system, after the completion of the start, the charging process is controlled the software, The running state of the charging machine is testing, Running state control system work mode, software system structure diagram as shown in Fig. 4.

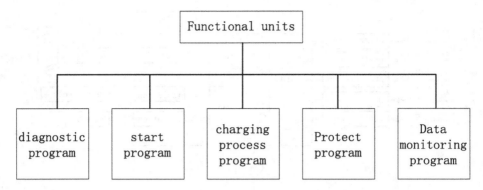

Fig. 4. Structure diagram of the software

(1) The boot process control principle

After the system is powered on, diagnosis system to check whether the input overvoltage, undervoltage, battery status is normal, whether overheating, whether or not Reverse connection, after self-checking normal, enter the start working mode. Startup process determines the amount of overshoot the Boost circuit, the reliability of the inverter bridge, and whether the output relay can work reliably. the flow diagram of start is as shown in Fig. 5.

(2) Charging process control structure principle

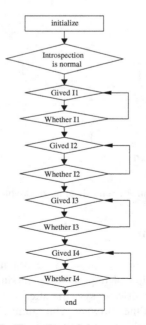

Fig. 5. Flow chart of the start process

After the start-up process, current charging is 16 A constant, outer ring for the current loop, when the charging voltage is 400 V, constant voltage charging is begined, until after the charging current is less than 0.5 A charging is complete, system safety is shutdown, charging process control principle diagram is shown in Fig. 6.

I_{ref} is a given output current value, I_0 is the feedback current value, the output of the current loop as the reference voltage loop, U_0 is the feedback voltage value.

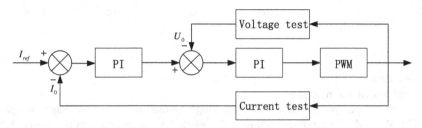

Fig. 6. Block diagram of double closed loop control

5　The Test Results and the Analysis of Data

According to technology requirements for car charger of a certain type of electric vehicle, we make the prototype, when single phase alternating current Voltage is 178 V to 265 V, the technical indicators of charger was tested, and part of the waveform as shown in Fig. 7, the test data as shown in Table 1.

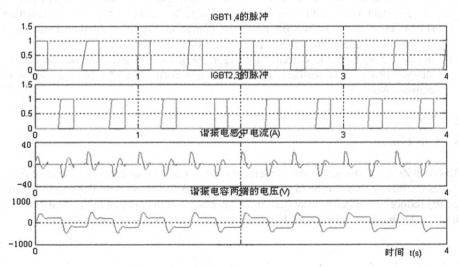

Fig. 7. Voltage and current waveform figure of Harmonic components

Table 1. Test data of car charger

Input voltage $u_{rms}(V)$	Input current $i_{rms}(A)$	Input power $P_1(kW)$	Output voltage $U_0(V)$	Output current $I_0(A)$	Output ripple $\delta(V)$
168.2	7.22	1.21	127.8	8.05	20
188	7.7	1.44	160.3	8.05	5.6
189.4	5.1	0.97	102.5	8.05	4.7
189	7.65	1.448	156.5	8.05	7.52
190.3	5.34	1.0	106.4	8.05	3.92
190.7	6.73	1.269	135.6	8.05	4.48

(2) Test datas

(3) Analysis of the results

Prototype power is 1500 w, single-phase ac input voltage range is 178 V ∼ 265 V, output dc voltage is 0 V–175.2 V, output current is 0 A–16 A, the power analyzer was used to this prototype, according to the test the following conclusions is resulted.

(a) When the load is weak capacitive, the inverter switching frequency for 1/2 of the natural frequency, if duty ratio of power devices is greater than half cycle duration of the resonant inductance current and is less than the negative half cycle, it can realize zero current of power device turn off.

(b) When the hybrid modulation method (PWM and PFM) is used, in regulating the charging machine power output zero current switching can be achieved;

(c) switch conduction constant pulse width ton is fixed, switch frequency is equal to or less than half of the resonant frequency, the pulse frequency modulation (PFM) change the switch off time, the operation condition of the circuit is in current intermittent, the resonant condition of is unchanged.

(d) the output voltage and current of charger charging is tested, the boot process of charger charging is realized, undisturbed transformation of constant-current to constant voltage.

6 Conclusion

Based on ZCS car charger in the implementation of power conversion at the same time, makes the power switch tube in the condition of zero current switch. For commutation, greatly reduce the switch tube switch stress, improve the efficiency of the system running, the vehicle charging machine high efficient, small switch stress, high reliability.

References

1. Wan, K., Feng, Y.: Discuss of fast charging technology. J. China Agric. Univ. **12**, 62–67 (2006)
2. Perreault, D.J., Selders, R.L., Kassakian, J.G.: Frequency-based current-sharing techniques for paralleled power converters. IEEE Trans. PE **13**(4), 626–634 (1998)
3. Malesani, L., Tenti, P.: A novel hysteresis control method for current controlled VSI. IEEE Trans. Ind. Appl. Part I **26**(1), 88–92 (1990)
4. Zhao, Q., Chen, Z., Wu, W.: Improved control for parallel inverter with current-sharing control scheme. In: CES/IEEE 5th International Power Electronics and Motion Control Conference, IPEMC 2006, pp. 1–5 (2006)
5. Yan, X., Lipei, H., Sun, S., et al.: Novel control for redundant parallel UPSs with instantaneous current sharing. In: IEEE PCC Conference Recordings, pp. 959–963 (2002)
6. Wang, Z., Wei, Y.: Principle and Application of the Soft Switching Power Supply, p. 4. Electronic Industry Press, Beijing (2006)
7. Yang, S., Xing, Z., Zhang, C.: Inverter parallel technology research based on droop. New Technol. Electr. Power **2**, 7–10, 80 (2006)
8. Zeng, J.: Single phase double conversion on-line UPS and its parallel operation. Huazhong University of Science and Technology (2003)
9. Chen, L., Lan, X., et al.: Double closed loop control of voltage source inverter parallel system circulation characteristics research. J. Electrotechnics **5**, 21–24 (2004)

Pocket Printer - A Novel Idea and Implement About Printer

Peng Kang[✉], Qi Zhou, Wei-Qiang Chen, and Mei-Rong Pan

School of Mobile Information Engineering,
Sun Yat-sen University, Guangzhou, China
{kangp3, zhouq66, chenwq39, panmr}@mail2.sysu.edu.cn

Abstract. Nowadays, normal printers in the market are very big and heavy, which is likely not convenient for personal office and tends to decline the efficiency of our work. To solve this problem, the demand for a mini, smart and wireless printer is rapidly increasing. And our pocket printer, which tends to be small enough to fit into a usual pocket could move itself and print letters wirelessly on any size of paper. This kind of printer could be just as big as a cup, which is very convenient to carry and efficient in printing.

Keywords: Pocket · Smart · Wireless · Printers · Personal office · Efficiency

1 Introduction

Printer in people's daily life plays a very important role. It can help enterprise personnel print office documents and business contracts, can help print student graduation thesis, learning materials and so on. A lot of people has been inseparable from it. The birth of mobile technology, it seems that any product is about the mobility and portability, and the printer is also quietly changing, becoming smaller and smaller, more and more portable.

The traditional printer has some disadvantages. As we know, the traditional printer is big, so it is impossible to be carried around. We have to go to somewhere with a printer when we need to print something, which is very inconvenient and inefficient. For another hand, the size of paper for traditional printer is fixed, that is to say, the kinds of paper size we can use are limited. Finally, the traditional printer is more expensive and has a more complex structure, which results in a higher maintenance cost. To solve these problems, a mini smart printer is developed. Our mini smart printer is a new kind of printer that is easily carried, not limited by the size of paper and cheaper than the traditional printer.

At home and abroad, there is no any successful products like this kind of mini smart printer. There have been two kinds of mini printer in the market. However, one kind of them is the ink-jet printer. It can be only used to print receipts. Its function is limited. The other one is a kind of dye sublimation printer. However, this kind of printer has high requirements in paper. It is expensive in maintenance.

Both of these two kinds of mini printer are limited by the size of paper, which is a big difference from our mini printer. A mobile way is used by our mini printer to print

X. Zhang et al. (Eds.): ESTC 2015, CCIS 572, pp. 118–129, 2015.
DOI: 10.1007/978-981-10-0421-6_12

words, that is to say, our printer can move when prints words, so our mini printer can work on any size of paper. In addition, the wifi is used to access the printer system. Once we need to print something, we only need to put our mini printer out from our pocket, and send a file in mobile phone or computer to the printer system to print out [1, 2]. A new printing method used by our pocket printer is different from the traditional ways. When the pocket printer works, the printer itself moves in a straight line on the paper, and the printing head fixed within the printer prints characters. And these two functions - moving and printing work in parallel.

The paper is organized as follows: Sect. 2 is the hardware system design. In Sect. 3, we present the software system design. Then, we perform the experiment and illustrate the results in Sect. 4. Finally, the conclusion is demonstrated in Sect. 5.

2 Hardware System Design

The pocket printer should work in a mobile way, so to control the printing head and the movement of the printer is needed. The printer can communicate with a mobile phone or a computer in a wireless way. As for the key component which is used for printing, ink jet printing head should be chosen carefully.

2.1 Circuit Design

The whole circuit which is showing in the Fig. 1 consists of four parts: Arduino connections, Supply voltage management, 20 V boost converter, Ink driver.

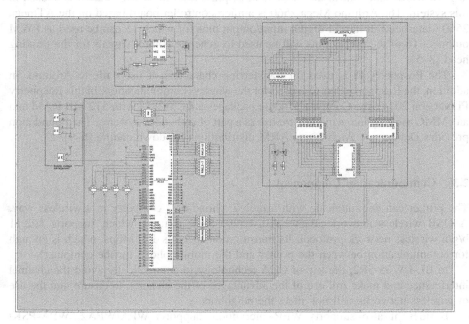

Fig. 1. The whole circuit consists of four parts: Arduino connections, supply voltage management, 20 V boost converter, Ink driver

Arduino connections part is the control component. It consists of an Arduino board and a Raspberry Pi. Control signals will be generated by the Arduino board to control the printing head to print words and control the movement of the printer. The Raspberry Pi is used to send characters of the file users want to print to the Arduino.

Supply voltage management part supplies power for the control component. Because the working powers of the control component and the printing head are different, we need different power providers. The Supply voltage management part is used to provide the control component with 5 V power.

20 V boost converter is for another power provider. It is used to provide stable power at 20 V for the printing head. To protect the circuit, we make it to be a separate component.

Ink driver is an important transmission component. It is used to transmit the control signals from the control component to the printing head and transmit the power from the 20 V boost converter to the printing head. There are totally 16 output ports to receive the control signals, which are corresponding to the ports on the printing head.

2.2   Control Component

The pocket printer should work in a mobile way, so to control the printing head and the movement of the printer is needed. The control component consists of two parts: an Arduino board and a Raspberry Pi.

Control signals will be generated by the Arduino board to control the printing head to print words and control the movement of printer. Arduino Mega 2560 is chosen in this system. The Arduino Mega 2560 is a microcontroller board based on the ATmega 2560 (datasheet). It has 54 digital input/output pins (of which 15 can be used as PWM outputs). 16 of the output pins will be used to generate control signals for the printing head [3–5].

The Raspberry Pi is used for transferring characters of users file to Arduino. In addition, the Raspberry Pi is also used for the wireless communication. In this Raspberry Pi (version 2014), the Compute Module packages a BCM2835 with 512 MB RAM and an eMMC ash chip into a module for use as a part of embedded systems. The Foundation provides Debian and Arch Linux ARM distributions for downloading [6–9].

2.3   Communication Component

The printer can communicate with a mobile phone or a computer in a wireless way. A USB wireless network adapter (BL-LW05-5R2) is used, which supports 802.11 b/g/n wireless network protocol. Its transmission speed is 150 Mbps, which is enough for communication between the printer and the mobile phone (or the computer).

In BL-LW05-5R2, the use of CCA technology to automatically avoid the channel interference and make full use of the advantages of the channel, to ensure that the use of wireless networks will not affect the neighbors.

Besides, it also supports WEP encryption, supports WPA/WPA2, WPA-PSK/WPA2-PSK and other advanced encryption and security mechanism. Wireless network provides a much more convenient way in the communication between the pocket printer and the mobile phone (or the computer).

2.4 Printing Head

In this system, ink jet printing head is chosen as the actuator. And the HP-C6602A is chosen, because this kind of printing head satisfies the printing requirements, and it is easier to control and cheaper than other printing heads.

HP-C6602A is a dot matrix printing head. Dot matrix printing is a type of computer printing which uses a print head that moves back and forth, or in an up and down motion on the page and prints by impacting and striking an ink-soaked cloth ribbon against the paper, much like the printing mechanism on a typewriter. However, unlike a typewriter or daisy wheel printer, letters are drawn out of a dot matrix, and thus, varied fonts and arbitrary graphics can be produced [10, 11].

The advantage of dot matrix is that they can produce graphical images in addition to text; however the text is generally of poorer quality than impact printers that use letterforms [12].

2.5 Moving Platform

To make a perfect product, all of these parts should be put on a moving platform including Arduino, raspberry pi, supply voltage management, 20 V boost converter, and Ink driver. And all of these parts should be integrated to minimize our product. At present, in terms of testing and efficiency, we just use Lego to make a simple platform. And we fix our printing head under the platform and our voltage management and integrated part on the platform. With four wheels making a crisscross pattern, our printer could move in a straight line on the paper driven by the Arduino and print letters clearly. This is the main difference between our pocket printer and other printers in the shopping mall.

3 Software System Design

In order to implement the function of pocket printer, we tend to design a robust software system. With this system, pocket printer could receive characters from the file which user want to print, and then it controls its printing head to spray ink and moves on the paper. From the description, it concludes that three parts are included in our software system. Firstly, a shell script needs to be implemented on the raspberry pi which means that users could log on the pocket printer and print files wirelessly. Moreover, an Arduino file needs to be written to control its printing head to spray ink. In the end, in order to realize print a file clearly, we would need to combine printing with moving and make these two functions work in parallel. In the Fig. 2, it displays the flow chart of our whole software system design.

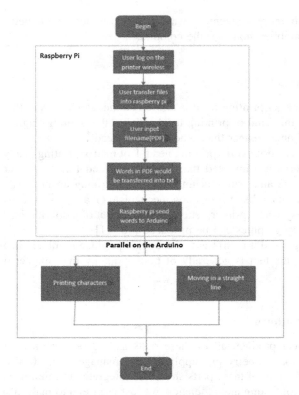

Fig. 2. The flow chart of pocket printers software system design

3.1   Upper Monitor - A Shell Script on the Raspberry Pi

As an upper monitor, it would interact with users through a shell script. And this script is like an application which users could click and run to print their files. In the meanwhile, in order to print PDF files, an important Linux command C pdftotext needs to be used when we write and implement this shell script. This command is an open source command-line utility for converting PDF files to plain text files. [13, 14] **upper monitor – a shell script** is our shell script which can transfer the characters of users pdf into output.txt, and then use the python file C transfer.py to send all the words of output.txt to Arduino.

UPPER MONITOR - A SHELL SCRIPT

```
1 #! /bin/bash
2 echo –n "Enter your filename (PDF):"
3 # user input the file they want to print
4 read filename
5 pdftotext $filename output.txt
6 python transfer.py
```

Moreover, transfer.py could send all of words in output.txt to Arduino. Code for Transfer.py illustrates how it complete this function.

CODE FOR TRANSFER.PY

```
1 import serial, time, sys
2 arduino = serial.Serial ('/dev/ttyACM0', 9600,
3 timeout = 1)
4 arduino.open ()
5
6 file = open("output.txt")
7
8 While True:
9    line = file.readline()
10   If not line:
11      break
12   For letter in line
13      arduino.write(letter)
14      time.sleep (1)
```

After transferring, Arduino shield needs to control printing head to print each word of users' pdf.

In addition, the reason why we use raspberry pi is that it can help our printer realize the function of wireless. Users could log on the raspberry pi through wireless network. That means our users could log on our printer wirelessly and transfer their files into raspberry pi and print them wirelessly.

3.2   Lower Computer - Control Printing Head

In order to print all kinds of characters, firstly a library needs to be created which tends to contain various words we would use to express in our daily life. And a matrix called font is used to contain these characters whose ASCII are between 32 and 96. Each character is represented with a matrix which has ten rows and 18 columns. And in every row, the first two codes 0b stand for control signal, the next two codes 00 mean low voltage level, the following two codes 00 are stored and the remaining 12 codes are used to control whether the printing head will spray ink or not (1 represents spraying ink and 0 represents not). An example is showing in the following Fig. 3 which stands for the character E and F.

Then Arduino Mega is initialized on pin 2 and its frequency is set to be 9600. And after that, if there are characters in the buffer of Arduino which means Arduino receives the words transferred from the raspberry pi, Arduino will judge which character it is and use the function "spray letter" to print these words. Following that, if these characters are recognized to be lowercase letters, they need to be transformed into uppercase letters, because our character library only has letters whose ASCII are between 32 and 96.

Next we need to focus on how to realize the function of "spray letter". In these function, it firstly uses #ASCII of letter we want to print to find its beginning row in the

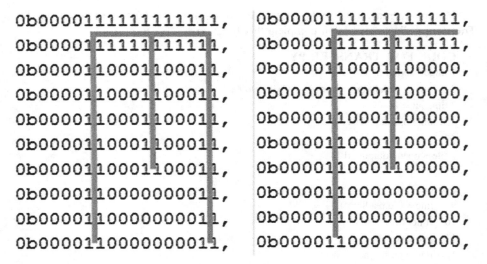

```
0b0000111111111111,    0b0000111111111111,
0b0000111111111111,    0b0000111111111111,
0b0000110001100011,    0b0000110001100000,
0b0000110001100011,    0b0000110001100000,
0b0000110001100011,    0b0000110001100000,
0b0000110001100011,    0b0000110001100000,
0b0000110001100011,    0b0000110001100000,
0b0000110000000011,    0b0000110000000000,
0b0000110000000011,    0b0000110000000000,
0b0000110000000011,    0b0000110000000000,
```

Fig. 3. Character E and F representing with matrixes

matrix "font". Then it uses loop function for ten times (each letter is represented by a matrix with ten rows) and uses the function "spray ink" to print each row of the letter. Finally, this pocket printer could print a complete letter we want to print.

Furthermore, we should pay attention to realizing the function of "spray ink". From existing information, our printing head is an ink printing head. If we want this printing head to spray ink, pulse signals should be given to the corresponding channels of this printing head. And each letter is actually controlled by 12 channels (2 of 14 channels are stored). Then pulse signals are given to the corresponding channels based on the digits from the right to the left of each letters matrix row. If Arduino reads 1, then pulse is given to that channel, or it will not receive the pulse signal. One example is displaying in the Fig. 4. In this figure, we just use Row 3 to demonstrate our idea.

```
0b0000111111111111,
0b0000111111111111,
0b0000110001100000,
0b0000110001100000,
0b0000110001100000,
0b0000110001100000,
0b0000110001100000,
0b0000110000000000,
0b0000110000000000,
0b0000110000000000,
```

Firstly, Arduino reads a zero, then it does not need to give a pulse to channel 1. Next another four zeros are read. Then Arduino gets a 1, and a pulse should be given to channel 6. And channel 6 will spray ink. Channel 7, 11 and 12 also spray ink because their positions are represented by 1.

Fig. 4. Arduino reads the matrix of letter F and calls the function "spray_ink"

Pseudocode of the function "spray ink" is showing like this:

PSEUDOCODE OF "SPRAY INK"

```
1 Input: ROW (a row of letter's matrix)
2 Output: DigitalWrite (Pulse, i)
3 For (i = 0; i < 12; i + +)
4     //left shift and judge whether that position is 1
5     If (ROW & 1 << i)
6        DigitalWrite (Pulse, i)
```

3.3   Lower Computer - Control Printing Moving

In order to print more clearly and wirelessly, our printer needs to learn how to move around. Unlike general printers, they all need paper to move forward. Our printer, however, needs itself to move in a straight line. So the function of moving needs to be implemented in the Arduino. And to complete it, a platform, which contains all the components our printer need, is built and printing head would be fixed under the platform which may be good for printing.

Implementation of the function moving is showing in the **Code for moving** (moving in a straight line and one motor is used to drive two parallel wheels):

CODE FOR MOVING

```
1 #define m1a 5
2 #define m1b 6
3 void ahead(){
4     digitalWrite(m1a, LOW);
5     digitalWrite(m1b; HIGH);
6 }
7 void Stop(){
8     digitalWrite(m1a, LOW);
9     digitalWrite(m1b, LOW);
10 }
11 void setup(){
12     Serial.begin(9600);
13     pinMode(m1a, OUTPUT);
14     pinMode(m1b, OUTPUT);
15 }
16 void loop(){
17     ahead();
18     delay(50);
19     Stop();
20     delay(50);
21 }
```

3.4   Lower Computer - Printing and Moving in Parallel

Because the function of printing and moving need to work in parallel on the Arduino and Arduino cannot schedule these tasks automatically, a methodology needs to be used to complete it. After doing some research and finding some information on the website, a fantastic project called Arduino-Task-Scheduler [15] from the Github is recognized as a simple and excellent way to solve this problem. This project is just like a library and provides some useful functions to us to schedule different tasks on the Arduino.

Firstly, Sch.init() and Sch.start() are put into the function setup(), and then Sch. dispatchTasks() is located into the function loop(). In these two steps, Sch.init(), Sch. start() and Sch.dispatchTasks() are the functions offered by that project. And then, the implement of function printing and moving are added at the end of codes. Finally, Sch. addTask() is called between Sch.init() and Sch.start() to add tasks into the task scheduler, like the following example in the **Example code for task schedule**.

With this library and these useful functions, Arduino could schedule the printing function and moving function through adjusting different parameters and use the most appropriate parameters to make these two tasks work perfectly in parallel. And all of these things will make our printing more clearly, neatly and wirelessly.

EXAMPLE CODE FOR TASK SCHEDULE

```
1 void setup(){
2    //code…
3    Sch.init();
4    //Add printing task.
5    //Starts at the 0th ms, and runs every 1 ms
6    Sch.addTask(printing, 0, 1, 1);
7    //Add moving task.
8    //Starts at the 1th ms, and runs every 2 ms
9    Sch.addTask(moving, 1, 2, 1);
10   Sch.start();
11 }
```

4   Test and Results

The process of testing is divided into four parts, the first part is to test whether Arduino could give pulse signals to ports of the printing head when codes which are used to print some letters such as I and E are compiled on the Arduino, the second part is to test whether Arduino could receive letters of users files from raspberry pi and give pulse to ports of the printing head, the third part is to test whether printer could move while Arduino is receiving letters of users files from raspberry pi and giving pulse to ports of the printing head, and the final part is to test whether our printer could print a line of words wirelessly which are in the users files and transferred from raspberry pi and at the same time the moving platform is driven by the Arduino.

In the first part, codes which are used to print letter I are written and compiled on the Arduino, and then 2 of 14 ports of ink driver are connected with the oscilloscope and observed whether there will be some wave patterns showing on the screen of oscilloscope. And the testing result is showing in the Fig. 5(a).

In the second part, users log on the printer through the raspberry pi wirelessly, and then they run the shell script and input the name of the file they want to print. And in the following steps, Arduino receive the letters of this file and give pulse to the corresponding ports of ink driver. And then 2 of 14 ports of ink driver are connected with the oscilloscope and observed whether there will be some wave patterns showing on the screen of oscilloscope. And the testing result is showing in the Fig. 5(b).

In the third part, users log on our printer through the raspberry pi wirelessly, and then they run the shell script and input the name of the file they want to print. And in the following steps, Arduino receive the letters of this file and give pulse to the corresponding ports of ink driver. And then 2 of 14 ports of ink driver are connected with the oscilloscope and observed whether there will be some wave patterns showing on the screen of oscilloscope. At the same time, the printer should schedule the function of printing and moving perfectly. This means that it is necessary to test that whether the moving platform could move in a straight line on the paper during the process of printing.

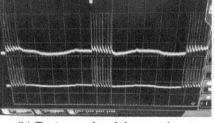

(a) Testing results of the first part   (b) Testing results of the second part

Fig. 5. Testing results of the oscillograph

After testing, the wave patterns are like the waves displaying in the Fig. 6 and the moving platform (printer) can move during the process of printing. And the moving platform is showing in the Fig. 7.

In the final testing part, it is important for us to test whether our printer could spray ink and print a line of letters. And a file filled with a lot of Is is chosen and used to test whether our printer could print a line of Is or not. The final result is showing in the Fig. 7(a). And it proves that our printer is able to print letters of the users' files in reality. Besides, we print a file filled with number 7 as well and its results are showing in the Fig. 7(b). It is clear from these two pictures that our printer could print these characters clearly, although I and 7 are very similar.

Fig. 6. Actual picture of moving platform

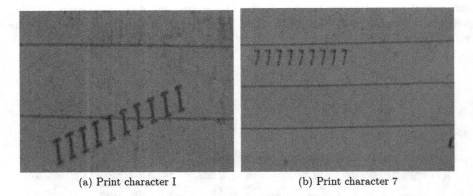

(a) Print character I   (b) Print character 7

Fig. 7. Testing results of our product

5   Conclusions

From the results of these tests, we tend to conclude that our printer could print as clearly as other inkjet printers and it is very different from traditional printers. Our printer could print wirelessly on the different paper with various sizes and the volume of our printer could be smaller than any other printers in the market. In the near future, with the improvement of integration of our printer, we would make it become a printer which can be really put in your pocket.

References

1. Technology C How it works - ZINK - Zero Ink. In: ZINK. Accessed 2 November 2012
2. Zable, J.L., Lee, H.C.: An overview of impact printing. J. Res. Dev. **41**(6), 651–668 (2007). (IBM)
3. Arduino - Introduction. In: arduino.cc
4. Arduino - FAQ. In: Arduino.cc
5. The arduino source code. In: The arduino source code
6. https://en.wikipedia.org/wiki/Raspberry_Pi
7. Brose, M.: Broadcom BCM2835 SoC has the most powerful mobile GPU in the world? In: Grand MAX, 30 January 2012. Archived from the original on 13 April 2012, Accessed 13 April 2012
8. Model B now ships with 512 MB of RAM. In: Raspberrypi.org. Accessed 15 October 2012
9. Verified USB Peripherals and SDHC Cards. In: Eben Upton.2012. Elinux.org. Accessed 6 May 2012
10. Commodore Business Machines, Inc.: VIC-1525 graphics printer user manual. In: Commodore Computer. Accessed 22 February 2015
11. Zerillo, S.D.: Dot matrix printing device employing a novel image transfer technique to print on single or multiple ply print receiving materials. In: 1980-03-25, Nashua, NH. Accessed 16 July 2009
12. https://en.wikipedia.org/wiki/Printer_(computing)#Modern_print_technology
13. https://en.wikipedia.org/wiki/Pdftotext
14. http://linuxappfinder.com/package/poppler-utils
15. https://github.com/blanboom/Arduino-Task-Scheduler

System and Network

Research on Trusted Computing Technology for Embedded Real-Time Operation System

Ming-di Xu[1(✉)] and Fan Zhang[2]

[1] Wuhan Digital Engineering Institute, Wuhan 430205, Hubei, China
mingdixu@163.com
[2] School of Mathematics and Computer Science, Wuhan Polytechnic University,
Wuhan 430023, Hubei, China

Abstract. The trusted computing technology (TCT) is an effective way to solve embedded real-time operation system (ERTOS) security. However, the existing TCT is hard to satisfy the properties of real-time and low power consumption directly. Based on vxworks kernel, this paper put forward a solution of trusted computing by designing embedded real-time trusted computing module and trusted software stack, which could realize the chain of trust by using integrity measurement certificate. Experiments show that the average execution time of commands on trusted platform module saves 65.81 % execution time compared with SW-TP, which can meet the ERTOS requirements of real-time property and low power consumption as a whole.

Keywords: Embedded real-time operation system · Trusted computing · Integrity measurement certificate · Real-time schedule

1 Introductions

With the deep integration of information technology and industrialization, in embedded systems and industrial control area, information security issues become increasingly serious. Such as the stuxnet virus occurred in Iran nuclear power plant in 2010. For industrial control system, there are lots of potential security risks, such as operating system security vulnerabilities, effective management and control for I/O port, old-version anti-virus software, as well as a large number of open universal communications protocol, commercial software.

According to reference [1], the common security requirements of embedded system include user authentication, network authorization access, communication security for terminal to terminal, secure storage of person's private information, content security of system files, and availability of system functions. The same as traditional PC system, in the early design of industrial control system, the security and safety are not considered which result that industrial control system is difficult to resist the existing advanced persistent attacks.

In the aspect that enhancing information system security, trusted computing is a new technology that provides an effective system-level security enhancement method for PC, server, mobile terminals through carrying platform integrity, identity authentication, data protection, etc. Intel, AMD, IBM, Microsoft, Nokia and other companies had introduced

© Springer Science+Business Media Singapore 2015
X. Zhang et al. (Eds.): ESTC 2015, CCIS 572, pp. 133–138, 2015.
DOI: 10.1007/978-981-10-0421-6_13

trusted products supporting trusted computing technology, such as processor supporting trusted execution technology (TXT), trusted platform module (TPM) built-in the chipset, and software-based trusted platform module (SW-TPM), Win10 operating system integrated with trusted computing, and trusted mobile phones. Meanwhile, trusted computing group (TCG) issued a white paper for security of embedded platform [2] in 2012, which provided solution ideas for the security of embedded devices.

Vxworks is an embedded RTOS (Real-Time Operating System) made by wind river company. It has the characteristics of high performance, scalability, et al., and is widely used in various fields. Different from other general embedded operating system, vxworks does not have security features, such as trusted computing, authentication, etc. On the other hand, vxworks system does not support trusted computing technology. Moreover, the existing trusted computing technology could not be migrated to vxworks considering the requirements of real-time and low power consumption, which needs rebuild traditional trusted computing technology.

This paper designs real-time embedded trusted platform module (RE-TPM) and real-time embedded trusted software stack (RE-TSS) by rebuilding vxworks kernel based on integrity measurement certificate.

2   Related Work

The white paper of trusted embedded platform released by TCG points that implementing TCG's trusted computing technology to embedded devices directly would cause many problems. Because embedded system is different with PC platform in terms of architecture, operating mode, etc.

In the respect of constructing trusted computing base (TCB) for embedded devices, Johannes from IAIK institute integrated trusted computing technology with TrustZone to build a embedded trusted computing platform for linux [3]. TrustZone technology reclaims a trusted area in embedded OS kernel to achieve system security, the reclaimed area runs in the processor's security zone. IBM presents PERSEUS for PDA's security architecture, which could isolate the different level applications by using virtual machine [4, 5]. However, architecture based on virtual machine requires a higher system resource overhead and is not applicable to restricted resource, strong real-time embedded system.

Aiming at data leakage and unexpected information flow issures, Lucas and Christoph put forward a method for constructing trusted virtual domain in 2011. The method could isolate different security domain and configure security properties automatically [6]. Denk et al. designed lightweight boot loader Das U-boot [7], which could validate the kernel image of operating system to prevent malicious code execution.

3   Trusted Vxworks

3.1   RE-TPM and RE-TSS

For resource-constrained embedded systems, using TPM chip will bring more time and energy consumption. Aiming at this problem, reference [8] pointed that the TPM chip

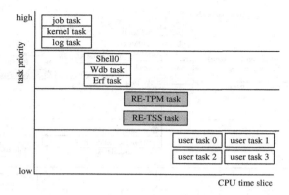

Fig. 1. RE-TPM and RE-TSS tasks

is not suitable for resource-constrained embedded systems and thought that SW-TPM running in protected hardware area is a better choice. To meet the low-power and real-time requirements of vxworks, this paper put forward RE-TPM and RE-TSS, which are all running in kernel mode in vxworks as shown in Fig. 1.

Both RE-TPM and RE-TSS are given higher task priority in order to ensure real-time response to user task. In the meanwhile, RE-TPM and RE-TSS respectively replace SW-TPM [9] and Trousers [10] by removing a lot of the commands that does not suit to embedded system and replacing RSA algorithm with ECC algorithm for reducing execution time.

3.2   Chain of Trust Based on Integrity Measurement Certificate

The chain of trust is to provide local trust evidence for platform remote attestation, while resource-constrained and low-power determine that chain of trust and platform remote attestation of TCG could not be used in embedded system directly. This paper refers reference integrity metric (RIM) certificate structure proposed by TCG mobile working group [11].

```
struct TPM_RIM_CERTIFICATE_STRUCT
{
TPM_STRUCTURE_TAG              tag;
BYTE                          label[8];
UNIT32                        rimVersion;
MTM_COUNTER_REFERENCE         referenceCounter;
TPM_PCR_INFO_SHORT            state;
UNIT32                        measurementPcrIndex;
TPM_PCRVALUE                  measurementValue;
TPM_VERIFICATION_KEY_ID       parentId;
BYTE                          extensionDigestSize;
BYTE         extensionDigestData[extensionDigestSize];
UNIT32       integrityCheckSize;
BYTE         integrityCheckData[integrityCheckSize];
}
```

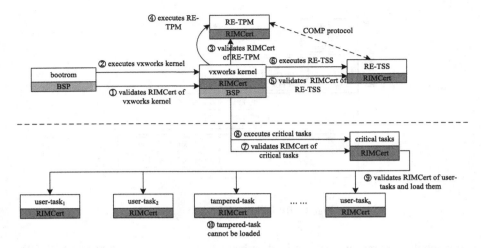

Fig. 2. Chain of trust for vxworks based on integrity measurement certificate

Different from traditional public key certificate, the parentid and integrityCheckData in RIMCert are used for certificate validation. The measurementValue is used for extending specific platform configuration register (PCR).

Different from the RTV authentication mode, as shown in Fig. 2, this paper achieve chain of trust transfer structure based on integrity measurement certificate in vxworks. Vxworks kernel, critical tasks, user tasks must be validated before running. The measurement values are stored into PCR of RE-TPM. Because the entity's RIMCert are all signed by RE-TPM in advance, the attacker is hard to obtain the sign key and forge the valid RIMCert. The assertion could ensure the integrity and authentication of code and environment of vxworks. The scheme is also suit to software running measurement. Meanwhile, TSS device driver layer (TDDL) of RE-TSS communicates with the RE-TPM through specific COMP protocol of vxworks, which ensure the reliability of trusted computing task.

4   Experiments

4.1   Performance Analysis for Commands

The testing platform is composed of Intel i7 2.5 G processor, 2 GB RAM, 500 GB hard disk, vxworks 6.6. Testing object is RE-TPM and SW-TPM [10] which is software-based trusted platform module developed by Strasser. Testing commands include PCR read and write, TPM authorization protocol, TPM key management, TPM encryption and sealed storage. The comparison results are shown in Table 1.

Since RE-TPM is running in vxworks kernel that has more higher task priority, the wind kernel has a better schedule for RE-TPM, which makes RE-TPM significantly better than SW-TPM in encryption and decryption, sealed storage, etc. The average time savings rate is 65.81 %, as shown in Fig. 3.

Table 1. Comparison of command execution time between RE-TPM and SW-TPM

Commands	SW-TPM(ms)	RE-TPM(ms)
TPM_PCRRead	6.69	6.10
TPM_Extend	12.46	6.40
TPM_OIAP	0.21	12.67
TPM_OSAP	0.82	24.00
TPM_TakeOwnership	28619.00	17098.50
TPM_CreateWrapKey	16938.00	12465.30
TPM_LoadKey	5367.00	423.90
TPM_ReadPubek	1.22	9.90
TPM_EvictKey	14.78	166.10
TPM_Sign	902.00	67.70

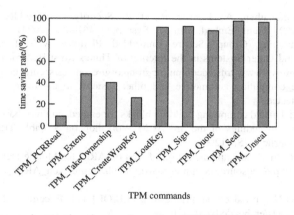

Fig. 3. Command execution time savings rate of RE-TPM compared to SW-TPM

4.2 Performance Analysis for Real-Time Scheduling

According to the characteristics of wind kernel scheduling mechanism, in order to ensure the reliability of trusted computing functions running in wind kernel, this paper uses task priority allocation mechanism for RE-TPM and RE-TSS as follows: RE-TPM is a simulation of TPM hardware chip and so RE-TPM Task must run with a higher task priority to satisfy the real-time response for application. RE-TSS is the middleware where applications access RE-TPM. In order to prevent the occurrence of priority inversion phenomenon, RE-TSS task dynamic inheritances the task priority of RE-TPM's. As shown in Fig. 1, in wind kernel, job-task, exec-task and log-task run at the highest task priority (priority is 0), and Shell0, wdb-task and erf-task run at the second highest task priority (priority less than 10), task priority of RE-TPM task (priority less than 50) is higher than the kernel driver, task priority of RE-TSS task is between RE-TPM Task and kernel driver (priority less than 70).

5   Conclusion

Embedded real-time operating system is the basic guarantee for security of industrial control system, and therefore the security of the system itself is the hot spot of present research. For issues how to implement trusted computing in vxworks, this paper starts from wind kernel and designs the embedded real-time trusted platform module and trusted software stack, and achieves chain of trust based on integrity measurement certificate. Experiment results show that this scheme can meet the real-time and low power consumption requirements of embedded systems. The next work is to to study how to establish standard security configuration for embedded systems.

References

1. Ravi, S., Raghunathan, A., Kocher, P., et al.: Security in embedded systems: design challenges. ACM Trans. Embed. Comput. Syst. 3(3), 461–491 (2004)
2. Trusted Computing Group. Secure Embedded Platform with Trusted Computing: Automotive and Other Systems in the Internet of Things Must Be Protected [EB/OL] (10 June 2012). https://www.trustedcomputinggroup.org/resources/secure_embedded_platforms _with_trusted_computing_automotive_and_other_systems_in_the_internet_of_things_ must_be_protected
3. Johannes, W.: Trusted computing building blocks for embedded linux-based ARM trustzone platforms. In: Proceedings of the 3rd ACM Workshop on Scalable Trusted Computing. ACM Press, Fairfax, USA (2008)
4. Secure Architecture and Implementation of Xen on ARM for Mobile Devices [EB/OL] (21 April 2007). http://xensource.com/files/xensummit4/Secure_Xen_ARM_xen-summit-04_07 _Suh.pdf
5. Embedded XEN Virtualization Framework [EB/OL] (11 December 2012). http://sourc eforge.net/projects/embeddedxen/
6. Lucas, D., Alexandra, D., Christoph, K.: Trusted virtual domains on OKL4: secure information sharing on smartphones. In: Proceedings of the 6th ACM Workshop on Scalable Trusted Computing. ACM Press, Chicago, USA (2011)
7. Das U-boot—The Universal Boot Loader [EB/OL] (08 December 2010). http://sourceforge. net/projects/u-boot/
8. Aaraj, N., Raghunathan, A., Jha, N.K.: Analysis and design of a hardware/software trusted platform module for embedded systems. ACM Trans. Embed. Comput. Syst. 8(1), 1–31 (2008)
9. Strasser, M., Stamer, H.: A software-based trusted platform module emulator. In: Proceedings of the 1st International Conference on Trusted Computing and Trust in Information Technologies. IEEE Press, Heidelberg, Germany (2008)
10. The Open-source TCG Software Stack [EB/OL] (11 October 2008). http://trousers. sourceforge.net/
11. Trusted Computing Group. Mobile Trusted Module (MTM) Specification, Version 1.0 [EB/OL] (14 June 2008). http://wwwtrustedcomputinggroup.org/resources/mobile_phone_ work_group_mobile_trusted_module_specification_version_10

Multi-hop Broadcast for Warning in Urban VANETs

Xiufeng Wang, Chunmeng Wang$^{(\boxtimes)}$, and Gang Cui$^{(\boxtimes)}$

Harbin Institute of Technology, Harbin, China
{wxf,wcm,cg}@hit.edu.cn

Abstract. Traditional directional broadcast protocols cannot efficiently provide data dissemination in urban Vehicular Ad Hoc Networks (VANETs) due to constructions at intersection. To improve dissemination toward all directions and decrease retransmission, in this paper, MBW (Multi-hop Broadcast for Warning) protocol in urban VANETs is proposed. With the MBW protocol, the road is classified into four directions according to the area in which vehicles are, they are east, south, west and north. Relay node at the intersection is decided by following rules: (1) one node records itself is at intersection if it has neighbor nodes from two or more different road direction, and distance between node and neighbor is more than road width. (2) and its ID is the smallest among the nodes at the intersection. Relay nodes at intersections prioritize to forward messages without waiting. On the road, relay nodes are selected according to a waiting time equation, message is broadcasted if waiting time ends, message is propagated in both directions on the road. With relay node selection strategy, The number of relay nodes is decreased, and the number of retransmissions is decreased. Simulation results show that MBW offers better coverage ratio, low delay, low forwarding nodes ratio and lower overhead comparing to exiting broadcasting protocols in urban VANETs.

Keywords: VANETs · Position-based broadcast · Data disseminate · Diverse traffic density

1 Introduction

Multi-hop broadcast technology provides various services including emergency warning and traffic information services in vehicular ad hoc network (VANET) [1]. In order to maximize the propagation of emergency messages along the road or in the relative area, multi-hop broadcast becomes the core technology for providing such services in VANETs. However, multi-hop broadcast is often interfered and affected by contention. If the selected relay nodes are unsuitable for multi-hop broadcast, rebroadcast hops and time will increase, this results in message redundancy and message packet collision. Contention also appears when accessing MAC, hence a broadcast storm will take place [1]. There are some solutions to alleviate the broadcast storm problem in MANET [2–5]. However, such solutions are not fully suitable for resolving the broadcast storm problem in VANET. There is a need for special methods to alleviate broadcast storm in VANET, methods that are based on the characteristics of VANET.

© Springer Science+Business Media Singapore 2015
X. Zhang et al. (Eds.): ESTC 2015, CCIS 572, pp. 139–152, 2015.
DOI: 10.1007/978-981-10-0421-6_14

There are several types of mitigate methods for broadcast storm such as probability-based broadcast, counter-based broadcast, distance based broadcast, neighbor knowledge broadcast and position-based broadcast [6]. The above mentioned schemes limit the relay node numbers for forwarding message, so hops of a message are reduced, the redundancy of a message is decreased, and the broadcast storm is migrated.

In position-based scheme, the neighbor node farthest from the broadcast node is selected as the rebroadcast node. The rebroadcast node for each hop is selected determinately and uniquely, therefore, the position-based schemes have relatively lower broadcast redundancy and latency. At present, most of position-based broadcast protocols which assume that vehicles travel on straight roads in urban VANET, but practical urban scenario consists not only of intersection with traffic lights and buildings but also changes in the density of traffic. So it will decrease message forwarding efficiency at intersection due to miss intersection. In [7–9], ROI (Region of Interesting) dissemination protocol is presented, these protocols consider intersection of the road, it causes network overhead increasing by using maintaining two-hop neighbor information. In this paper, we propose MBW protocol for forwarding messages to a large region around the accident site. The proposed protocol fully considers traffic lights and buildings in practical urban scenarios at the intersections. The goal of this paper is to inform approaching vehicles from all directions to adjust their route for avoiding collision. The contributions of this work are shown as follows:

(1) We establish a cartesian coordinate system for every relay node, the direction of the road is classified into east, south, west and north according area in which vehicles are, if the relay node has neighbors from two or more different direction, and the distance between relay node and neighbor is more than the road width, it will records itself at intersection, and if ID of the node is the smallest among all nodes at intersection, it is defined relay node at intersection. The relay node at intersection prioritized to forward message without waiting time.

(2) On the road, relay node is decided by WT(waiting time) formula, this formula is decided by factor of forwarding probability of receiving node. Relay node forwards message when WT is end, the first node which forward message is defined relay node. In addition, data can be forwarded in both direction on the road.

2   Related Work

Broadcast is the key technology of message dissemination for VANET, however, blind broadcast suffers from redundant transmissions, especially under dense networks. Many solutions for this issue based on position are designed, some of them aim at message dissemination on straight roads without intersections [6, 10–12].

In [6], Wu et al. propose PMB (position-based multi-hop broadcast), which decreases message redundancy and increases real time of message transmission, ACK message will increase network overhead. Yang et al. proposed PAB broadcast protocol where distance between sender and receiver [10], speed of vehicle and angle are considered. This protocol uses opposite vehicle as relay node for forwarding. It does not show how long a channel is occupied, it will message collision.

In [11], Liu et al. propose relative position based (RPB) address model without infrastructure, it adopts directional greedy broadcast routing approach to forward messages. This work uses ACK scheme, so overhead is high. In [12], Bi et al. proposed PMBP (A Position Based Multi-hop Broadcast Protocol) model for emergency, PMBP selects the furthest most node to source node in dissemination direction to forward message at each hop and BRTS/BCTS handshake is used, so it cause network overhead to increase. In [9, 13], selection of relay node for rebroadcast at intersection is addressed, a corresponding broadcast scheme is proposed, so dissemination of messages for an area is realized, there are infrastructure requirements in [13], this increase hardware overhead. No infrastructure requirements in others [14].

In directional broadcast UMB (Urban Multi-hop Broadcast Protocol) RTB/CTB broadcast mechanism is proposed and it enhances the reliability of broadcast by ACK between broadcast nodes and relay nodes [13, 15]. Peer-to-peer communication is only between broadcast node and the farthest node, others nodes only receive messages, this paper sets channel occupation time according to distance between receiving node and broadcast node. The farther node from broadcast node occupies the channel for longer time, that is, the farther node from broadcast node will be selected as relay node. This limits the number of relay nodes and suppresses message retransmission, thereby reducing broadcast storm. However, it is not easy for the protocol to achieve convergence in the dense section of the road by RTB/CTB mechanism selecting relay nodes. This leads to duration and overhead increase and network throughput degradation. The iterative process is simplified in RTB/CTB [16, 17] of UMB by averagely divided area of broadcast node coverage.

In [16], the contention windows are set so that they do not overlap each other on different sections of the road. This ensures that a farther node is prioritized to handshake with the broadcast node. In [17], for the contention window overlaps that node selects in every section of the road, it is impossible to guarantee the most furthest node from broadcast node as relay node, it suffers from more collision. In [18], the researchers use RTB/CTB broadcast handshake mechanism in UMB to choose the farthest node as the relay node. IFS is inversely proportional to distance from broadcast node, IFS is shorter if the position is farther.

Tung et al. propose road-based directional broadcast protocol [19], it classifies vehicles into groups based on roads they are on and select a relay node with the best line-of-sight for each group. It decreases message reliability and redundancy due to wrong group. Road topology in includes obstacles at intersections which improves efficiency of transmission and reliability.

Broadcast protocol in [7–9] propose forwarding messages in ROI without infrastructure. Viriyasitavat proposed Urban Vehicular Broadcast (UVCAST) [7], UV-CAST has broadcast suppression regime and store-carry-forward regime. Local one-hop neighbor information is used for determining the regime that should be operated. To achieve this, it uses mapping information to determine whether it is at an intersection or not, and calculate WT to rebroadcast message if it should operate under suppression regime. To achieve store-carry-forward regime, UV-CAST protocol rules that boundary nodes store and carry message around until they encounter uninformed neighbors. This protocol uses periodic beacons to identify uninformed vehicles. The drawback of this protocol is that, upon receiving a beacon from an uninformed neighbor a vehicle immediately rebroadcasts the message without any coordination with other vehicles in the neighborhood. This increases redundant messages, especially under dense network scenarios.

In [8], Maia et al. proposed HyDiAck broadcast protocol, this protocol is operated under dense and sparse scenarios. HyDiAck combines the forwarding zone concept with a timer-based broadcast suppression approach to limit the rebroadcast nodes. Forwarding zone is area that message can cover by each hop. HyDiAck selects vehicle inside a forwarding zone to rebroadcast messages to further vehicles in dense scenarios. Under sparse scenarios, the protocol employs implicit acknowledgments to guarantee robustness in message delivery. Both [7] and [8] are suitable for dense and sparse networks. BSM broadcast protocol extends AMB [9], and improves the overhead and forwarding node ratios in comparison with AMB [20].

3   Proposed MBW Protocol

Main goal of broadcast protocol is disseminate message in a large region around the accident site with low delay, low overhead, high reachability and low forwarding node ratio under diverse traffic flow density environment. To maximize the number of vehicles that receive the warning message per transmission, the mechanism of selection of the relay nodes is very important. Two different methods are presented for the intersections and on the straight road respectively. For employing these two methods.

We establish a rectangular coordinate system for relay node, The origin of coordinates is O(x, y), which is relay node, as shown in Fig. 1. The scope that relay node cover by transmit with one-hop is averagely classified into 4 parts, angle of every part is $\frac{\pi}{2}$, According to the direction of the counterclockwise, $\alpha \in [\frac{\pi}{4}, \frac{3\pi}{4})$, $\beta \in [\frac{5\pi}{4}, \frac{7\pi}{4})$, $\gamma \in [\frac{3\pi}{4}, \frac{5\pi}{4})$, $\theta \in [-\frac{\pi}{4}, \frac{\pi}{4})$. We shows four directions definition of the of east, west, south and north.

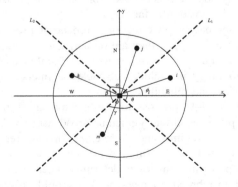

Fig. 1. The road directions

Definition 1. $\forall$ node i, Angle between the sender and receiver is ϕ_i, the node is in the east of the road if $-\frac{\pi}{4} \leq arctg\phi_i < \frac{\pi}{4}$.

Definition 2. $\forall$ node j, Angle between the sender and receiver is ϕ_j, the node is in the north of the road if $\frac{\pi}{4} \leq arctg\phi_j < \frac{3\pi}{4}$.

Definition 3. $\forall$ node k, Angle between the sender and receiver is ϕ_k, the node is in the south of the road if $\frac{5\pi}{4} \leq arctg\phi_k < \frac{7\pi}{4}$.

Definition 4. $\forall$ node m, Angle between the sender and receiver is ϕ_m, the node is in the west of the road if $\frac{3\pi}{4} \leq arctg\phi_m < \frac{5\pi}{4}$.

The node is at intersection if a relay node has neighbors from two or more different directions of the east, west, south and north, and distance between node and neighbors is greater than the road width.

MBW is implemented by MBW1 and MBW2 methods respectively. MBW maintain neighbor list for recognizing road intersection. MBW1 maintains neighbor list to select relay node at intersection when emergent accident happen, so hello beacon is drastically decrease, MBW1 can effectively decrease network overhead. MBW2 periodically maintain neighbor list. Both of them adopt hello beacon to maintain neighbor list, hello packet contains <Hello, Position, Direction, Hop, SID, MID, VID>.

Hello: hello packet,

Position: vehicle position,

Direction: records direction of vehicle to last relay node (east, south, west, north),

Hop: hello packet hop number,

SID represents source ID,

MID: source node message ID,

VID: field records vehicle ID.

Every node save the MID and SID in pairs when they receive the hello packet with Hop marked 0. Hello bacon is 1 Hz. We explain two methods in detail.

MBW-ONE forwarding messages strategy:

- Source node broadcast hello beacon that Hop field is 0, nodes which receive this hello beacon send hello beacon which Hop field is set 1 only once in one second, those nodes receiving this hello beacon broadcast respond packet only once in 1 s, limiting times of hello beacon and respond can decrease network overhead, respond packet contains Respond field and Position field, those nodes receiving respond calculate distance between itself and neighbors, if distance is more than road width in two or more direction, it marks itself at intersection and records VID minimum if its VID is less than other VID, otherwise, node does not do anything.

- After a node broadcasts hello with Hop field 0 and waits tms, it broadcasts data packet, if nodes at intersection receive data message, they broadcast hello packet with Hop field 0, nodes receiving hello with Hop field 0 broadcast hello beacon with Hop field 1, and then those nodes receiving this hello packet broadcast respond, then the node with least VID forwards data message immediately without waiting. So this node is selected as relay node.

- If all nodes on the road receiving hello beacon with Hop field 0, those nodes after they receive data packets calculate WT and wait, a node receives hello packet with Hop field 0 from other nodes if its WT is not end, then it does not broadcast hello with Hop field 0, if a node receives hello packet with Hop field 0 from other nodes after it have sent hello with Hop field 0, it will compares the SID and MID that it saves with the hello packet's SID and MID, if all the SID and MID it saves are different from the hello packet's SID and MID, it does not receive message duplicate, so it broadcasts hello packet with Hop field 1 only once in 1 s, then nodes receiving this hello beacon broadcast respond packet only once in 1 s, nodes receiving respond packet update intersection mark. If a node receives a hello packet with the same SID and MID as it saves, it compares their VID value, if its VID is more than other node's VID and Direction value is same, it will cancels forwarding data, otherwise, it will forward data message. Therefore, forwarding node is defined relay node on the road.
- MID is adds 1 after source node broadcasts data packet.

MBW-TWO forwarding messages strategy:

- A node updates neighbor list when it receives a hello bacon whose 'Hop' field is 0, it calculates the distance between itself and neighbor nodes, it will mark itself at intersection if the distances between itself and neighbors in two or more directions are more than road width, meanwhile, it also marks 'VID' minimum if its 'VID' is less than 'VID' that it receives hello bacon, otherwise it will not do anything.
- Source node immediately broadcasts data message if accident happens, we adopt the node that VID is the least
- to forward message without waiting if nodes at intersection receive message, so it is also selected as relay node. Data packet contains information <Data, Position, Direction, TS, SID, MID, Data>. 'Data' field represents data packet, 'Position' is position of node, 'Direction' is direction(east, south, west, north) relative to last relay node, 'TS' is time sending packet time, 'SID' represents source node ID, 'MID' is message ID, 'Data message' field represents warning message.
- When nodes on the road receive data packet, these nodes calculate their WT and wait. If WT is not end, a node receives data packet from other node and their 'Direction' value are the same, then it cancels forwarding message, so nodes in different direction relative to source node also forward data message. When WT expires, data packet is forwarded, so forwarding node is defined relay node.
- 'MID' is added 1 after source node broadcasts data packet. Both strategies can be used for forwarding different messages at the same time. MBW broadcast protocol limits the number of times of the messages retransmission by select the minimum relay node sets. Therefore, it can reduce message redundancy and contention, this also decreases the broadcast storm.

3.1   Waiting Time Calculation

To limit the number of vehicles that broadcast a message, calculating WT for forwarding message scheme is researched in previous works. Typical WT calculation method in position based broadcast protocol is adopting some factors to design waiting time function, such as wireless transmission R of broadcast vehicle, distance between sender and receiver, the number of neighboring vehicles and vehicle velocity etc. In [6], the wait time is referred to as defer and the computing function is given by the following expression:

$$T_{defer} = \left| T_{\max} * (1 - \frac{R_j - R_i + d_{ij}}{R_{\max}}) * \alpha + T_{rand} \right| \tag{1}$$

$$\alpha = 1 - \exp(-\lambda * (1 - \frac{R_j - R_i + d_{ij}}{R_{\max}})) \tag{2}$$

In above formula, R_i and R_j is the transmission range of the two nodes i and j, respectively. d_{ij} is the distance between the nodes i and j. Such a relationship between WT and distance is not obvious, a similar WT function in [9], BSM broadcast protocol proposed the wait time Wt calculation expression as:

$$Wt = (1 - \frac{dsr}{R})^{nn} * Wt_{\max} \tag{3}$$

Here dsr is the distance between sender and receiver, nn is the number of neighboring vehicles. It is obvious that such an expression is not a linear function, however, in [8], HyDiAck broadcast protocol proposes WT calculation expression as:

$$T_{S_{ij}} = S_{ij} * t \tag{4}$$

$$S_{ij} = \begin{cases} \left\lfloor N_S \times (1 - \lceil \frac{\min(D_{ij}, R)}{R} \rceil) \right\rfloor & \text{if in } forwarding \ zone \\ \left\lfloor N_S \times (2 - \lceil \frac{\min(D_{ij}, R)}{R} \rceil) \right\rfloor & \text{otherwise} \end{cases} \tag{5}$$

It can be seen in the above expression that the wait time $T_{S_{ij}}$ is a linear function of D_{ij} where D_{ij} is the distance between sender and receiver. N_S is the number of available time slots for each of the two zones. In [7], UV-CAST protocol shows waiting time function as:

$$\tau_i = \begin{cases} \frac{1}{2}(1 - \frac{d_{i,j}}{R})\tau_{\max} & \text{if } i \text{ is at an intersection} \\ \frac{1}{2}(2 - \frac{d_{i,j}}{R})\tau_{\max} & \text{otherwise} \end{cases} \tag{6}$$

The above equation is a linear function of τ_i and $d_{i,j}$, and τ_i is the waiting time and $d_{i,j}$ is the distance between the sender and the relay node. We can conclude that the vehicle which is farther away from the sender has a higher probability of forwarding the message. We firstly show the probability expression with respect to distance between sender and receiver, in which the distance is divided by wireless transmission radius.

$$P_i = \frac{d_i}{r} \tag{7}$$

P_i is the probability of a receiver rebroadcasting a message, d_i is distance of the receiver from the sender, and r is the wireless transmission radius. A vehicle waits for a shorter time before it forwards a message if it has a higher probability value, therefore in this paper, we adopt P_i factor to establish the exponential and linear WT calculation formula. The expressions (8) and (9) show the WT for exponential and linear respectively.

$$WT = WT_{max} \times (1 - exp(-(1 - P_i))) \tag{8}$$

$$WT = WT_{max} \times (1 - P_i) \tag{9}$$

WT_{max} is set at 100 ms in this study. The duration will be increased if WT_{max} is too high, and if WT_{max} is too short, many vehicles broadcast before they receive duplicate packets. Figure 2 shows a comparison between formula (8) and (9). When distance between sender and receiver is farther, waiting time of WT formula computing is more shorter, in particular, when distance is more 200 m, value of linear and exponential WT is very closed, however, when distance is less than 200 m, WT value that exponential formula calculate is less than linear formula, to forward message quick, we adopt exponential formula (8).

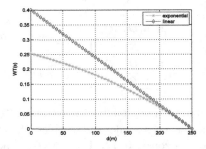

Fig. 2. Exponential and linear WT curve

Formula (8) is used for calculating WT on the road, but to the relay node at the intersection, upon it receiving message, it will forwards and not wait time, other nodes which receive messages cancel forwarding. Therefore, The WT calculating formula for a relay node is concluded as follows (10), which is used not only at intersections but also on the road.

$$WT = \begin{cases} 0 & if\ i\ at\ intersection \\ WT_{max} \times (1 - exp(-(1 - P_i))) & otherwise \end{cases} \tag{10}$$

3.2 Implementation of Message Propagation

To implement data message dissemination we use message labeling techniques [21]. When a message is sent, it has the source node ID, message packet ID and vehicle ID attached. In this study the dissemination of message is done by adopting MBW1 and MBW2 respectively, the dissemination of message procedure follows two flow charts as follows Figs. 3 and 4.

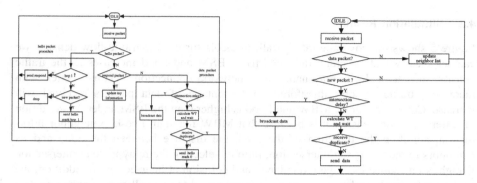

Fig. 3. MBW1 flow   **Fig. 4.** MBW2 flow

4 Performance Analysis

4.1 Simulation Parameters

To assess the performance of MBW, a series of simulations are performed by using the NS2 simulator. The MBW is compared to the related BSM [9] and flood. All protocols are evaluated under low, normal and high traffic density conditions, the vehicles density ranges from 800 vel/h to 4000 vel/h, speed ranges from 0 to 60 km/h. We adopt a 1500 m^2 grid road topology for the simulations, each road is 2-way and has 3-lanes for each direction. The vehicles run follow traffic signals at the intersections, traffic signals includes red lights, green lights and yellow lights. During simulation straight green light and red light is 30 s and 70 s respectively, yellow light is 3 s, left turn green light is 20 s, left turn red light is 80 s, left turn yellow light is 3 s, the whole traffic light cycle is 100 s. The obstacle is set at intersection. To simulate realistic vehicle movements, we use the mobility model defined by the VISSIM simulator. A vehicle positioned at the middle of certain road is responsible for generating a warning message which is propagated in the region around.

Veins 2.0 network model in IEEE802.11p standard has defined the link and physical layers [22], we set the bit rate to 3 Mbps for the broadcast protocol, we set the message packets size to 512 bytes and the hello beacon packets size to 25 bytes and are generated every 1 s [23], respond packets size is 9 bytes. Simulation time is 500 s. The following four metrics are used to evaluate reliability, efficiency and scalability. Coverage ratio, it is percentage of the number of vehicles that receive the data packet in the simulation area. Higher coverage ratio means that MBW select relay node reliably and the protocol has high tolerance to different traffic density. Delay, it means the average time that it takes data packet from source node to intended node, this metric measures the efficiency of the data transmission. Overhead, it is equal to the number of data packets received by each vehicle during simulation. This metric is used to measure the scalability of network. Forward node rate, it is the proportion of vehicles to rebroadcast the data packet from the source node in the network.

4.2   Simulation Results

Figure 5 shows the coverage ratio of all protocols for diverse traffic flow density, we can see clearly that coverage ratio of MBW, BSM and flood increases as the traffic density increases. It is reasonable that network connection become better with increasing traffic density, therefore, the percentage of data packets received will increase. Coverage ratio of MBW and flood is higher than the BSM under the condition of different traffic density, it is because that MBW maintain two-hop neighbor information, adopting the direction of the road, the distance between the node and its neighbors to recognize the intersection, ratio of selecting the relay node at intersection is high, so it reduce message redundancy and collision at intersection. In addition, the farthest node can be selected on the road, it reduces message collision, it enhances data transmitting reliably, therefore, coverage ratio is higher than BSM's. Coverage ratio of flood is high since all nodes which receive message forward message, so nodes receiving message are more than BSM's. Coverage ratio of BSM is low since it has no scheme to recognize intersection, it reduce the chance to forward message toward all direction at the intersection, and it selects relay node with more neighbors, so it is not necessary to select the farthest node, it will cause message redundancy and collision. Coverage ratio of BSM is averagely lower 6 % than MBW1's. Coverage ratio of BSM is averagely lower 15 % than flood's. Coverage ratio of BSM is averagely lower 20 % than MBW2's.

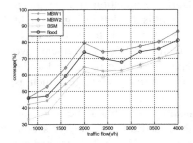

Fig. 5. Coverage rate

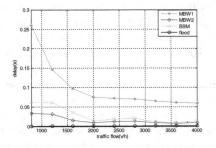

Fig. 6. Delay

Figure 6 shows delay comparison for BSM, MBW and flood protocol. As can be observed, delay becomes short as density of nodes increase, it is since that network connection become better when the nodes increase. Delay of flood is the lowest among them for all nodes which receive data packets forward message, so message is forwarded to the whole simulation area soon. Delay of BSM is averagely higher 2373 % than flood's. Delay of MBW2 is lower than BSM's and MBW1's, this is for it always maintain neighbor list during simulation, so it uses the shortest time to find the relay node at intersection and forwards message to other nodes. BSM's delay is averagely higher 60.2 % than MBW2's. However, it is lower than MBW1's delay, BSM's delay is averagely lower 73.9 % than MBW1's, it is for MBW1 only maintains neighbors list when emergency accident happen, so it wastes some time to find relay node.

MBW proposes that message is forwarded immediately towards all direction at the intersection without waiting time, and it can select the farthest node to forward message, and it reduces time for forwarding message. While BSM always maintains neighbors information for density of nodes, it select relay node with high density, so it is not necessary to select furthest node to forward message, so its delay is long than MBW2's.

Figure 7 presents forwarding node ratio. As already discussed, message redundancy and contention decrease as the number of forwarding nodes is few, therefore, broadcast storm correspondingly decrease. Forwarding node ratio of flood is the highest among them for all nodes receiving message forward message, BSM's forwarding node ratio is averagely lower 51 % than flood's and averagely higher 75 % than MBW1's respectively, BSM's forwarding node ratio is averagely lower 12 % than MBW2's. MBW2's forwarding node ratio is higher than BSM's for it always maintain two-hop neighbor information, recognition ratio of intersection is high, so relay node at intersection is right found, and relay node can also be selected right on the road by WT, so its forwarding ratio is high. MBW1's forwarding node ratio is lower than BSM's for it maintains neighbor list only emergent accident, and its forwarding node ratio decrease as traffic density become large, this is because network connection becomes good, so relay node on the road can be selected in the furthest position, so its forwarding node ratio decrease. When traffic density become high, it is not necessary for BSM to select farthest relay node, so the number of forwarding nodes will increase. In conclusion, the method of selecting relay node is right, it decrease message redundancy, so message is transmitted reliably and efficiently.

Figure 8 shows that overhead of MBW, flood and BSM under diverse traffic density. Overhead of MBW1 and flood is lower than BSM's, MBW2's overhead is higher than BSM's. Overhead of BSM is averagely higher 37 % than MBW1's and averagely lower 6 % than MBW2's respectively, and averagely higher 355 % than flood's. MBW1's overhead is lower than BSM's for it maintain neighbor list only emergent accident, and scheme of selecting relay nodes at intersection and on the road limits the number of relay nodes, so data packets transmitting is reduced, overhead of network is decreased. Flood does not maintain neighbor list, so overhead is lower than others. MBW2 also maintain two-hop neighbor information during simulation, so its overhead is higher than others. Overhead of MBW slightly increase as traffic density become, so scalability of this protocol is better than BSM's in high traffic density, it is because MBW limits relay node numbers efficiently, therefore, the rebroadcast duplicates are suppressed when traffic density becomes high.

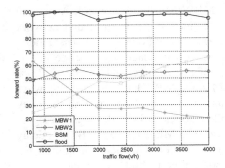

Fig. 7. Forwarding node ratio

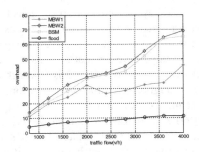

Fig. 8. Overhead

5 Conclusion

In this paper, we propose MBW protocol based on position, a warning message propagation protocol for urban VANETs with diverse traffic flow density. The protocol classifies the direction of road into east, west, south and north. It maintains neighbors list, the node records itself at intersection if the distance between neighbor and itself is more than road width in two or more different road direction. If there are much vehicles at the intersection, the node with smallest ID is selected relay node at intersection, the relay node prioritize to forward message toward all direction without waiting time. It supports data disseminate in both directions on the road. So it improves coverage ratio, its coverage ratio and decrease delay. Due to efficiently limit the number of the relay node by using different selecting scheme on the road and at the intersection, so it improves the forwarding ratio and reliability of data dissemination under dense network conditions. It performs with a better overhead than BSM because it selects the farthest node for forwarding message.

In conclusion, MBW protocol is suitable for resolving safety application broadcast under diverse traffic flow density environment with low overhead, low delay and high coverage ratio.

References

1. Li, F., Wang, Y.: Routing in vehicular ad hoc networks: a survey. IEEE Veh. Technol. Mag. **2**(2), 12–22 (2007)
2. Ni, S.-Y., Tseng, Y.-C., Chen, Y.-S., Sheu, J.-P.: The broadcast storm problem in a mobile ad hoc network. In: Proceedings of the 5th Annual ACM/IEEE International Conference on Mobile Computing and Networking, Series MobiCom 1999, pp. 151–162 (1999)
3. Tseng, Y.-C., Ni, S.-Y., Shih, E.-Y.: Adaptive approaches to relieving broadcast storms in a wireless multihop mobile ad hoc network. IEEE Trans. Comput. **52**(5), 545–557 (2003)
4. Hu, C., Hong, Y., Hou, J.: On mitigating the broadcast storm problem with directional antennas. In: 2003 IEEE International Conference on Communications. ICC 2003, vol. 1, pp. 104–110, May 2003

5. Qayyum, A., Viennot, L., Laouiti, A.: Multipoint relaying for flooding broadcast messages in mobile wireless networks. In: Proceedings of the 35th Annual Hawaii International Conference on System Sciences. HICSS 2002, pp. 3866–3875, January 2002
6. Wu, X., Song, S., Wang, H.: A novel position based multi-hop broadcast protocol for vehicular ad hoc networks. JNW 6(1), 112–120 (2011)
7. Viriyasitavat, W., Tonguz, O., Bai, F.: UV-CAST: an urban vehicular broadcast protocol. IEEE Commun. Mag. 49(11), 116–124 (2011)
8. Maia, G., Villas, L., Boukerche, A., Viana, A., Aquino, A., Loureiro, A.: Data dissemination in urban vehicular ad hoc networks with diverse traffic conditions. In: 2013 IEEE Symposium on Computers and Communications (ISCC), pp. 459–464, July 2013
9. Najafzadeh, S., Ithnin, N., Razak, S., Karimi, R.: Bsm: Broadcasting of safety messages in vehicular ad hoc networks. Arab. J. Sci. Eng. 39(2), 777–782 (2014)
10. Yang, Y.-T., Chou, L.-D.: Position-based adaptive broadcast for inter-vehicle communications. In: 2008 IEEE International Conference on Communications Workshops. ICC Workshops 2008, pp. 410–414, May 2008
11. Liu, C., Chigan, C.: RPB-MD: a novel robust message dissemination method for VANETs. In: 2008 IEEE Global Telecommunications Conference. IEEE GLOBECOM 2008, pp. 1–6. IEEE, November 2008
12. Bi, Y., Zhao, H., Shen, X.: A directional broadcast protocol for emergency message exchange in inter-vehicle communications. In: 2009 IEEE International Conference on Communications. ICC 2009, pp. 1–5, June 2009
13. Korkmaz, G., Ekici, E., Özgüner, F., Özgüner, Ü.: Urban multi-hop broadcast protocol for inter-vehicle communication systems. In: Proceedings of the 1st ACM International Workshop on Vehicular Ad Hoc Networks, Series VANET 2004, pp. 76–85 (2004)
14. Li, D., Huang, H., Li, X., Li, M., Tang, F.: A distance-based directional broadcast protocol for urban vehicular ad hoc network. In: 2007 International Conference on Wireless Communications, Networking and Mobile Computing. WiCom 2007, pp. 1520–1523, September 2007
15. Korkmaz, G., Ekici, E., Ozguner, F.: Black-burstbased multihop broadcast protocols for vehicular networks. IEEE Trans. Veh. Technol. 56(5), 3159–3167 (2007)
16. Chiasserini, C., Gaeta, R., Garetto, M., Gribaudo, M., Sereno, M.: Efficient broadcasting of safety messages in multihop vehicular networks. In: 2006: 20th International Parallel and Distributed Processing Symposium. IPDPS 2006, p. 8, April 2006
17. Fasolo, E., Zanella, A., Zorzi, M.: An effective broadcast scheme for alert message propagation in vehicular ad hoc networks. In: 2006 IEEE International Conference on Communications. ICC 2006, vol. 9, pp. 3960–3965, June 2006
18. Taha, M., Hasan, Y.M.Y.: VANET-DSRC protocol for reliable broadcasting of life safety messages. In: 2007 IEEE International Symposium on Signal Processing and Information Technology, pp. 104–109, December 2007
19. Tung, L.-C., Gerla, M.: An efficient road-based directional broadcast protocol for urban VANETs. In: 2010 IEEE Vehicular Networking Conference (VNC), pp. 9–16, December 2010
20. Korkmaz, G., Ekici, E., Ozguner, F.: An efficient fully ad-hoc multi-hop broadcast protocol for inter-vehicular communication systems. In: 2006 IEEE International Conference on Communications. ICC 2006, vol. 1, pp. 423–428, June 2006
21. Little, T., Agarwal, A.: An information propagation scheme for VANETs. In: Proceedings, 2005 IEEE Intelligent Transportation Systems, pp. 155–160, September 2005

22. Jiang, D., Delgrossi, L.: IEEE 802.11p: towards an international standard for wireless access in vehicular environments. In: 2008 Vehicular Technology Conference. VTC Spring 2008, pp. 2036–2040. IEEE, May 2008
23. ITS Standards Fact Sheets: IEEE 1609-Family of Standards for Wireless Access in Vehicular Enviroments (WAVE)

Dependable Data Management in the IoT Traceability System

Hu Yuan[(✉)] and Tao Pin

Tsinghua National Laboratory for Information Science and Technology (TNList),
College of Computer Science, Haidian, Beijing 100084, China
Anruohy@gmail.com

Abstract. The IoT traceability system based on RFID asks the high reliability of the data management, each data item is valuable and indispensable. A RFID based organic food traceability system is introduced in this paper, and some deepgoing discussion about data reliability is given on the following three segment, the data collection, data uploading and data management. RFID encryption and other techniques are used to improve the data legality in the data collection segment. The uploading task is designed as a standalone process to enhance the stability of data uploading, and the data will be kept in the terminal reader device for several days to deal with the server disaster. The data managed in the server is physically deleting prevented as the user may do the misoperation, and the backup server can further improve the data dependability.

Keywords: IoT · Traceability system · Data management · Reliability

1 Introduction

In order to strengthen the food safety, the government are constantly strengthening the management of food traceability and tracking [1, 3]. Safety supervision of meat product is an important part of strengthening food safety, and it can improve the management level of meat product traceability effectively with the IoT technology. For a long time, most of our livestock are in the statues of natural backyard, small-scale captive, small size and low level of production and management, and the management of livestock products traceability is not yet well established [4]. Product quality had the problem of potential safety hazard that had seriously restricted the development of China's animal husbandry. To solve these problems better, the relevant departments have been gradually carried out a lot of work, for example, Chinese Ministry of Agriculture issued immunized identity management approach on animals, China AQSIQ carried out China barcode to promote the project, on 69 kinds of key products affixed mandatory product quality electronic supervision code, etc. These efforts have laid a good foundation for further improving the quality of Chinese products and the establishment of food safety traceability system.

For organic traceability system, electronic tags had been worn on tracked live animals for one year to ten years, and can be read many times for the tag information through the terminal reader device in the life cycle of the livestock. The tag information will be uploaded to server's database for subsequent inquiries. This system of typical

X. Zhang et al. (Eds.): ESTC 2015, CCIS 572, pp. 153–160, 2015.
DOI: 10.1007/978-981-10-0421-6_15

IoT is based on collecting information of electronic tag. In the above process, the information that collected by the terminal reader device is related with the final consumer. What is more, organic product management and the final consumer concern and need the information. Therefore, every piece of information is important and indispensable. In the above process, how to ensure information not to be lost is such an important challenge which the design of IoT system faces.

This article describes the development of traceability system for the organic livestock products which the authors involved in. Content of this article shows the design of the framework of the system and focuses on introducing the reliability of the data security technology, from the following three segment, the data collection, data uploading and data management. In the link of the data collection, RFID tags may face forgery, multi-label confusion, label difficult to read, etc. Therefore, protection mechanism needs to be set on the electronic tags and reader devices, so that it can guarantee the correctness and uniqueness of the tag information is read by the terminal reader device. In the link of the data uploading, the operation of data uploading may conflict with user's operation on the Data Terminal, and the process of uploading data may failed for the reason of the abnormal network. Even after the data is being uploaded, the data may lose due to the failure of server system. How to consider all above problem and guarantee data integrity is an important challenge while designing the system. In the link of the data management on server, authorized users such as system administrator have certain privileges to modify data and delete data. How to avoid the user's misoperation in the work process, and how to recovery data after user's misoperation must be considered while designing the system.

Firstly, Sect. 2 shows the design framework of the organic traceability system. Then, the third quarter elaborates the data reliability on the following three segment, the data collection, data uploading and data management, and discusses about the safeguards in the Iot system. At last, Sect. 4 gives the system implementation and conclusion.

2 System Design

In this paper, the IoT organic traceability system mainly supervise the breeding link in supply chain of livestock products. Breed link is the starting point at guaranteeing the quality of livestock products and is the key to guarantee the safety of products. Making use of farm production management system to record all the information of livestock from birth to slaughter, it can eliminate the quality and safety issues of livestock products, and provide evidence for assessment grade and traceability product quality.

The chart of the IoT organic traceability system is shown in Fig. 1.

IoT is the network of physical objects. Firstly, the core and foundation of IoT aais still the internet, and it is extension and expansion of the network based on internet. Secondly, the client of IoT has extended and expanded to all items, and can deal with information awareness, swapping and communication. The function of this IoT system based on RFID electronic tag introduced in this paper. RFID is a Radio Frequency Identification. The RFID tag is used widely to mark and manage all kinds of things, and

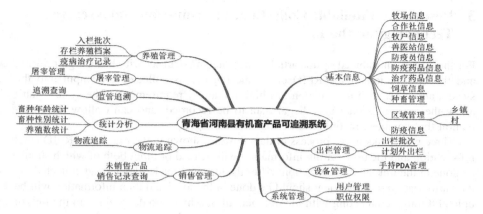

Fig. 1. The chart of the IoT organic traceability system

there are usually two kinds of RFID tags; Active and Passive tags. Block diagram of organic traceability system around the RFID electronic tag is shown in Fig. 2.

In the IoT organic traceability system, the electronic label has the core position, and it uses the terminal reader device to collect the related information including immune, quarantine and migration in the process of growth from birth. People can't identify cattle individuals in a group of livestock, so that we need the help of equipment to collect the label information and ear tag to be worn on the livestock's ear for the purpose that the collected information can be refined to each individual livestock, and based on the RFID label to further supply and improve the individual's attribute information, description information, pictures information, etc. All information will be transmitted to the data center server through the 3G network. Finally, the management department and the consumers can query and retrieve each livestock individual information through the network to achieve products' traceability.

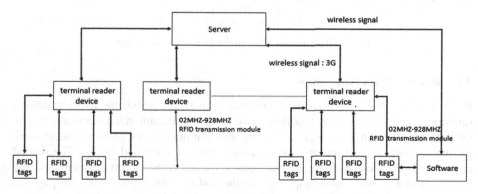

Fig. 2. Block diagram of organic traceability system around the RFID electronic tag

3   Research on Reliable Collection, Transmission and Archive Technology in the IoT

For the system introduced in this article, guaranteeing data security has a high priority, and the information of the RFID electronic tag that is collected and input into the system and other data information has high reliability requirements. The system can't allow the erroneous data and illegal data to be recorded, and can't allow the information that has been recorded to be lost and damaged.

Three main links in the process of data flow are shown in the Fig. 3, the RFID label information and the user-setting information will be read or input,both of which should be done in the link of data collection; After the terminal reader device had collected the data information, Pretreatment should be done in the local,and then information will be upload through connecting with the internet, all of which should be done in the link of data uploading; After the information had been uploaded, users can do the operation including modifying data, deleting data and querying data through visiting the server on the internet. That is the link of data management on the server. The follows will introduce the three main links and describe the possible problem of data reliability and the solutions to the problem.

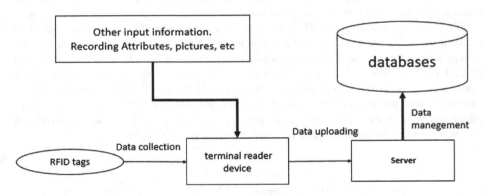

Fig. 3. Three main links in the process of data flow

3.1   Reliable Data Acquisition

In the link of data collection, there are two main issues while the actual system is running. The first problem is that there may be illegal, unauthorized electronic tag. In view of this situation, the legality of tag information needs to be checked and verified, for the purpose of ensuring that the data collected is correct and lawful. The second problem is that there may be multiple tag in the actual work environment, thereby confusing one-to-one relationship between the collected information and the physical objects (livestock). Therefore, the system must check the situation whether there is a plurality of electronic, and guarantee uniqueness of data.

(1) Encryption-encoding on RFID tag

As a unique identification label, the data stored in the electricity tags is call Label. The label is in accordance with international standards in different versions, and the all standards request that there are bit areas in the electricity tags used to store the user-defined and user-encoded label. Length of bit area are different, for example, 96 bits, 128 bits, etc. In the design of this system, in order to be compatible with most of the actual electronic tags, the information area of 64-bit is chosen to set up rules that how the label in the electricity is encoded. Specific encoding rules is associated with the realization of the actual system, not repeat them here. However, we use a byte to mark the rules of encoding and encrypting label, which can guarantee the legitimacy, the correctness and the future expandability of the system data collected in the link of the data collecting, and optimize the program to guarantee the data security in case of emergency.

In the way of reserving a byte to mark the rules of encoding and encrypting the label, the label information is allowed to store in encrypted manner, at the same time, the label information can be encrypted according to different encryption algorithms. This system temporarily uses two encryption, key XOR encryption and DES encryption.

It can effectively prevent counterfeit electronic tag information and the physical (livestock) getting into the system through the label information is encrypted and stored in the RFID tag, which play a significant role in guaranteeing that organic products are certified from the source to prevent counterfeiting. Moreover, due to the presence of the encryption algorithm, encryption algorithms objective guarantees that only the correct label information can be correctly decoded, and prevent the terminal reader device collecting the wrong tag information. Finally, the byte of identification encoding can also be seen as an information of the coded version, so that the improving of future encoding could be achieved. Improving encoding can play a role in the emergency protection when the original encryption-encoding system is attacked.

(2) Alarm while reading multi-tag

In actual operating system environment, the situation that multi-tag will be read simultaneously often occur, for example, there are several livestock in the reading area, the operators of the terminal reader device carry other electronic tags. In the above case, system can't build the one-to-one relationships between the physical world objects (livestock) and the information world, which will result in data confusion. The best solution to this problem is that the appropriate measures should be token to prevent the problem at the source of the information collected. The terminal reader device itself has the ability to read multiple tags simultaneously. Therefore, the software can be set up on terminal reader device, so it makes alarm information and reports error to the user, and at the same time any of the electronic tag information just be read should be abandon. After receiving the alarm message, users will try to eliminate possible errors until the terminal reader device read the only label information. After reading the information correctly, the software will establish one-to-one relationship between the label information and other related information, and store all information in the terminal reader device. The measures can ensure the uniqueness and the correctness of the data collection.

3.2 Dependable Data Uploading

After the information of the RFID tags and other properties have been collected into the terminal reader device successfully, the terminal reader device has local cache with a certain capacity so that the collected data will be kept while network fail to work. Then, data kept in the local cache will be uploaded to server once network works.

While designing the Software of the terminal reader device, the device is a multi-task concurrent system that have to deal with the local data and complete the task of input and output, and the task of data uploading has important priority and reliability, so that the feature of data uploading is designed as a separate function module running in a separate process. The module of data collection and data uploading communicate with each other via a sample pro-defined interface.

Uploading mechanism for dependable data: Firstly, the data will be stored in local SQLite database after the module of data uploading received the information from the module of data collection. There are three data segments that include collection time, uploading time and uploading flag, and this three data segments are spliced onto the data which had been stored in the local databases. Before writing each animal information to the SQLite database, it must plus an integer type of flag information. As shown in Table 1, the uploading flag used to identify whether the data successfully uploaded and the times of uploading failures. Principle design of uploading flag: The initial value of the flag data is 1, if the upload is successful, the flag data becomes 0 from 1; if the upload failed, flag data automatically plus 1 on the prior basis. The purpose of this design is to take a threshold value K according to the actual situation, you can control the priority of the data depending on whether the flag value exceeds the threshold K and determine whether the data is successfully uploaded.

Collection time and uploading time are consistent with the data on servers, so that these information should be synchronized with the service. But for the uploading flag just working for the module of data uploading, it will be removed from the information which should be uploaded. The module of data uploading will scan data stored in the local database according to the inspection mechanism, and according to the data priority, will make repeated attempts to upload the data that is not successfully uploaded until uploading successfully. Table 1 shows local database field of the terminal reader device.

Table 1. Local database field of the terminal reader device

Data itself	Collection time	The uploading flag	Uploading time
Data 1	Time 1	0	Time 01
Data 2	Time 2	1	–
Data 3	Time 3	10	–
Data 4	Time 4	20	–
...	...	...	...

In the software design of the terminal reader device, the module of data uploading not only repeatedly executes the command of uploading data that is not uploaded successfully, but also saves the data that was uploaded successfully within a certain period of time. So that, it can avoid losing data completely that was caused by errors or anomalies on the server program. This measure adds a protective mechanism for guaranteeing the safe and reliable system data, and plays an important role in the actual operation of the system.

3.3 Reliable Data Management

Terminal reader's data will be written to the database system of the server after being uploaded successfully. For the data in the server database, system administrator and user with a certain authority have the permission to add, delete, modify and query information. Authorized users can legally modify or even delete valuable data through the Internet. Since authorized users have higher authority on the system's data, authorized users can modify or delete some artificial errors in the process of acquisition through the above interface, so these modified or even deleted operations are legal. But this users may make some misoperation during work, it may lead to appearing Error removal, if this situation happens (very likely to happen), it will result in valuable data being deleted mistakenly, and bringing irreparable damage. So all these modified or deleted operations through network in the system's design do not really delete database's data actually, they only plus modified or deleted identification. In this way, data administrators of higher level will be reported through the process of system management after authorized users making misoperation, it contributes to recovery error removal data successfully, and increases data's security in the whole system.

In addition, architectural design of server also adopt two mechanisms of setting up specialized database server and adding backup of data server, data security will be further guaranteed. Specialized database server can let the data store in an independent physical server by the separation of data access load and other Web application load, lifetime network security and stability of data is improved. Data disaster recovery can be guaranteed by setting up backup of data server, and it can reduce the risk of the loss of valuable data stored by server, which is caused by natural disasters and other abnormal causes.

4 System Implementation and Conclusion

In this paper, the design of IoT traceability system for the organic livestock products implement data security technology in the link of data acquisition, data uploading and data management according to requirements of data reliability in application. At present, the system has been applied in the traceability system of organic livestock products in Qinghai Province, it has been dealt with the risk of multiple data's loss in the actual system and protected data security in this IoT system. The experience of the actual system operation shows that this paper's technical scheme is effective.

References

1. Huang Jing (黄静): Research and Implementation of Traceability System in the Beef Safety Production Chain. Northeast Agricultural University (东北农业大学), Heilongjiang (2011)
2. Wan Shuo (万硕), Zhang Xifeng (张西峰), Xia Ping (夏萍): Study and application of the traceability system of agricultural products quality and safety. Liaoning Agric. Sci. (辽宁农业科学) **2011**(5), 68–71
3. Kong, H., Li, J.: Application review of the global identification system (EAN·UCC system) in the traceability of the food safety supply chain. Food Sci. **2004**(6), 49
4. Luan Peixian (栾培贤), Wang Hongbing (王洪斌), Xiao Jianhua (肖建华), Xu Qiang (徐强), Chen Xin (陈欣): The design of information traceability system for pork breeding field system. Heilongjiang Anim. Husbandry Vet. (黑龙江畜牧兽医) **09**, 73–76 (2011)
5. Li Jintao (李锦涛), Guo Junbo (郭俊波), Luo Haiyong (罗海勇): Radio frequency identification (RFID) technology and its application. Inf. Technol. Express (信息技术快报) **11**(02), 1–10 (2004)
6. Wang, S.Y., Dong, C.L., Liu, Y.D.: Research and implementation of aspect-oriented programming. Appl. Res. Comput. (11), 220–223 (2004). (in Chinese)
7. Berg, L.: Animal identification. Farm Ind. News **39**(1), 82–86 (2006)
8. Hou Chunsheng (侯春生), Xia Ning (夏宁): Applied research on RFID technology in China's agricultural products quality and safety traceability system. China Agric. Sci. Bull. (中国农学通报) **26**(03), 296–298 (2010)
9. Jiao Yabing (侯春生): Building MIS for internet of things based on RFID/EPC technologies. Packag. Eng. (包装工程) **31**(23), 116–120 (2010)
10. Gan Yong (甘勇), Zheng Fue (郑富娥): Application of the IoT in supply chain based on EPC technology. Market Modernization (商场现代化) (16), 10–11 (2006)

Novel Congestion Avoidance Mechanism ZigBee-Based Wireless Sensor Network

Zhibing Peng, Zhibin Zhang$^{(\boxtimes)}$, Yingdong Ma, Lianhe Fu,
Shixiang Qiu, and Fengqi Wei

School of Computer, Inner Mongolia University, Hohhot 010010, China
ZhiBingPeng2015@163.com,
{cszhibin,csmyd,cswfq}@imu.edu.cn,
{2631119357,100512898}@qq.com

Abstract. In a larger scale ZigBee wireless sensor network, congestion will be an inevitable issue. Especially, in many environment monitoring or industry applications, it is impossible to omit the case. Thus, there is realistic motivation to address this fundamental problem. In the paper, we improve the transmission fashion of synchronization mechanism in IEEE802.15.4/ZigBee protocol with one random method, and pose a time-sharing transmission fashion to avoid congestion. Experimental results indicate that the two proposed methods can significantly reduce collision and, as a result, congestion avoidance can be implemented. The validity of proposed strategies is intuitively demonstrated through an experimental test-bed based on open-source implementation of IEEE802.15.4/ZigBee protocols.

Keywords: ZigBee · Random transmission · Congestion avoidance · Time-sharing

1 Introduction

ZigBee wireless sensor networks (WSNs) has been widely employed in monitoring harsh environment sits and controlling in industry application [1–3]. ZigBee WSNs is easy to deploy because of features such as wireless and low energy consumption. These features make it more popular in a wide range of areas including monitor, control and military application. As more and more network nodes are deployed widely, the system needs to handle a large amount of data, which might cause network congestion. Network congestion will impact on overall network performance and application objective, for example, packet loss, increased latency, excess retransmission load, and lopsided energy depletion. In a typical case, terminal nodes send a large amount of packets to father node by concurrent transmission. Instead of real-time handing of these packets, the father nodes usually deal with a relatively slow rate. As a result, the buffer of father node may overflow in this case. This is the typical reason of network congestion [4]. Another reason can be link level condition such as contention, interference and bit error. Furthermore, sensor network's traffic pattern may also lead to congestion, in which traffic is event driven and would be burst [5]. All nodes are activated simultaneously in IEEE802.15.4 beacon enabled mode, which might give rise to data collision.

© Springer Science+Business Media Singapore 2015
X. Zhang et al. (Eds.): ESTC 2015, CCIS 572, pp. 161–168, 2015.
DOI: 10.1007/978-981-10-0421-6_16

One of the challenges for ZigBee wireless sensor network is to reduce congestion [6]. In current study, there are four direction to deal with congestion scene, including re-adjusting rate, contention-based, medium access control protocol and transmission protocol. In many open literatures, congestion control strategies have been proposed. In [4, 6–8], the authors achieve traffic control when network congestion has occurred instead of congestion avoidance which can prevent congestion occurring and induce better network performance without other overhead. Thus, congestion avoidance is a better policy than congestion control. However, congestion avoidance in wireless sensor network has not received serious study until recent [9]. In [9], the authors build a congestion avoidance topology to improve performance. The proposed retrieval strategy is complex and unrealistic to embed into the resource-constrained ZigBee network. In [10], in order to avoid congestion, the authors propose a re-routing method to reduce traffic load in specific link/node. However, the algorithm wastes expensive computation resource. [11] reduces packet collision by fusion of slotted CSMA/CA and TDMA techniques and using multi-path data propagation for collision avoidance. However, the proposed method will disable in a mobile scene. [12] provides a Multi-Channel scheme for collisions avoidance in IEEE802.15.4/ZigBee protocol. The proposed method needs to partition the network into many sub networks. However, it only can eliminate inter and intra-sub network collision.

There are few researches in the ZigBee protocol stack. Researchers prefer to use stimulation tool such as NS-2, OPNET, and OMNET etc. In the paper, we aim to avoid congestion in ZigBee wireless sensor network based on the open-source implementation of IEEE802.15.4/ZigBee protocols. We propose two methods to achieve congestion avoidance in ZigBee application layer (APL) and operating system abstraction layer (OSAL) in IEEE802.15.4/ZigBee protocol stack. The experiment results show that the proposed methods are better candidate scheme.

2 Materials

ZigBee wireless sensor network comprises three potential components. These components are called as ZigBee coordinator, ZigBee router, and ZigBee terminal respectively. Different types of nodes have different roles within a network. In ZigBee sensor network, there is only one coordinator node. Coordinator node is responsible for initializing and maintaining the network. Router nodes are capable of receiving and passing on message in a network, as repeater that can expand the scope of network. There are three different types of topology possible for ZigBee network: star topology, tree topology and mesh topology. Tree topology holds as a stationary structure, becoming a preferred scheme for our experiment. In order to remove the effect of link change, a tree network topology is considered. We adopt CC2530 chip which include sensor module, processor module, wireless communication module, power supply module and antenna module [9]. As shown in Fig. 1, every terminal node is connected with five kind's sensor including carbon dioxide concentration, air temperature and humidity, moisture content, light intensity. Meanwhile five kind's data are packaged in a command as show in Table 1. Terminal nodes are connected to sensor and responsible for collecting sensor data and sending them to router node. Router nodes, acting

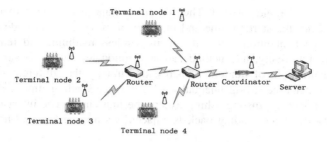

Fig. 1. Experiment deployment scheme

as repeater, are responsible for dealing with sensor data from terminal node. All sent packet are converged to coordinator which is directly connected to PC by USB serial port. In Fig. 1, nodes are randomly distributed in laboratory section and remain stationary after deployment. To achieve the goal of comparison, the topology structure also holds as stationary in all experiments. Other parameters such as the distance and location of nodes will be constant.

3 Congestion Avoidance

In this section, we propose two methodologies for congestion avoidance in ZigBee WSN: random transmission mechanism (RTM) and time-sharing transmission mechanism (TSTM). The first method tries to avoid congestion occurrence with random driving fashion. However, the time-sharing transmission employs a time division method to avoid channel contention.

3.1 Random Transmission Mechanism

The fundamental incentive for the random transmission mechanism is designed to avoid terminal nodes holding channel simultaneously. Meanwhile, it is a proactive mechanism for congestion avoidance. We adjust intervals of terminal nodes in order to avoid collision. In Fig. 1, suppose terminal nodes 1, 2, 3, 4 intend to send data. In IEEE802.15.4/ZigBee protocol beacon-enabled mode, all terminal nodes will be activated simultaneously. Then, terminal nodes use a constant for interval supposes 3000 ms to transmit data synchronously. In the mode, we propose rand transmission mechanism which sets interval as T. Thus, the interval of node i, denoted as T_i, can be given as

$$T_i = I + rand() \ \& \ 0xR \tag{1}$$

where I is the initial interval within node i, $rand()$ is random function, R is a constant jointly random function generating random value which varies in preset range. A greater R can generate bigger T_i. In experiment, I is preset as 3000 ms, and R is preset as $0 \times FA0$. Afterwards, in next interval, terminal nodes transmit data with different starting time and interval. Though, all terminal nodes are activated simultaneously. However, the starting time and intervals of every terminal node are different which can avoid contention and collision in wireless medium, and reduce retransmission times. Intuitively, the method can accommodate the packet surge. Figure 2 illustrates the principle of random transmission strategy that different nodes access channel in distinct time, using unequal access during. Sending time and interval of three terminal nodes are distinguishing except the first circle. The interval is the time difference between twice sending packets adjacent within one terminal node.

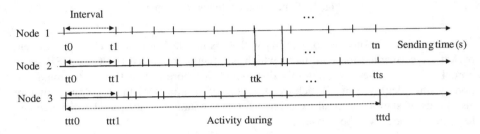

Fig. 2. Time-sharing schematic diagram

Additionally, random function has a drawback which generates identical values. In some cases, for instance at tk in the Fig. 2, the starting time and intervals of terminal nodes will be identical. The situation degrades the performance of random transmission mechanism by bringing in more contention. In the case, the network can resort to the time-sharing transmission method which is presented in the next subsection.

3.2   Time-Sharing Transmission Mechanism

In the subsection, we propose a time-sharing transmission method to improve channel contention in IEEE802.15.4/ZigBee protocol. The scheme can be presented in detail as follows:

- Step 1: When network is constructed successfully, we store all jointed network node i in a array denote as $node[]$, $node[j] = Network\_Address_i$, $j \subseteq [0, k]$, where k + 1 is the number of the overall network nodes. The array of $node[j]$ can be applied to check for network topology. Coordinator node, router nodes and terminal nodes are marked as 0, 1, and 2 respectively. Terminal nodes are stored in a temporary array and their flag is equal to 2, denoted as $temp[l]$. The number of terminal nodes is $l + 1$.
- Step 2: Define regular time variable denoted by Δt, $\Delta t = \dfrac{interval}{l + 1}$, $l \geq 0$.
- Step 3: Define a new starting time of each node denoted as $start\_t_i$; $start\_t_i = interval + \Delta t * j$ where interval is the original one, j is the index of array.
- Step 4: Invoke nodes at $start\_t_i$. The interval is constant and identical within terminal nodes.

Figure 3 illustrates the principle of time-sharing schedule. As shown in Fig. 1, there are four terminal nodes in network. The interval is preset as 3 s. As show depicted in Fig. 3, four terminal nodes take turn holding channel to transmit packet.

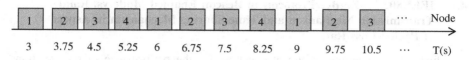

Fig. 3. Time-sharing mechanism

4   Experimental Results

Experiments are conducted in the laboratory where the maximum range is 25 m (the range of visibility of industrial grade CC2530 exceeds 500 m). Thus, we need to unplug the antenna to avoid forming star network topology. In all experiments, we evaluate the performance of network by using two criterions: packet loss rate and end-to-end delay. In literatures [10, 11], the authors find that the network performance will be affected by some external factors such as moisture, location, wind etc. Thus, in order to eliminate the external factors interference, all experiments are conducted in a similar environment. The environment parameters is controlled as follows: temperature 25 °C, air moisture content 0.73 %, in a unattented environment. In order to construct a tree topology depicted as Fig. 1, the antennas need to be unplugged on the terminal nodes. We use serial port debugging tool to deal with packet in PC, and define the command format as follows:

Table 1. Command format

Head	Operation code						
Head	Recnum	Node number	MAC	Network address	Father node	Data	Senum
4	2	1	6	2	2	10	2

In Table 1, recnum and senum are the number of received and sent packet respectively. Packet loss rate denoted as PLR is defined as:

$$PLR = \frac{senum - recnum}{senum} \tag{2}$$

The unit is Byte in the command format. In the experiments, we collect five types of data which contain CO_2 concentration, air temperature, light intensity, humidity and air moisture content. Two Bytes are consumed by every type. The head field consumes four Bytes and is designed to achieve different functionalities, including sending collection data instruction, statistic PLR instruction, clearing previous statistic result and checking network topology instruction. In the experiments, each PLR is calculated every an hour. In the next two subsections, we demonstrate the experimental comparisons between proposed methods and native ZigBee protocols.

4.1 IEEE802.5.4/ZigBee Protocols in Beacon Enabled Mode vs. Rand Transmission Mechanism and Time-Sharing Mechanism in Aspect of Packet Loss Rate

The first set of experiments aim at checking for the performance of random transmission mechanism and time-sharing mechanism in aspect of packet loss rate. In Fig. 4, x-axis stands for index of sampling data groups. Every sample is computed every an hour. Figure 4 indicates that the packet loss drastically decreases by executing the proposed RTM and TSTM. The result implies that the proposed mechanisms under synchronization mechanism can be two good candidates for ZigBee wireless sensor network in congestion scene, especially being applied immensely in harsh and perilous environments such as crops growth monitoring etc. The maximum threshold of interval must considerate the timeliness of the specific application. When adopting a TI CC253 chip, we suggest that the minimum threshold of interval is set as 3 s.

In Fig. 4, the means of packet loss rate between RTM and TSTM are 2.1974 %, 1.8853 %, respectively, and the variances of both are 0.7756, 0.2215, respectively. Obviously, the curve of loss packet rate of RTM is more volatile than that of TSTM, shown as in Fig. 4. In nature, the volatility of RTM is directly related to the random values.

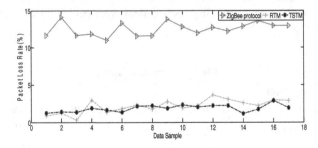

Fig. 4. Comparisons among ZigBee protocol, RTM and TSTM in aspect of packet loss rate

4.2 IEEE802.15.4/ZigBee Protocols in Beacon Enabled Mode vs. Rand Transmission Mechanism and Time-Sharing Mechanism in Aspect of End to End Delay

The second set of experiments is used to compare our proposed methods with native ZigBee protocol in the end-to-end delay. In the experiments, the interval is preset as 3 s.

In Fig. 5, x-axis represents the index of groups. Every group is computed every one hour. The two proposed methods obtain less end-to-end delay than ZigBee raw protocol. The end-to-end delay of TSTM and RTM are less than 400 microseconds. However, in most case, the latencies are over 400 microseconds, shown as in Fig. 5.

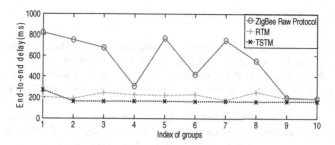

Fig. 5. Comparisons among ZigBee protocol, RTM and TSTM in aspect of end to end delay

In Fig. 5, the end-to-end delay of TSTM is approximate 200 microseconds. That to say, every terminal nodes hold on channel approximately 200 microseconds. In TSTM, if Δt is greater than 250 microseconds, the mechanism can achieve favorable performance. When the scale of network is enlarged, in order to ensure the performance of TSTM, it is necessary to increase the interval. In RTM, when there are many nodes in ZigBee network, in order to ensure the mechanism to obtain ideal effect, we need to expand the value of R. When the value of R becomes bigger, the collision probability will become smaller.

5 Conclusion

In general, in synchronized protocols of ZigBee, all nodes are simultaneously activated. In the paper, we propose two strategies to avoid congestion. Terminal nodes send data by the random driving fashion and the time-sharing fashion which alleviate the pressure of routing nodes. The intervals of terminal nodes are updated as random values under RTM mode. The possibility of collision will degrade properly. It is more advisable to avoid congestion with random intervals than fixed interval. Under RSTM mode, terminal nodes transmit packets with different transmission period to take turns transmitting packets. These strategies are compatible with ZigBee protocols. We compare our propositions to synchronization mode of ZigBee. The results show that our schemes are superior to IEEE802.15.4/ZigBee protocols somewhat in the aspect of packet loss rate and end-to-end delay. For instance, the packet loss rate in IEEE802.15.4/ZigBee beacon enabled mode varies from 10.98 % and 14.068 %. However, the packet loss rate varies from 0.325 % and 3.67 % for RTM, and from 1.25 % and 2.9 % for TSTM.

Acknowledgment. This work is supported by the National Nature Science Foundation of China (No. 31160253; No. 31360289; No. 61461039), Innovation Experiment Program for University Students (No. 201410126043), and Inner Mongolia natural science foundation (No. 2013MS0903), SPH-IMU (No. 30105-125130). The authors wish to thank the anonymous reviewers for their helpful comments in reviewing this paper.

References

1. Fucheng, X.U., Minghua, Z.H.U.: Design and implementation of library monitoring system based on ZigBee. J. Comput. Inf. Syst. **9**(13), 5281–5289 (2012)
2. Chavan, C.H., Karande, M.P.V.: Wireless monitoring of soil moisture, temperature and humidity using ZigBee in agriculture. Int. J. Eng. Trends Technol. (IJETT) **11**(10), 493–497 (2014)
3. Qiu, W., Dong, L., Wang, F., et al.: Design of intelligent greenhouse environment monitoring system based on ZigBee and embedded technology. In: 2014 IEEE International Conference on Consumer Electronics-China, pp. 1–3. IEEE (2014)
4. Yun, D.S., Cho, S.H., Seo, D.W., et al.: An efficient and reliable data transmission control method for relaxing congestion problem in ZigBee network. In: Proceedings of the 2nd International Conference on Ubiquitous Information Management and Communication, pp. 533–537. ACM (2008)
5. Borasia, S., Raisinghani, V.: A review of congestion control mechanisms for wireless sensor networks. In: Shah, K., Lakshmi Gorty, V.R., Phirke, A. (eds.) ICTSM 2011. CCIS, vol. 145, pp. 201–206. Springer, Heidelberg (2011)
6. El Rachkidy, N., Guitton, A.: Congestion reduction using a MAC scheduling. J. Commun. **9** (10), 751–761 (2014)
7. Liu, Q., et al.: An enhanced routing algorithm for congestion control in a home energy management system. In: 2013 IEEE 2nd Global Conference on Consumer Electronics (GCCE), IEEE (2013)
8. Jeong, W.S., Cho, S.H.: Congestion control for efficient transmission in ZigBee networks. In: 5th International Conference on Wireless Communications, Networking and Mobile Computing, 2009 (WiCom 2009), pp. 1–4. IEEE (2009)
9. Dasgupta, R., Mukherjee, R., Gupta, A.: Congestion avoidance topology in wireless sensor network using Karnaugh map. In: Applications and Innovations in Mobile Computing, 2015 (AIMoC 2015), pp. 89–96. IEEE (2015)
10. Khaliq, K.A., Akbar, M.S., Qayyum, A., et al.: Congestion avoidance hybrid wireless mesh protocol (CA-HWMP) for IEEE802.11s. Procedia Comput. Sci. **32**, 229–236 (2014)
11. Mantri, D., Prasad, N.R., Prasad, R., Scheduled collision avoidance in wireless sensor network using ZigBee. In: 2014 International Conference on Advances in Computing, Communications and Informatics (ICACCI), pp. 2129–2134. IEEE (2014)
12. Sahraoui, M.: Collisions avoidance multi-channel scheme for the protocol IEEE802.15.4. In: 2012 International Conference on Information Technology and e-Services (ICITeS), pp. 1–9. IEEE (2012)
13. Abbasi, A.Z., Islam, N., Shaikh, Z.A.: A review of wireless sensors and networks' applications in agriculture. Comput. Stan. Interfaces **36**(2), 263–270 (2014)
14. Ruiz-Garcia, L., Barreiro, P., Robla, J.I.: Performance of ZigBee-based wireless sensor nodes for real-time monitoring of fruit logistics. J. Food Eng. **87**(3), 405–415 (2008)
15. Shuaib, K., Alnuaimi, M., Boulmalf, M., et al.: Performance evaluation of IEEE802.15.4: experimental and simulation results. J. Commun. **2**(4), 29–37 (2007)

Congestion Alleviation Method ZigBee-Based Wireless Sensor Network

Zhibing Peng, Zhibin Zhang[✉], Shixiang Qiu, and Lianhe Fu

School of Computer, Inner Mongolia University, Hohhot 010010, China
ZhiBingPeng2015@163.com, cszhibin@imu.edu.cn,
{100512898,2631119357}@qq.com

Abstract. In the ZigBee wireless sensor network, the congestion will deteriorate the network performance and yield potential burst event. Especially, in a large-scale network, it is impossible to omit the situation. In this paper, we propose an effective congestion detection without consuming significant computational resource in the resource-constrained ZigBee wireless sensor network. Simultaneously, we propose a novel congestion alleviation with a flexible congestion level in Application Layer and Operating System Abstraction Layer of IEEE 802.15.4/ZigBee protocol stack. Furthermore, in order to adjust the data flow of the network, we combine the congestion alleviation with a random driven fashion. Our test-bed is based on an open-source ZigBee protocols stack. Experimental results show that our algorithm outperforms the native ZigBee protocols in a spect of packet loss rate.

Keywords: Zigbee · Congestion detection · Congestion relief

1 Introduction

ZigBee is one of the most prominent communication technologies for low-power consumption, low-rate, low-cost, short-distance, and it works in 2.4 GHz band. ZigBee wireless sensor networks (WSNs) has been applied in many fields extensively such as environment monitoring, danger alarm and disaster rescue etc. [1–3]. In these applications, in order to avoid the packet loss, ZigBee protocol is embedded in an acknowledgement and retransmission [4]. However, when network congestion has occurred, the repeated retransmission and acknowledge degrade the network efficiency [5]. Accordingly, the congestion control has an achievable expected effect for congestion scene. In a typical case, the transmission rate of packet is slow than receiving rate of packet, and then the buffer of node falls into an overflow state, and the abnormal packets are discarded. This is how the typical network congestion occurs [6]. In many literatures, the congestion or traffic control methods have been studied. In [7], the authors proposed a new MAC scheduling mechanism to relief congestion by dividing nodes into many groups. At any time, either all nodes are inactive, or all groups of nodes are active except one group. And the method ignores a practical case that the congestion has local characteristic that the congestion may only occur in some interlinking nodes instead of all links. In [6], authors did not take into account the acknowledgement and retransmission mechanism. Firstly, the time interval is set as a fixed value which neglects the congestion degree. Secondly,

X. Zhang et al. (Eds.): ESTC 2015, CCIS 572, pp. 169–178, 2015.
DOI: 10.1007/978-981-10-0421-6_17

the authors confirm that the network congestion will occur when the terminal nodes fail to receive the acknowledgement frame. In general, it is possible that the acknowledgement frame loss can show the packet loss because the ZigBee protocol is equipped with a build-in confirm and retransmission mechanism. Only when the third loss of acknowledgement frame arrives, we can confirm the packet loss. How to tackle the network congestion, there are some common stages: the congestion avoidance, the congestion detection, the congestion notification or the congestion confirm and the rate adjustment [8]. However, the existing detecting methods are not precise and have complex calculations. The performance of the congestion control is also restricted. There are few theoretical researches in the ZigBee protocol stack. Researchers prefer to use a stimulation tool to demonstrate the valid of proposed hypothesis instead of designing in Z-Stack. In the paper, we outline our design to relief the congestion in the ZigBee wireless sensor network. We improve the congestion detection and propose an effective traffic control method in ZigBee application layer (APL) and operating system abstraction layer (OSAL).

2   ZigBee Elementary Technologies

IEEE 802.15.4/ZigBee devices can be categorized according to their functionalities: full function devices (FFD), reduced function devices (RFD) [9]. In the ZigBee network, FFD is a network center, managing the overall network. RFD is capable of forwarding frame, and also has its child nodes connecting to it. In our experiment, the ZigBee coordinator represents FFD, and the ZigBee router and the ZigBee terminal stand for RFD. The terminal nodes as data source are responsible for collecting sensor data and transmitting message to the upstream node, and talk to the router or the coordinator. The ZigBee Alliance extends the generic star topology to tree topology and mesh topology [10]. It is possible that different network structures are oriented to different application objects. The tree structure has advantage in high connectivity and low routing overhead, which is suitable for stationary performance analysis [11], and is a good choice for our experiment.

3   Congestion Control

3.1   Congestion Detection

In [12], the authors define the congestion level is a ratio between the number of inputting packets and the number of outputting packets within node. However, the buffer which store packet is invisible in Z-Stack 2006. And meanwhile, the structure of network may also alter. Thus, the number of inputting or outputting packets is uneasy to be counted within the intermediate nodes. We use a computational simple and effective statistical method without consuming excessively computational resources of CC2530 chip. To achieve this goal, we selectively focus on the terminal nodes and the coordinator node.

Packet loss rate is a valid criterion and indicator of network congestion, providing guidelines in performance optimization. In order to calculate precisely the packet loss rate, we do the following works. All nodes are labeled and can be identified by the MAC address which is assigned by a tool called SmartRF Flash Programmer. Table 1 illustrates the relation between the MAC address and the label. We design a statistical function to calculate the number of sending or receiving packet. In the terminal node, when sending a packet, the statistical function calculates the number of the corresponding nodes. In the coordinator, when receiving a packet, the statistical function calculates the number of the corresponding nodes. Intuitively, the computation about packet loss is simple without redundancy head.

Packet loss rate, denoted as PLR, is computed based on the following formula [7]:

$$PLR = \frac{\textit{the number of sending packet} - \textit{the number of receiveing packet}}{\textit{the number of send packet}} \quad (1)$$

Detection interval denoted as DI is preset as DI_0. A larger DI value degrades the timeliness of detection method. On the contrary, a relatively smaller DI value, the coordinator will frequently send uncast notification message to the corresponding terminal node, adding redundant load which will weaken the performance of network.

We define the congestion level as depicted in Table 2, where P_i is a threshold for the packet loss rate. I_i represents an interval and the difference of the adjacent I_i should be greater than or equal to one second. We predefine five degrees about the congestion, and r is a random value uniformly distributed in the range (0, 1). We set a dynamic interval according to the corresponding congestion level. This scheme is helpful to reduce the collision probability compared with setting a constant for the interval. It is possible that terminal nodes have identical congestion level. And this is undesirable, causing collision. However, in this case, our method will achieve significant advantage by adding random value for I_i. In general, the random values are different. Thus, no matter what the terminal node's congestion level, the probability that the intervals are identical is tremendous small. And so, the possibility of collision will degrade properly.

Suppose there are three nodes called as node 1, 2, 3 respectively. Unfortunately, the three nodes are in the identical congestion level. Then, the random value r can be remarked as r_1, r_2, r_3, respectively. Nevertheless, in a small-scale ZigBee network, r_1, r_2, r_3 are unequal. Thus, the method is superior to using a fixed value somewhat.

Table 1. The relation of MAC address and label

MAC Address	0 × FFFFFFFFFFFF0000	0 × FF … FF0001	0 × FF … FF0007	…
Label	0 × 0	0 × 1	0 × 7	…

Table 2. The relation among PLR, congestion level and interval

PLR's range	$[0, P_1]$	$(P_1, P_2]$	$(P_2, P_3]$	$(P_3, P_4]$	$(P_4, 1]$
Congestion level	mild	mild + +	medium	medium + +	intense
Interval(s)	0 × $(I_1 + r)$	0 × $(I_2 + r)$	0 × $(I_3 + r)$	0 × $(I_4 + r)$	0 × $(I_5 + r)$

3.2 Congestion Relief

For a plain description to a congestion relief (CR) mechanism, we present some related definitions of elementary terms firstly [13].

- Define 1 (**Depth**): For a terminal node i in ZigBee wireless sensor network transmitting sensing data to a coordinator passing through path $\{s_0 = i, s_1, s_2 \ldots s_d = d\}$, the number of nodes on this path excluding the coordinator is called as the depth of the node i to the coordinator, denoted by **Depth**$(i) = d$.
- Define 2 (Father node and child node): For a node i in ZigBee wireless sensor network, if it is directly linked to a node j and the node i sends sensing data to the node j directly. Then, the node i is called as the j's children node, the node j is called as i's father node.
- Define 3 (**Correlation**): For every node i in ZigBee wireless sensor network, if its data comes from the node j directly or indirectly, and the node j must be a terminal node. Then, the two terminal nodes are called as "having correlation". The number of these terminal nodes is called as correlation, denoted by **Correlation**$(i) = s$.

The basic procedure of congestion alleviation is that when the coordinate detects a congestion arrival, it sends an interval to update message to execute full-fledged control operation by unicast transmission to corresponding terminal nodes.

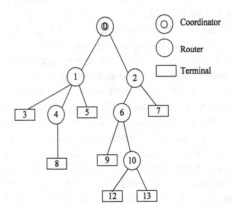

Fig. 1. Schematic diagram of the congestion alleviation

Figure 1 shows the principle of the proposed algorithm in this paper. And the coordinator is responsible for the kernel tasks. When DI expires, the coordinator calculates the PLR, and then compares with its range to in order to obtain a congestion level. When the congestion is unequal to the previous one, the coordinator sends a new interval to the corresponding terminal node to re-adjust the interval. For instance, if the node 0 detects PLR of the node 3 ($PLR \in (0, P_1)$), the coordinate sends an updating interval to the node 3, notifying it to transmit a packet per $I_1 + r$ second during the next DI. In general, if a packet of the node 3 is lost, it may be overflowed within the node 1.

Thus, if the interval of the node 3 is prolonged, the number of the packets within the node 1 will decrease. If the value of **Depth** and **Correlation** of a terminal node is relatively bigger, such as the node 12, the cause of packet loss is complicated. Suppose *PLR* of the node 12 is greater than zero, and there are many some potential causes for this congestion scenario, including the packets overflow within the node 2 or the node 6 or the node 10, or the node 2, 6, or the node 2, 10, or the node 6, 10, 2, or the node 6, 10. However, no matter what the reasons may be, as long as the coordinator updates the interval of the node 12 according to the congestion level, the number of packet within the communication link (12-10-6-2-0) will reduce. Thus, we can avoid assessing a variety of congestion situations and complex computing. Because, when the packets overflow within the node 2, it is possible that the node 6 and the node 7 cause the congestion. Unfortunately, the node 6 has its child nodes which are connected with the node 9 and the node 10. Furthermore, the node 10 also has its child nodes. Thus, the reason is intricacy that leads to the packet loss of the node 2. Therefore, we propose a conjecture to reduce calculation, which can avoid considering the effect of intermediate node in the communication links. And the correlation and the interval of node are regarded as main considering factors, which mirror the number of sending packets. In fact, if the depth and the degree of nodes become bigger, the possibility of the congestion occurrence will significantly rise. For instance, **Depth**(1) = 1 and **Depth**(2) = 1, but **Correlation**(1) = 3 less than **Correlation**(2) = 4. That is, when the intervals of terminal nodes are identical, the congestion possibility of the node 2 will bigger than the node 1. If we judge all possibilities in a congestion situation, it is inevitable to induce redundancy computing, and weaken network performance. Thus, the new method proposed in this paper only considers the number of sending packet within the terminal nodes, and the number of receiving packet of the coordinator node, and it can avoid the intermediate node and some specific causes, being advisable.

ZigBee protocols achieve acknowledgement and retransmission mechanism. However, because network congestion has occurred, it is possible to lose the updating message. We find that when the updating interval message is lost, the congestion alleviation approach will be disabled during the next *DI*. Thus, in order to improve the control efficiency, it is necessary that the coordinator confirms whether the next interval is updated successfully after the updating interval message is sent. If the message is lost, the coordinator needs to retransmit the message. In the experiment, we set the maximum of retransmission times as 3, and then, acknowledge the updating message after approximate 400 ms. In some cases, if the network fails to update the interval after three times, we adjust $DI = \frac{DI}{3}$. When the interval is updated successfully, *DI* is re-adjusted as DI_0.

In the OSAL of the coordinator, we can achieve good congestion alleviation operation by calculating the *PLR* and its congestion level. We implement the congestion relief strategy in OSAL (called as CR), and avoid triggering event in APL. CR achieves the following functionalities:

- assessing congestion level for all terminal nodes.
- sending update message to terminal node by unicast.

In order to simplify the description, the terminal node is denoted as TD_i, i is the index of terminal node. In our experiments, the CR strategy, the values of I_i and P_i are depicted in detail as follows:

- Step 1: Define an interval, DI_0 is preseted as 60 s. The default is 3 s for the interval.

$$buf\_rate\,[i],for\ i \subseteq [0,4]$$
$$buf\_rate\,[0] = 0x(4+r), buf\_rate[1] = 0x(5+r)$$
$$buf\_rate[2] = 0x(6+r), buf\_rate[3] = 0x(7+r)$$
$$buf\_rate[4] = 0x(a+r)$$

- Step 2: Define different congestion levels. The range is partitioned by the threshold $P_i(i = 1,2,3,4)$, corresponding to 0.05, 0.1, 0.15, and 0.25, respectively. That is, there are five ranges including [0, 0.05], (0.05, 0.1], (0.1, 0.15], (0.15, 0.25] and (0.25, 1], marked as *mild, mild + +, medium, medium+ +, intense*, respectively. These thresholding values are related directly to the performance of the network. In the experiment, we find a trend that if the thresholding values are relatively smaller, the performance of the network becomes relatively better.
- Step 3: For every terminal node, computing PLR_i, $i \subseteq [1,m]$. the variable m is the number of terminal nodes.
  Compare PLR_i with the congestion ranges. Confirm the interval or *rate*

$$rate = buf\_rate[j],\ j \subseteq [0, m-1]$$

- Step 4: Send a unicast updating interval to TD_j by invoking the function, SendData $(TD_j, rate, 2)$ which then calls AF_DataRequest().

In order to further improve the network performance, we let the terminal node to transmit packet with the *CR* mechanism jointing a random driven fashion (see another paper in this proceedings). This hybrid mechanism called as *CR+* can be embedded successfully in ZigBee protocol.

4 Experimental Results

We chose a microcontroller (Texas Instruments CC2530) with a sensor module, a processor module, a wireless communication module, a power supply module and an antenna module to achieve experimental verification. The sensor module is connected with different types of sensors sensing carbon dioxide concentration, air temperature and humidity, moisture content and light intensity, respectively. Our test-bed is based on the Texas Instruments ZigBee protocol stack 2006 (Z-Stack 2006). The terminal nodes and the router nodes are randomly distributed in a rectangular section (5 m, 25 m). Meanwhile, the coordinator is connected to PC by a USB serial port as a communication bridge. Data packets from every node flow into the coordinator. The coordinator can control forwards messages to all its descendants in the network [11]. In order to do experiment comparisons, the tree-structured is bound to keep the same as the previous one.

The network performance will be interfered by some environment parameters, WiFi and other factors [14–16]. Thus, in order to pave the way of the ideal solution, the experimental environment remains the same. A serial port debugging tool is used to receive data and send different control instructions. And the instruction format is described as follows:

Table 3. Instruction format

Head	Operation code						
Head	recnum	Node number	MAC	Network address	Father node	Data	senum
4	2	1	6	2	2	10	2

In Table 3, the recnum, the senum is the number of received packet, or sent packet, respectively. The unit is Byte in the instruction format. In the experiments, each datum sample is calculated periodically every an hour. We can see the topology structure of network by checking the network address of a node combines with father node in the experiments. The field for node number consumes one Byte. That is, the number of nodes ranges from 0 to 255. The head field is used for controlling network behavior. In this following subsection, we check if our schemes work well as we expected.

4.1 Native IEEE802.15.4/ZigBee Protocol in Beacon Enabled Mode vs. Congestion Relief

The first set of experiments was performed to verify the performance of the congestion alleviation compared with the ZigBee raw protocol. We burned the native ZigBee protocol code into the ZigBee nodes of the network designed in our experiments, and then, calculated the packet loss rates every one hour. In contrast, we burned the ZigBee protocol code equipped with the congestion relief mechanism proposed in this paper into the same ZigBee nodes. Seventeen groups of packet loss rates were obtained in the experiments. The results are shown as in the Fig. 2.

In Figs. 2 and 3, x-axis stands for the index of groups which is the number of packet loss rate. From the Fig. 2, we can see that the *CR* mechanism has significant

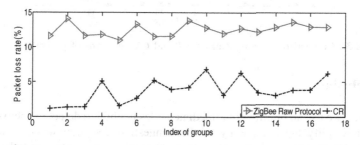

Fig. 2. Comparisons between *CR* and ZigBee raw protocols in terms of packet loss rate

performance improvements over IEEE 802.15.4/ZigBee protocol in beacon enabled mode. In this way, the smooth congestion operation is maintained without many packet losses, and the packet loss rate has been reduced sharply. The result shows that the low sampling rate has favorable effect on reducing the number of packets in ZigBee wireless sensor network.

4.2   Hybrid Mechanism of Random Driven Fashion and Congestion Alleviation

The second set of experiments was designed to validate the hybrid mechanism above mentioned. The procedure of experiment included to burn the ZigBee's raw protocol code equipped with the random driving fashion and congestion alleviation into the ZigBee nodes of network designed in this paper. Then, we build the same network as shown in the Fig. 1 and calculated a packet loss rate every one hour. We obtained seventeen groups of data in all. The results are plotted in Fig. 3. We can observer the fact that the *CR* mechanism has salient effect on the congestion scenario. However the *CR+* has advantage over *CR*. Figure 3 displayed that the packet loss rate varies from 1.167 % to 6.3 % for the *CR* mechanism, and from 0 % to 1.28 % for the *CR+* scheme in the experiments. Thus, the performance of *CR+* is superior to *CR* somewhat. In fact, the difference between *CR* and *CR+* is distinguishing. *CR+* has two functionalities: the congestion avoidance and the congestion relief, and *CR* is only the congestion relief. Unlike the *CR* mechanism, *CR+* is designed for avoiding the congestion occurrence in advance. When the congestion arrives, *CR* is activated. Therefore, the hybrid mechanism designed in our experiment can finish simultaneously the functionalities such as congestion avoidance and congestion mitigation. As depicted in Fig. 3, the results show that the hybrid mechanism is a better alternative candidate for the congestion scene.

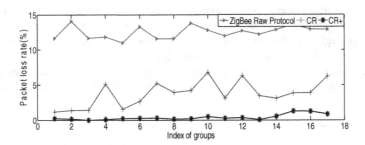

Fig. 3. Comparisons among ZigBee, *CR* and *CR+* in terms of packet loss rate

5   Conclusion

In this paper, we use an omitting intermediate nodes method to detect the network state, which can simplify the complexity of the congestion detection without consuming excess calculation resource. Then, we improve the congestion control with the multiply congestion levels and a random driven fashion. These strategies are compatible with ZigBee protocols. Experimental results display that the proposed algorithm in this paper can significantly relief the network congestion, compared with the original one.

Acknowledgment. This work is supported by the National Nature Science Foundation of China (No. 31160253; No. 31360289), Innovation Experiment Program for University Students (No. 201410126043). The authors wish to thank the anonymous reviewers for their helpful comments in reviewing this paper.

References

1. Ren, X.P., Zhang, H.: Design of gas alarm system based on Zigbee network. Comput. Technol. Autom. (2014)
2. Xu, F., Zhu, M.: Design and Implementation of library monitoring system based on ZigBee. J. Comput. Inf. Syst. **9**(13), 5281–5289 (2012)
3. Jiang, F., Zhao, W.: ZigBee technology application in disaster rescue. Adv. Mater. Res. **605–607**, 2358–2361 (2013)
4. Jeong, W.S., Cho, S.H.: Congestion control for efficient transmission in ZigBee Networks. In: 5th International Conference on Wireless Communications, Networking and Mobile Computing, 2009 (WiCom 2009), pp. 1–4. IEEE (2009)
5. Kurose, J., Ross, K.: Computer Networking: A Top Down Approach Featuring the Internet. Addison Wesley, Reading (2001)
6. Yun, D.S., Cho, S.H., Seo, D.W., et al.: An efficient and reliable data transmission control method for relaxing congestion problem in ZigBee network. In: Proceedings of the 2nd International Conference on Ubiquitous Information Management and Communication, pp. 533–537. ACM (2008)
7. El Rachkidy, N., Guitton, A.: Congestion reduction using a MAC scheduling. J. Commun. **9**(10), 751–761 (2014)
8. Raisinghani, V., Borasia, S.: A review of congestion control mechanisms for wireless sensor networks. In: Shah, K., Lakshmi Gorty, V.R., Phirke, A. (eds.) ICTSM 2011. CCIS, vol. 145, pp. 201–206. Springer, Heidelberg (2011)
9. Tennina, S., Koubâa, A., Daidone, R., et al.: IEEE802.15.4 and ZigBee as enabling technologies for low-power wireless systems with quality-of-service constraints. Springer Science & Business Media, Heidelberg (2013)
10. Jiang, F.C., Wu, H.W., Yang, C.T.: Traffic load analysis and its application to enhancing longevity on IEEE 802.15.4/ZigBee Sensor Network. J. Supercomput. **62**(2), 895–915 (2012)
11. Huang, K.L., Yen, L.H., Wang, J.T., et al.: A backbone-aware topology formation (BATF) scheme for ZigBee wireless sensor networks. Wirel. Pers. Commun. **68**, 47–64 (2013)
12. Liu, Q., Qian, H.W., Wang, B.W., et al.: An enhanced routing algorithm for congestion control in a home energy management system. In: 2013 IEEE 2nd Global Conference on Consumer Electronics (GCCE), pp. 438–439. IEEE (2013)
13. Hao†, X., Liu, B., Jia, N., Dou, J.: A transmission-effective congestion-cognized routing protocol for wireless sensor networks. J. Comput. Inf. Syst. **6**(8), 2592–2636 (2010)
14. Ruiz-Garcia, L., Barreiro, P., Robla, J.I.: Performance of ZigBee-Based wireless sensor nodes for real-time monitoring of fruit logistics. J. Food Eng. **87**(3), 405–415 (2008)

15. Casey, P.R., Tepe, K.E., Kar, N.: Design and implementation of a testbed for IEEE 802.15.4 (Zigbee) performance measurements. EURASIP J. Wirel. Commun. Netw. **2010**(23), 1–11 (2013)
16. Mardini, W., Khamayseh, Y., Jaradatand, R., et al.: Interference problem between ZigBee and WiFi. In: International Proceedings of Computer Science and Information Technology, pp. 133–138 (2012)

The Design and Implementation of Process Copy and Memory Sharing on SeL4

Jian Zhang[1(✉)], Qiao Kang[2], Zhoujian Yu[2], Lei Wang[1], and Cangzhou Yuan[2]

[1] School of Computer, Beihang University, Beijing 100191, China
buaacszj@qq.com, wanglei@buaa.edu.cn
[2] School of Software, Beihang University, Beijing 100191, China

Abstract. SeL4 is the newest member of the L4 microkernel family. It is also the world's first (currently the only one) general-purpose operating system which has passed the formal verification. However, as the micro-kernel system, seL4 currently provided little library function interface. RefOS is a typical multi-tasking operating system which built on seL4. This paper achieves the mmap function, providing memory mapping and sharing, as well as process copy which is similar with the fork function on RefOS. The child process can share the memory region which is marked as SHARED by mmap with its parent process. Our job provides support for implementing the POSIX standard interfaces on RefOS, as well as a lower-level interface for the development of parallel programs.

Keywords: SeL4 · Refos · Memory sharing · Process copy

1 Introduction

L4 kernels are a serial of operating system kernels which are based on the microkernel architecture [1]. In 2009, the NICTA created a new version of L4 kernels, called Secure Embedded L4. SeL4 was announced to be the world's first general-purpose operating system which had passed formal verification [2]. In July 2014, NICTA made it open-source.

Formal verification provides an unprecedented level of security guarantee for seL4. SeL4 is designed for the real-time applications. And it has broad prospects in those industries which have high demand for security, such as military and medical industries.

RefOS is a typical multi-tasking operating system which built on seL4 and provided by NICTA.

As a microkernel system, seL4 provides few application interfaces, which leads to developers having great difficulty developing applications on seL4. RefOS has enriched library functions of seL4 to some extent, but not enough. Especially the lack of mmap [3] and fork [4] makes it difficult to develop parallel programs, which limits its application. This paper achieves the mmap function, providing memory mapping and sharing, as well as process copy which is similar with the fork function on RefOS. The child process can share the memory region which is marked as SHARED by mmap

© Springer Science+Business Media Singapore 2015
X. Zhang et al. (Eds.): ESTC 2015, CCIS 572, pp. 179–188, 2015.
DOI: 10.1007/978-981-10-0421-6_18

with its parent process. The innovation of our job is that we provide not only the function of process copy, which is not supported by seL4, but also the function interface of memory sharing between processes. Mmap and fork functions that we provide may have many applications when people develop parallel programs on seL4, such as implementing the standard POSIX interface.

2   Related Works

In 2009, NICTA presented seL4, which was the world's first (the only one currently) general-purpose operating system which had passed formal verification. Formal verification had been achieved in small kernels, but this was the first time to achieve it in operating system kernel which can perform complex tasks. Studies found that those common attack methods were completely ineffective to seL4, such as buffer overflows.

SeL4 is based on L4, which provides virtual address spaces, thread and inter-process communication [5].

Affected by the design of EROS [6] /KeyKOS [7], the seL4 microkernel provides a capability-based access-control model. Access control governs all kernel services; in order to perform an operation, an application must invoke a capability in its possession that has sufficient access rights for the requested service. Capability is designed for improving the security of operating system.

The creation and use of the high-level kernel services is achieved by the creation, manipulation, and combination of kernel objects, such as Thread Control Blocks, Virtual Address Space Objects and so on. Kernel objects can only be accessed by capability. The relationship between capabilities and kernel objects to be accessed is just like the relationship between file descriptors and files.

RefOS is a multi-server operating system, which built on seL4 and provided by NICTA. The aim of RefOS is to provide a reference to design a microkernel based operating system on seL4. Therefore, the interface functions provided by RefOS are limited. For parallel programming support, only a proc_clone function for copying thread and a proc_new_proc function for loading a designated elf file to run are provided. There are serious problems to develop parallel programs on RefOS, by the reason of it neither supports process copy, nor supports memory sharing.

3   Relevant Content in RefOS

3.1   The System Structure of RefOS

RefOS embraces the component-based multi-server OS design. The two main components are process server and fileserver. Servers are normal processes which provide interfaces for applications and keep the seL4's implementation details from those application developers. The hierarchical structures are shown as Fig. 1.

The process server runs as the initial thread, and is responsible for starting up the rest of the system. Other components of the system can be anything from clients, device drivers, file servers, terminal programs, tetris...etc.

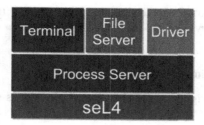

Fig. 1. Components concept of RefOS.

The process server is the most trusted component in the system. It runs as the initial kernel thread and does not depend on any other component (this avoids deadlock). The process server also implements the dataspace interface for anonymous memory, and acts as the memory manager [8].

3.2   Key Data Structures

RefOS has a process control block structure to store process related information. There is a variable named vspace for the whole virtual space of the corresponding process.

There are also two structures—window and dataspace—for managing virtual memory and physical RAM. The window structure is just like the vm_area_struct structure in linux, which is a contiguous section of virtual memory that has the same access permissions. For example, when a new elf file is loaded, every section (data section, text section and so on) corresponds to a window in the new process. The virtual spaces in RefOS are managed by the form of windows.

The dataspace structure in RefOS is managed by the process server. A dataspace is a memory space, a series of bytes, representing anything from physical RAM to file contents on disk to a device or even to a random number generator. The concept is analogous to UNIX files.

Therefore, a mapping relation between a window and a dataspace can be considered as a mapping relation between virtual memory and physical RAM. Actually the most immediate way for a process to use its own virtual memory space is creating a dataspace and a window and then building a mapping relation between them.

4   The Implementation of Process Copy and Memory Sharing

Process copy and memory sharing are implemented by two functions—mmap and fork. The current mmap function that RefOS provides can only be used to allocate a space anonymously, just like the malloc function. It can neither map a file to memory, nor map in shared mode.

The new mmap function this paper achieves sees a dataspace as a file. It maps the dataspace to memory with a shared flag or a private flag according to its parameters. Then the fork function will traverse the current process's whole address space.

According to the flag that mmap sets to determine whether the child process shares certain chunks of memory with the parent process.

4.1   The Implementation of Mmap

The execution flow of original mmap that RefOS provides is shown as Fig. 2.

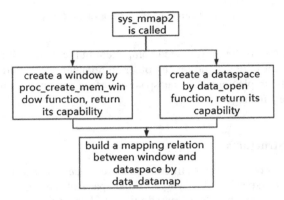

Fig. 2. The original mmap of RefOS.

We can see that the original mmap function only open a new dataspace, creates a new window in current process and establishes the mapping relations between them. It can neither map an existing dataspace to memory, nor mark whether the window is shared or private.

In our design, the new mmap realizes those functions above. The execution flow of new mmap is shown as Fig. 3.

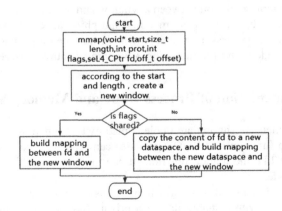

Fig. 3. The execution flow of the new mmap.

4.2   The Implementation of Fork

The implementation of fork is more complex than mmap. The execution flow of the fork function we design is shown as Fig. 4.

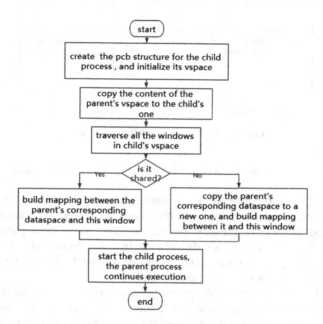

Fig. 4. The execution flow of fork.

When the fork function is called, firstly it will create the child process and initialize related structures. Then the fork function will traverse all the windows of the parent process and create corresponding windows in the child process. If a window in the parent process is shared, the corresponding window in the child process will share the same dataspace with its parent. If not, it will create a new dataspace and copy the content of its parent's dataspace to the new one.

The memory structure of the parent and the child is shown as Fig. 5.

So the implementation of fork is divided into two parts: process copy and memory sharing. In addition, our fork function is a bit different from the fork function that linux implements: our fork function does not return twice. The child process will execute a particular function specified by fork. So we need add a third part: passing parameters to the child process and invoking a new function.

Process Copy. The virtual space is managed by many windows. When the fork function is called, firstly it will traverse all the windows of the parent's virtual space, and find the corresponding dataspace. For every window of the parent process, a same window will be created in the same position of the child process. Then according to whether the window is shared or not, the child process will share or copy the parent's

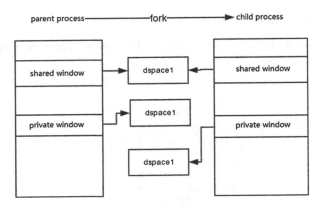

Fig. 5. The memory structure after fork.

dataspace. Finally the mapping relation between the new window and the dataspace will be built.

In addition, there is a special window—static parameter area—in the virtual space of RefOS. When loading a new process, RefOS's process server will allocate a physical page in a fixed position of the new process to store some static parameters. This window is special because there is only one page in this window and it does not have a corresponding dataspace. So we cannot copy its content by copying or sharing its dataspace, which is the way to copy other windows.

This special page is located in the parent process's virtual space and the target area is in the child process's virtual space. While the fork function is called by the process server and the process server cannot access the two virtual spaces directly.

For the above problems, the paper's implementation is that firstly we map the special page of the parent process to the current process and create a anonymous dataspace, and then copy the content of the special page (which has already mapped to the current process) to the anonymous dataspace. Secondly we create a window with the size of a page in the particular position of the child process (the same position of the special page in the parent process) and build the mapping relation between the window and the anonymous dataspace.

Then the parent process's copy is completed.

Memory Sharing. According to the semantics of the mmap and the fork function defined in linux, the child process created by the fork function should share those files that mapped with shared mode by the mmap function with its parent process. In RefOS, those files should be replaced by dataspaces.

As a result, on the one hand, the mmap function needs to mark whether the window it creates is shared. On the other hand, the fork function needs to determine that whether the child process should share the corresponding dataspace with its parent according to whether the window is shared.

So we add a flag in the current window structure of RefOS. This flag can be set as shared or private. And add judgement in the fork function: If the flag is shared, the child process will share the same dataspace with its parent and build a mapping relation between its own window and the dataspace. If the flag is private, it will create a new dataspace and copy the content of its parent's dataspace to the new one and then build a mapping relation between its own window and the new dataspace.

Passing Parameters and Calling Functions. The child process created by our fork function will execute a particular function. Suppose the particular function is defined like this:

```
void child_func(void* arg)
{
    ...
}
```

When the child process has been created, the address of the child_func function will be assigned to the pc pointer. In this way, the child process will begin execution at child_func's first instruction.

The implementation of passing parameters is different because of different architectures. This paper focuses on ARM.

When compiling the code of child_func, the complier doesn't know whether the function is called normally or called by assigning an address to the pc pointer. The complier handles all function calls in the same way.

The first few instructions of a function call will push the return address onto the stack and get the arguments of the function. The child_func function has only one parameter. According to the ABI of arm architecture [9], this parameter will be stored in register r0. And then the child_func function will get the parameter from register r0.

Therefore, the fork function writes the parameter to register r0 and assigns the child_func's address to pc pointer. In this way fork can pass the parameter to the child process and call a specified function.

5   Functional Test

To test mmap and fork, this paper designs a serial of test cases, which are used to test the correctness and validity of every part.

5.1   Functional Test of Mmap

The test of mmap is relatively simple. The major part is testing whether the mapping relations between dataspace and window can be built, and, whether the physical memory can be accessed through virtual address after mapping.

The execution flow of test function is shown as Fig. 6.

When a dataspace is passed in as an argument, mmap will create a window mapped to the dataspace and return the window's address. Then the address can be operated just like an ordinary pointer.

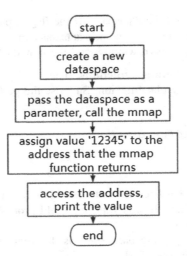

Fig. 6. The execution flow of mmap's test.

The output results are shown as Fig. 7. The value '12345' means the test function executes correctly.

```
test_mymmap function start!
in test_mymmap: dspace created
shared mmap2 caught!
in test_mymmap: window and dspace mapped
in test_mymmap: 12345 writed to window
Now, read from window: 12345
```

Fig. 7. The output of mmap's test.

5.2 Functional Test of Fork

The test of fork is relatively complex. It is divided into several parts: process copy, memory sharing and make the child process execute a specified function with specified parameters. The test procedure is shown as Fig. 8.

Firstly we map a dataspace with shared mode to a window, and map another dataspace with private mode to another window. Their addresses in parent process are vaddr1 and vaddr2. The value in vaddr1 is set to 1, and the value in vaddr2 is 2. Secondly two fork functions are called, one uses vaddr1 as a parameter and another uses vaddr2. So the child processes generated by fork can access the two addresses. By judging whether the values of the two addresses are equal with their values in parent process, we can confirm whether process copy is achieved. Then we change the values in vaddr1 and vaddr2 in child processes. Whether the two values are changed in parent processes determines whether memory sharing is achieved.

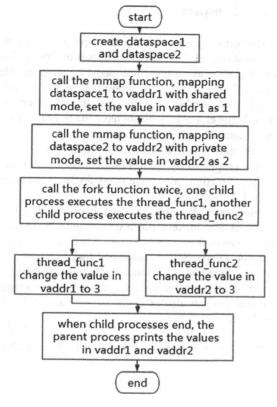

Fig. 8. The execution flow of fork's test.

The test results are shown as Fig. 9.

From the test results, we can see that each child process copies the parent process successfully. And the changes to shared area in child process do affect its values in parent process, but the changes to private area do not affect the parent process. That means the fork function executes correctly.

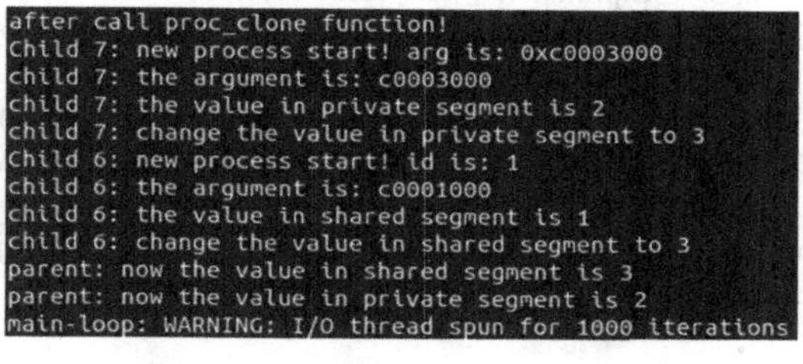

```
after call proc_clone function!
Child 7: new process start! arg is: 0xc0003000
child 7: the argument is: c0003000
child 7: the value in private segment is 2
child 7: change the value in private segment to 3
child 6: new process start! id is: 1
child 6: the argument is: c0001000
child 6: the value in shared segment is 1
child 6: change the value in shared segment to 3
parent: now the value in shared segment is 3
parent: now the value in private segment is 2
main-loop: WARNING: I/O thread spun for 1000 iterations
```

Fig. 9. The output of fork's test.

6 Summarize and Prospect

As the world's first (the only one currently) general-purpose operating system which has passed formal verification, seL4 has broad prospects in those industries which have high demand for security, such as military and medical industries. Nevertheless, there are few applications developed on seL4. An important reason for this situation is that seL4 only provides a limited number of APIs. And the reference multi-tasking operating system RefOS built on seL4 also does not have many library functions, especially for the development of parallel programs.

This paper achieves mmap and fork, which provides not only the function of process copy that is not supported by seL4, but also the function of memory sharing between processes. These functions may have many applications when people develop parallel programs on seL4.

RefOS has a terminal now. But the functions it provided is limited: it can only create a new child process and make it run a designated elf file using the exec command. And the exec command is synchronous, which means that you cannot do anything else but wait for it ends. So the mmap and fork functions we provides can be used to achieve a more complicated terminal, including executing commands asynchronously, the support of environment variables, the support of varieties of commands and so on. What's more, our job also provides strong support for implementing the POSIX standard interfaces.

Acknowledgments. This work was supported by Natural Science Foundation of China (No. 61272167).

References

1. Elphinstone, K., Heiser, G.: From L3 to seL4 what have we learnt in 20 years of L4 microkernels? In: Proceedings of the Twenty-Fourth ACM Symposium on Operating Systems Principles, pp. 133–150. ACM (2013)
2. Klein, G., Andronick, J., Elphinstone, K., et al.: Comprehensive formal verification of an OS micro-kernel. ACM Trans. Comput. Syst. (TOCS) **32**(1), 2 (2014)
3. Mmap(2) - Linux manual page
4. "POSIX". Standards. IEEE
5. Derrin, P., Elkaduwe, D., Elphinstone, K.: seL4 reference manual. In: NICTA-National Information and Communications Technology Australia (2006)
6. Shapiro, J.S., Smith, J.M., Farber, D.J.: EROS: a fast capability system. ACM (1999)
7. Hardy, N.: KeyKOS architecture. ACM SIGOPS Oper. Syst. Rev. **19**(4), 8–25 (1985)
8. Elphinstone, K., Cheng, A., Chen, X.: RefOS — Reference Design For A Microkernel Based Operating System. 2015.5.30
9. ARM Information Center (2008). http://infocenter.arm.com/help/index.jsp?topic=/com.arm.doc.subset.swdev.abi/index.html

Author Index

Printed in the United States
By Bookmasters

Printed in the United States
By Bookmasters